Alchemy, Jung, and Remedios Varo

Alchemy, Jung, and Remedios Varo offers a depth psychological analysis of the art and life of Remedios Varo, a Spanish surrealist painter. The book uses Varo's paintings in a revolutionary way: to critique the patriarchal underpinnings of Jungian psychology, alchemy, and Surrealism, illuminating how Varo used painting to address cultural complexes that silence female expression.

The book focuses on how the practice of alchemical psychology, through the power of imagination and the archetypal Feminine, can lead to healing and transformation for individuals and culture. *Alchemy, Jung, and Remedios Varo* offers the first in-depth psychological treatment of the role alchemy played in the friendship between Varo and Leonora Carrington—a connection that led to paintings that protest the pitfalls of patriarchy.

This unique book will be of great interest for academics, scholars, and post-graduate students in the fields of analytical psychology, art history, Surrealism, cultural criticism, and Jungian studies.

Dennis Pottenger is a Jungian-oriented psychotherapist and award-winning literary journalist based in the USA.

Rebecca Livingston Pottenger is a licensed psychotherapist, feminist scholar, and adjunct faculty member at Pacifica Graduate Institute, USA.

Research in Analytical Psychology and Jungian Studies Series

Series Advisor: Andrew Samuels, Professor of Analytical Psychology, Essex University, UK.

The *Research in Analytical Psychology and Jungian Studies* series features research-focused volumes involving qualitative and quantitative research, historical/archival research, theoretical developments, heuristic research, grounded theory, narrative approaches, collaborative research, practitioner-led research, and self-study. The series also includes focused works by clinical practitioners and provides new research informed explorations of the work of C. G Jung that will appeal to researchers, academics, and scholars alike.

Books in this series:

Symbolic Mental Representations in Arts and Mystical Experiences
Primordial Mental Activity and Archetypal Constellations
Giselle Manica

Jung's Technique of Active Imagination and Desoille's Directed Waking Dream Method
Bridging the Divide
Laner Cassar

The Cartesian Split
A Hidden Myth
Brandon Short

Psychogeotherapy
Revisioning Therapeutic Space
Martyna Chrześcijańska

Alchemy, Jung, and Remedios Varo
Cultural Complexes and the Redemptive Power of the Abjected Feminine
Dennis Pottenger

For more information about this series please visit: www.routledge.com/Research-in-Analytical-Psychology-and-Jungian-Studies/book-series/JUNGIANSTUDIES.

Alchemy, Jung, and Remedios Varo

Cultural Complexes and the Redemptive Power of the Abjected Feminine

Dennis Pottenger

Edited and introduced by
Rebecca Livingston Pottenger

Routledge
Taylor & Francis Group

LONDON AND NEW YORK

First published 2021
by Routledge
2 Park Square, Milton Park, Abingdon, Oxon OX14 4RN

and by Routledge
52 Vanderbilt Avenue, New York, NY 10017

Routledge is an imprint of the Taylor & Francis Group, an informa business

British Library Cataloguing-in-Publication Data
A catalogue record for this book is available from the British Library

Library of Congress Cataloging-in-Publication Data
A catalog record has been requested for this book

ISBN: 978-0-367-70421-6 (hbk)
ISBN: 978-0-367-70425-4 (pbk)
ISBN: 978-1-003-14623-0 (ebk)

Typeset in Sabon
by Newgen Publishing UK

For Rebecca,
It wasn't the pancakes I wanted, dear.

Contents

Figures

Acknowledgments

"Individuation," Jung wrote, "does not shut one out from the world, but gathers the world to itself" (1954/1969, para. 432). This research monograph grew from the ways in which Remedios Varo gathered the uncured wool of the world to herself, weaving from it a painted tapestry of love and transformation. My ability to notice what Varo was doing is due to my association with my wife, Rebecca. Rebecca is a gifted editor who restitched unwieldy threads of research into a cohesive form and, in depth psychological acts of midwifery, cooked the essence and meaning of Varo's work into an imaginal broth that nourishes our understanding of how the alchemical practice of painting helped the artist heal from trauma and protest problems associated with patriarchy. Rebecca's ability to see into and reflect upon psychological dynamics at work in culture are on full display in chapter 9 in her explication of Varo's painting, *The Encounter*, a work that features a woman who comes in from the dark wood of the unconscious with the knowledge that there is a secret held in her womb—a secret which has been silenced.

Two friends have supported me over the past decade as I have transitioned from magazine journalism to work as a Jungian-oriented psychotherapist and independent scholar. Thank you to Gail Lyons for not just talking about Jungian psychology but having the courage to live with the unconscious as you experience it. Thank you to Matthew Fike for patient, thoughtful sensitivity and for the unselfish ways you worked to open doors for me as a writer and scholar.

Three women have supported me in vital ways. My first editor, Cheryl Romo, encouraged me to *find the people* worth writing about. From Jean Palmer-Daley, a Jungian analyst and my thesis advisor at Pacifica Graduate Institute, her advice *less fire, more breathing* became an alchemical practice I work with in every aspect of my life. Inez Martinez, a longtime Board Member with the Jungian Society for Scholarly Studies, has affirmed the quality of my scholarship for more than a decade.

This look at alchemical psychology in the art and life of Varo started as a presentation at *Art and Psyche: The Illuminated Imagination*, a conference in Santa Barbara, California in the spring of 2019. Thank you to Jungian Analyst Linda Carter and the Art and Psyche Working Group for the invitation to speak. Thank you, also, to Devon Deimler, a curatorial assistant at Pacifica, who read and liked my proposal for a talk on Varo.

Generous people invested time and energy to help with research. I am grateful to Gioia Jacobsen and Mark Kelly at Pacifica Graduate Institute, who helped me find an important book, *Surreal Friends*, through interlibrary loan. Thank you, also, to Lorna Peachin and Heidi Boyson, at the Kristine Mann Library, housed at the Analytical Psychology Club in New York, who found the quote on cultural complexes by Ann Ulanov that appears in chapter 5. Richard Buchen, reference librarian at Pacifica, helped fact check an elusive quote on Freud's relationship with patriarchy. Brandon, in the interlibrary loan department at Heterick Memorial Library at Ohio Northern University, emailed a copy of Kelly Wacker's 1995 monograph on alchemy in the work of Varo and Leonora Carrington quoted in Part Two.

I am grateful to Melanie Cameron, Director of Gallery Wendi Norris in San Francisco, who gifted me use of a digital image of Remedios Varo's painting *Embroidering the Earth's Mantle*. I am also grateful to Hayley Blomquist, Licensing Executive at the Artist Rights Society for copyright permissions for Varo's and Leonora Carrington's paintings included in this text.

Last, but not least, thank you to Susannah Frearson, at Routledge, who referred me to a visionary colleague, Emilie Coin, without whose interest and openness to something different this book would not have come into being.

Reference

Jung, C. G. (1954/1969). On the nature of the psyche (R. F. C. Hull, Trans.). In H. Read et al. (Eds.), *The collected works of C. G. Jung* (Vol. 8, 2nd ed., 114–25). Princeton, NJ: Princeton University Press.

Prelude: Preparing the canvas

Artist Remedios Varo (1908–1963) wove psychological and alchemical processes within her paintings that point the way to both personal and collective healing and the unmaking of patriarchal "social structures and practices in which men dominate, oppress and exploit women" (Millett, cited in Jensen, 2017: 39). Varo found a kindred spirit and established an important friendship with artist Leonora Carrington (1917–2011), who, like Varo, engaged with the tradition of Surrealism in Paris in the 1930s. Because the paintings of Varo and Carrington embody a keen awareness of patriarchal influences, ingenious use of symbolism, and courageous exploration of the unconscious and the Feminine, their images reveal the relevance of both Jungian psychology and alchemy to help shift gender constructions that dehumanize women and occlude both our humanity and the life-giving presence of the archetypal Feminine.

We live in a time of paradox: In 2017, *National Geographic* published a special edition titled *The Gender Revolution* that provided a glossary including nonbinary gender terms; but in 2016 the first U.S. Black president left office, replaced in an election that heralded a desire among much of the U.S. population to return to misogynistic and racist values. Despite waves of feminist and civil rights movements in the Unites States, Black women still earn less than Black men, who earn less than white women, who earn less than white men for equivalent work (2017 U.S. Department of Labor Table). People with a female body, regardless of their gender identity or sexual orientation, remain at risk of sexual violence, with U.S. colleges now referred to as having a culture of rape.* The #metoo movement has shined a strong light on the persistent predominance of men's sense of entitlement to a woman's body as a reward of power and position.

Moreover, issues of racism and misogyny are international in scope. The United Nations Human Rights Council's working group on discrimination against women and girls reported that "the trends affecting the world of work and their impact on women required urgent attention from all. Without this, current gender inequalities and discrimination would not only be replicated but would be exacerbated" (Human Rights Council, 2020: para. 2). The #metoo movement is gaining ground internationally, unsilencing women across the globe. Sparked by racism, police brutality, and the Black Lives Matter movement in the United States, institutional racism is being recognized as a worldwide issue, and protests have spread across countries in Europe, Asia, Africa, and Latin America.

Carol Gilligan, a feminist psychologist known for her work on gender equality, and David Richards, an attorney and professor of law at New York University, have defined patriarchy as

> an anthropological term denoting families or societies ruled by fathers. It sets up a hierarchy—a rule of priests—in which the priest, the *hieros*, is a father, *pater*. As an order of living, it elevates some men over other men and all men over women. (2009: 22)

As argued in *Alchemy, Jung, and Remedios Varo*, patriarchy is an androcentric system of power and privilege. Psychologically, this system perpetuates a dynamic driven by the will to dominate and control that which is considered "other," from women, to people of color, to environmental resources.

Suggested in *Alchemy, Jung, and Remedios Varo* is the idea that to include the oppressed, dispersing their number throughout the hierarchical ranks may be progress—however, it remains progress *within* the patriarchal paradigm. With the optimum well-being of individuals, communities, and cultures in mind, inclusion of the oppressed is not enough because it ignores the influence exerted by unconscious cultural complexes—the deeper problems with patriarchy out of which oppression continues to arise. As Marion Woodman pointed out, patriarchy is fundamentally driven by a lust for power over (1993). Having split mind from matter, it is invested in what James Hillman called *delusional literalism*, a perspective that objectifies nature and the female body, supporting the patriarchal power drive (2010: 192). As this work points out, these psychological factors operate in the world as a defense against vulnerability, fear of the unknown, and powerlessness—complexes projected onto women and the feminine.

In their lives and art, and through their friendship, Varo and Carrington did not seek inclusion but rather struggled to free themselves from the androcentric patriarchal paradigm and then to look at it through female eyes and to imagine fundamentally different and transformative ways of engaging with self, world, and cosmos. To do this, these artists dipped their paint brushes into a brew of Jungian psychology, mythology, mysticism, intellect, imagination, and the courage to confront the unconscious. The art of Varo and Carrington asks us to challenge the structure of the world in which we live at deeper levels: Rather than struggling to compete, the work of these artists illuminates the unmaking of patriarchal structures of identity that create inequality, the revivification of the relational and imaginal, and the transformation of the fear of the unknown and powerlessness into love and partnership.

Although Varo did not label her work arts-based research, as analyzed in these pages, her paintings nestle nicely into this category. In this context, Varo's paintings are seen to create and convey meaning based in "sensory, emotional, perceptual, kinesthetic, embodied, and imaginal ways of knowing" (Leavy, 2017: 5). With these thoughts in mind, this study of Varo's work challenges the androcentric nature of alchemy and Jungian depth psychology. Our revolutionary intention is to look with new eyes at the psychological and sociocultural transformation evoked in Varo's work. New here is not only the application of Jungian concepts and methods to Varo's art and life, but also the application of Varo's painted perspectives to cultural complexes threaded into Jungian approaches to psychology and alchemy.

This work has been crafted in keeping with Varo's frequent use of both weaving and the spiraling path as images of the integrative, wholistic, and cyclical nature of the Feminine principle in psychic and physical life. Part I focuses on Varo, seeing through her life, dreams, and painted images the artist's psychological and alchemical attempts to transform forces of repression and oppression. Part II circles back around to Varo's friendship with Leonora Carrington. Our amplifications here aim to extract the animating essence from a friendship that served for both women as a cauldron of transformation—an alchemical vessel forged from the similarities in their experiences of war and imprisonment and a shared interest in the creative and psychological uses of mysticism for female healing. Part II illuminates the art of Varo and Carrington as a symbolic challenge to misogyny in both psychology and Surrealism, focusing in particular on Varo's re-imagining of the myth of the Minotaur.

We finger this thread again in Part III, where added to our reflections on the artist's unraveling of the myth of the male hero is Carrington's vision of the Minotaur's daughter and a depth psychological look at the portrayal of the divine Feminine in two paintings by surrealist Wifredo Lam. In Part III, the Jungian idea of the transcendent function as the resolution of opposites is freed from the binary paradigm of patriarchy and engages the multifaceted constituency of an archetypally Feminine perspective. In imaginal dialogue, Varo's and Carrington's images engage with each other, as well as with images of the distorted, dismembered, and dislocated feminine and the wounded masculine bereft of the feminine in the work of Lam. In the movement toward the central image of an opus that holds the potential to unmake the patriarchy, the threads of Jungian psychology, alchemy, and

Surrealism are woven throughout the fabric of the transformative response of the feminine to personal and collective wounding.

Rebecca Livingston Pottenger, M.A., M.F.T.

* Rape on college campuses has increased since 2015. See Association of American Universities Campus Climate Summary (2019)

References

Gilligan, C., & Richards, D. (2009). *Deepening Darkness: Patriarchy, resistance, and democracy's future.* Cambridge, NY: Cambridge University Press.

Hillman, J. (2010). *Alchemical psychology.* Putman, CT: Spring Publicaations.

Human Rights Council. (2020). Human Rights Council holds interactive dialogue with the working group on Discrimination Against Women and Girls. www.ohchr.org/EN/NewsEvents/Pages/DisplayNews.aspx?NewsID=26040&LangID=E

Jensen, R. (2017). *The end of patriarchy: Radical feminism for men.* North Melbourne, Australia: Spinifex Press.

Leavy, P. (2017). *Research design: Quantitative, qualitative, mixed methods, arts-based, and community-based participatory research approaches.* New York, NY: Guilford Press.

U.S. Department of Labor. (2017). *Earnings.* www.dol.gov/agencies/wb/data/earnings

Woodman, M. (1993). *Conscious femininity: Interviews with Marion Woodman.* Toronto, Canada: Inner City Books.

Part I

The death of Remedios Varo and the science of all things

First Matter

The dream of the executioner

Remedios Varo recorded ten dreams in her diary. The dreams are undated. Varo titled the last entry in the series, simply, "Dream 10." The dream:

> I had discovered an extremely important secret, something like a part of the "absolute truth." I don't know how, but powerful people and government authorities had found out that I possessed that secret and considered it extremely dangerous for society, since, if it were known by everyone, the entire existing social structure would collapse. So they took me prisoner and condemned me to death. The executioner took me to a place that seemed like the wall of a city. From either side of the wall an earthen slope dropped very steeply.
>
> The executioner seemed very pleased. I felt great fear and great distress. When I saw he was already preparing to behead me, I started to cry and pleaded with him not to kill me, it was still too soon to die and he should consider that I still had many years of life ahead of me. Then the executioner started to laugh and to mock me. He said, "Why are you afraid of death if you know so much? Having so much wisdom, you shouldn't fear death." Then I realized suddenly that what he was saying was true and that my horror wasn't so much of death, but instead because I'd forgotten to do something of the greatest importance before dying. I begged him to give me just a few more moments of life so that I could do something that would allow me to die in peace. I explained that I loved someone and needed to weave his "fates" with mine, since once this weaving was done, we would stay united for eternity. The executioner seemed to find my entreaty very reasonable and granted me some ten more minutes of life. So then, I acted fast and wove around myself (much as baskets and hampers are woven) a sort of cage in the shape of an enormous egg (four or five times larger than me).

The material I used to weave it was like ribbons that kept materializing in my hands and which, without seeing where they came from, I knew were his substance and my own. When I finished weaving that egg- like object, I felt at peace, but I kept on crying. Then I told the executioner that he could kill me at once, because the man I desired was woven with me for all eternity. (1997/2018: 94-6, emphasis in original)

Chapter 1

Varo's alchemical practice of painting and the problem of patriarchy

In the mid-1950s, Remedios Varo exhibited four paintings as part of a group show at the Galería Diana in Mexico City. In one of the paintings, *The Useless Science or the Alchemist*, a woman turns the handle of an alembic, a machine used in alchemy to separate liquids. A tower with three turrets looms above the alchemist, who sits on a stool, wrapped in a cloak that forms around her from the same black-and-white checkerboard material as the floor. Varo has cut the outer walls of the tower away to reveal an intricate mechanical labyrinth—a complex contraption of gears and pulleys powered by the woman turning the handle of the alembic. Attached to the apparatus, on the roofs of two of the towers, wheels turn, flags unfurl, bells sound. Rain falls from a golden cloud-filled sky, moisture collecting in upturned fluted baskets mounted on two walls of the tower. Down below, on a bench in a hidden alcove, rainwater drips into a bottle from a pipe connected to one of the fluted baskets. Four more bottles filled with green liquid sit on the bench, waiting to be filled with rainwater.

Alchemy, wrote Varo's biographer Janet Kaplan, had fascinated the artist "since childhood, both as a literal process of laboratory experiment (the chemical transformation of base metals into gold) and as a metaphorical process of psychic transformation" (1988: 124). In *The Useless Science or the Alchemist*, Varo imagines the extraction of the elements of a new world both for herself and for cultures plagued by the problems of male domination and misogyny. "In this painting," wrote Jungian analyst Mary Wells Barron, "the tower-like houses—which throughout her work suggest initiation huts—contain the mechanisms of energy, which are set in motion by the alchemist's hand" (2006, "About the Cover Art"). "The alchemist," Barron added,

> is evoked by the image of the woman at a spinning wheel—an apt image, since the work concerns the thread of life. The wheels inside the tower houses provide the energy for the process under way, namely, the extraction of essence, which appears as drops of moisture falling from above. ("About the Cover Art")

Alchemically, Varo's painting depicts the process through which a person distills the essence of the unconscious psyche into forms that can be used both for personal growth and for improving life at larger levels of community and culture. The painting relates psychologically and mythologically to Varo's dream of the executioner, for Varo's surrender to her own death, and her weaving of the egg, suggest that she placed infinite trust in what James Hollis called the "invisible plane that supports the visible" world (1995: 148). "Tracking the gods," Hollis wrote, "means paying feeling attention to the incarnation of ... archetypal images" (106). Through painting, Varo tracked the movement of the gods, both in herself and in the misogynistic cultures she lived in. Perhaps this devotion to "returning to the source, that is, to the reality of the psyche," is what the executioner, who would kill the vulnerable feeling part of himself that he projects onto a woman, finds so threatening about Varo (106).

With the interplay between human and divine in mind, the imagery in Varo's paintings and in the dream of the executioner speak to more than the aspects of the artist's personal life being worked on in the cauldron of her imagination. In particular, the dream of the executioner features imagery that evokes archetypal forces that transcend the ego. We can look first at the executioner as a representation of the patriarchal need to kill the feminine that threatens to undermine its power with the uncertainty of feeling. Secondly, and depth psychologically, the dream depicts the universal experience of dying and becoming, death being a process of transformation that offers possibilities of light (making room for something new) and casts a shadow that frightens the ego. The ego marks "the boundaries against death by not letting the energies flow, accumulating them instead as protection against the fear of death" (Akron & Banzhaf, 1995: 80).

Archetypally, Varo's surrender to her own death in the dream brings to mind the crucifixion of Christ. As a form of capital punishment, crucifixion, wrote an essayist in *The Book of Symbols*, was inflicted upon "slaves, foreigners, and political or religious enemies of the state" for a thousand years starting in the seventh century ("Crucifixion," 2010: 744). Crucifixion, in this extraverted sense, involves an experience of unbearable suffering:

> Apparently, the condemned was first stripped and scourged. Then his outstretched arms were fastened or nailed, probably through the wrists, to a horizontal beam that was raised to cross an upright stake... Death, most likely from dehydration and loss of blood, followed within a day or two, sometimes hastened by piercing the body or breaking the legs. (744)

Transitioning from crucifixion as a punitive practice designed to deter religious fervor to its symbolic equivalent in Varo's dream moves our amplifications into psychological spaces in which a person experiences "the most ... excruciating forms of psychic tension, where harrowing dualities and oppositions rend body and soul" ("Crucifixion," 2010: 744). From a Jungian perspective, there is a method to the madness: such an experience "evokes a radical, permanent reversal of the way things were, and an equally radical shift ... in the consciousness that mediated them" (744).

Injured by institutionalized misogyny and the traumas of war, Varo knew what it was like to carry her own cross—to take on the suffering of her life and mix it with the sweetness of divine love and the liberating energies of imagination. In service to the birth of a better way to live, Varo's paintings, and her dream of the executioner, evoke an important symbol: the *coniunctio*, often depicted in alchemical emblems as "the marriage and/or sexual intercourse between Sol and Luna or some other personification of the opposites" (Edinger, 1985: 217). In the dream of the executioner, Varo wove her destiny with her opposite, the man with whom she wished to be connected for eternity. We look later in more detail at the psychological presence and meaning of the man in the dream. Here we notice the crucial role crucifixion—the psychological experience that forces the ego to surrender into service to the deep Self—plays in preparing a person to bring their gift into the world.

Dietrich Bonhoeffer knew what would happen when he spoke out against Hitler's genocidal persecution of Jews. But how could the pastor and theologian live with himself if he did *not* speak out? Hollis wrote about the theological dilemma that tormented Bonhoeffer during confinement in Tegel prison and, later, Flossenbürg concentration camp, before his execution by the Nazis in the spring of 1945. "No one would choose such a dilemma, but something inside chooses for us and places us at the crossroads where only crucifixion of the ego can occur" (Hollis, 2004: 87).

Remedios Varo had her own dilemma to deal with: how to live fully as a woman in a world dedicated to the superiority and violence of men. A skilled seamstress who designed and made her own clothes as well as costumes for the theater, Varo faced her terrors by painting, her canvases the loom upon which she embroidered images of female imagination and empowerment. Having faced misogyny in religious and gender systems that did their best to stifle a woman's voice and very being, Varo turned to painting as a way to re-stitch the frayed contours of a life that included more than its share of upheaval and pain.

Psychologically, Varo followed a Jungian map of the soul. From a classical Jungian perspective, the ego's job is to recognize and support the designs of the deep Self. For the unconscious knows more than the ego does about who we are and what we are supposed to contribute to the world around us. Suffering exposure to one's shadow, and persevering in the face of the "everlasting indestructibility" of our complexes, is often not easy or pleasant (Hillman, 2005: 48). In Varo's case, healing from trauma may have been even more painful than the experience of being wounded was to begin with. But something happened as the artist painted her fantasies. Wounds healed, creating a clearing for love and wonder. She settled and came home to herself. Painting, as a symbolic and alchemical practice, helped the artist liberate the golden aspects of her personality from within the prison of unresolved trauma and unconscious psychological complexes.

Painting, for Varo, was also a numinous spiritual practice that brought her into an intimate working relationship with the deep Self, an upper-case metaphor Jungian psychology uses to refer to the "kind of energy in which the activity of divinity may be witnessed" (Hollis, 2004: 92). This meeting, this collaboration, is what a conscious life, and the practice of alchemical psychology, are all about (19). The aim of the alchemical work is to create something new from the remnants of the old form, destroying and reconfiguring it in a way that creates "more and more consciousness in the universe" (Edinger, 1985: 230).

For Varo, the idea that human beings are mirror reflections of the stars in the sky is a foundational metaphysical truth. For this artist, there is a reciprocal relationship between human life and the inexpressible mystery of the cosmos. This relationship is a thread that connects her personal life to the paintings she produced and the role of alchemy in her symbolic attempts to birth a world that embraces the imaginative power of women, the disavowed wisdom of the female body, and the archetypal Feminine.

In this alchemical work, we finger imaginal threads Varo stitched into her paintings and fantasies over the last decade of her life. One of these threads involves personal growth. For Varo, painting was an artistic practice that enabled her to express and symbolize the changes taking place within her psyche as she grappled with complexes and intensely frightening and traumatizing shadow material. For Varo, who read and studied Jungian psychology, painting furthered her personal work of individuation because it brought her into a healing and reciprocal relationship with the numinous archetypal forces that animate human life.

A second thread begins where the first leaves off, for growth and clarity not only helped Varo heal from injury and calm inner upset: Becoming more of herself helped the artist prepare to paint. Deep suffering may have been the price Varo paid to become conscious enough to create paintings that might best be looked upon not only as beautiful or iconic works of art but also as alchemical recipes with subversive intent. Varo painted visions of the person she was working to become. But Varo did more than make art for herself. Through painting, this alchemical seamstress also wove the garment of a world made new from the discarded fabric of a patriarchal system of male dominance built on violence, exploitation, and oppression. Varo's paintings, and her dream of the executioner, imagine the un-making of the patriarchy.

Throughout this monograph, we sift into the metaphoric messages Varo coded into her paintings. Our task is to engage with and understand the symbolic meaning of her meticulous imagery. Our wanderings make for a *circumambulation*, a walk around a mysterious center that cannot be known but only glimpsed through images and felt experience that reflect its unknowable and inexpressible nature.

Born in Spain, Varo lived the last 20 years of her life in exile in Mexico City. Uprooted from everything she knew, the artist lived and painted "in marginal spaces" where "she created some of the most extraordinary work in contemporary painting" (Agosin, 1998: 18). Beyond the bright lights of such a spotlight, the value of a psychological study of Varo's art and life may well come down to an invitation, for through her work the artist beckoned those who are devoted to living in concert with the archetypal presences who appear on her canvases. Their visitations hint at how we might address misogynistic cultural complexes and re-enchant the world as a place where courage and love, rather than fear and the will to power, reign.

There are still other threads we work to tease apart—painting as weaving, art as propaganda, the labyrinth as a metaphor for the search for the deep Self. Traveling into a world of metaphor and symbol, Varo's imagery invites us to transform ourselves as a first step toward the alchemical re-invention of a world that works for everyone, not just those with patriarchal privilege.

There is one thread that is especially important to finger as we descend with Varo into the suffering of her life in a bid to return from our journeys rejuvenated with meaning and new resources. This dark thread connects the artist's life and her death from a heart attack in the fall of 1963 with her dream of the executioner. From a Jungian perspective, we can consider Varo's dreamtime encounter with death as her psyche's way of expressing and responding to the annihilating presence of masculinity, distorted by fear and driven to acts of violence by the pathological need to destroy women as the projected containers for unconscious male powerlessness and shame.

In what follows, we track, with Varo, into unseen realms of dream and fantasy, symbolic spaces in which love and wonder blend with cruelty and death. To "roam her enchanted woods," and to "pace the parapets of her monasteries and castles," it is helpful to understand the medieval mindset that Varo brought to her art and life (Engel, 1986: 8). "To the medieval mind," wrote Peter Engel, "understanding the world was a matter of explicating an iconographic code in which each material object was not merely a thing in itself, but the symbolic emissary of a profound and otherworldly power" (8).

Steeped in spiritual growth, and devoted to using the images that formed on her canvas to evoke deeply held beliefs in the wisdom and healing capacities of a sacred universal order, Varo worked in her paintings to transform what is into what can be. The nature of such a process creates uncertainties. Working alchemically in one's deep inner life, questions destabilize the way things are in a bid to instigate a process of transformation aimed at recombining the unmade original elements in new ways.

Here, as we begin to engage with the artist and her imagery, we sense the numinous power of Varo's imaginal meeting with death. But the dream of the executioner also confounds and frustrates. Potential meanings lead in numerous directions. What, for example, is the relationship (if there is one) between Varo's dream of the executioner and the death of her physical body from a heart attack? What connection might there be between the dream of the executioner and the paintings Varo was making as she worked to highlight female empowerment and to expose the ways in which patriarchal misogyny harms women?

From a Jungian perspective, we are drawn into the story that unfolds in the dream not only because we want to find the answers to our questions but also because we are hoping, like Varo, for a glimpse of the sacred and transcendent. Our curiosity is crucial, for it matches the mischievous vitality Varo brought to art and to her life. Varo loved to ask questions. She loved to experiment, to play with possibilities. After her death, Varo's friend, poet Octavio Paz, imagined the artist saying of her work: "We are surprised, because I paint surprised" (Paz & Callois, 1966, 8).[1]

As we stoke the alchemical fire this artist once tended, we engage, as Varo did, in the practice of alchemical psychology. Alchemy, wrote Stephen Wilkerson, is "devoted to the process of transformation—changing, elevating, and purifying the human spirit" (2019: 10). "The modest aim of spiritual alchemy," Wilkerson added, "is progress: not omniscience, but simply to become more aware, to become increasingly more conscious, and to explore the unconscious as thoroughly as possible" (232).

Varo invites us to do this in her painting of the woman turning the handle of the machine built to take the stuff dreams are made of and transmute them into a form that can be used to remake a world that fails to work for everyone into one that does. In *The Useless Science or the Alchemist*, Barron wrote,

> Varo depicts the process of transformation symbolically through the black and white tiles on the floor. The rigid, flat surface becomes flexible, and rises to form the alchemist's robe. Is this not precisely what occurs when, through slow, constant, even repetitious work, rigid defenses or lifeless patterns dissolve in the *solutio* and give way to new life, a less complexed, more resilient way of being? (2006: "About the Cover Art")

If we linger in the presence of the woman extracting the essence of the divine mystery, a new psychological insight is possible.

> Upon reflection, the viewer realizes that it is Varo, the artist herself, who has assumed the role of the alchemist, and now sits on a three-legged

stool, like the Pythia at Delphi, bringing her unique feminine lunar consciousness to bear on the task at hand, supported in her work by Wisdom, the Divine Feminine.

(Barron, 2006: "About the Cover Art")

We track now into the symbolic world of a painter drawn to transforming the conflict between opposing forces. In Varo's imaginal world, images and symbols liberate the literal, and sometimes lethal, mind of the masculine. Softened into its own disavowed desire to feel, compulsive heroic force gives way to the surrendered power of understanding, empathy, and personal authority. From polarizing positions in patriarchal paradigms dedicated to suppressing emotions and the relationality that threatens to expose underlying vulnerability, Varo remakes the masculine and feminine into archetypal partners who can now combine to bring insight and guidance to human life. In Varo's inner world, men and women are no longer combatants in a war between the sexes. Instead, as Wilkerson pointed out in his look at the role of alchemy in Goethe's *Faust*, "women and men are and should be equal partners in a world animated by and understood through love" (2019: 352).

Alchemy and art as modes of deep inquiry

C. G. Jung sifted through the symbolic spaces of the soul much like an archeologist; Remedios Varo perfected an alchemical work of her own making: art as a mode of deep inquiry. For Varo, painting was a pigmented and paint-brushed search for self-discovery not only for her own benefit but for the betterment of the world around her. "In an attempt to forge a personal identity," wrote scholar Gloria Durán, women surrealist painters like Varo "explore the archetypes of Woman as alchemist, as scientist, as spinner and weaver of mankind's destinies, and above all as creator, spiritual guide, and visionary" (1988: 299).

Stifled by her Catholic upbringing, and later traumatized by the terror of two wars, Varo's life took her into dark regions. Varo's artistic response grew from the ground of her devoted study of mysticism, spirituality, and Jungian psychology. Varo was drawn to painting and to the devotional practice of working with images and symbols in a bid to engage with the numinous forces at work in the psyche and the world. In a painting she titled *Discovery*, for example, a group of explorers stand on a ship that has landed at a shore near a forest. In the distance, a "luminous small sphere or pearl" glows with a golden light (Varo, 1997/2018: 100). An image of wonder and reverence, the painting evokes a felt sense of a quest completed, of freedom found, a surrendered ego's recognition that there are living archetypal forces at work in our lives.

With her image of the explorers who have found the orb, a symbol for the divine light that glows at the center of the material world, Varo worked symbolically from a lineage of alchemical practitioners who depicted change through the union of opposites. A common image used by the alchemists to express the conjunction of opposing forces is intercourse between a red man and a white woman.

"The alchemists," wrote Dennis William Hauck, saw the process of bringing the soul and spirit together "as one of passionate lovemaking driven by the desires of archetypal masculine and feminine forces" (1999: 213). "On the psychological level," Hauck wrote, "conjunction is the constellation of a new belief system less tied to convention and more in line with higher truths" (214).

> During Conjunction, the major effort in one's life is the creation of a unified self that is true to both inner essences and universal truths and can withstand the onslaughts of ignorance, insensitivity, and illusion one encounters in the world. (215)

According to Hauck, the "alchemists associated the operation of Conjunction with the virile bull and assigned the astrological cipher of Taurus to signify this operation" (1999: 227). Astrologically, as an Earth sign, Taurus "is symbolic of masculine strength, virility, planning, and bull-headedness. The search of the Taurian is for meaning and value in life" (227). Unwavering in her efforts to engage with the healing powers of the unconscious, Varo featured bulls as symbols of the masculine in two paintings from 1962, the year before her death.

In *Tauro*, Varo painted a bull with the fur of incandescent orange and yellow. Varo's bull has wings that help the shimmering animal fly over the Taurus constellation in a mottled sky the artist has painted black with hints of gold. The sky itself grounds the painting in a depth psychological viewpoint that "sees the image of the star-studded sky as a visualization of the flickering sparks of consciousness within the dark vastness of the unconscious psyche" ("Sky," 2010: 56). The color of the sky is also important, alchemically speaking. By painting the sky black but infused with gold, Varo brought together the density and destruction of the operation that begins the opus, the *nigredo*, with the purified golden aspects one aims for in the *coniunctio* that culminates the work.

Varo's painting depicts the alchemical union of opposites through her inclusion in the bull's face of feminine features belonging to his unseen mate, the cow. For Barbara Hannah, the "penetrating, puncturing and aggressive power of the horns," along with the "toughness of the bull's hide," are two qualities that link the bull with the masculine (2006: 371). Psychologically, Hannah sees "in the cow the principles of serene docility, gentle acceptance, and a renunciation of the bull-headedness typical of certain men, the animus, and the ego in general" (385). From a Jungian perspective, the cow brings to the process of transformation the ability to embody "that type of docility marked by strength and integrity of character and a recognition of our own limitations" (380). "The cow," Hannah adds, "becomes the symbol of the attitude required to reach the middle, the quiet place in the center of the tension of the opposites" (380). As such, it represents the "path to the transcendent function," the psyche's tendency when the tension can be held to produce a third image or idea that transcends or unifies the opposites—a crucial movement in the process of individuation (380).

In the alchemical vessel—in Varo's case, a painting—when opposing factors are held together with the relational energies of Eros—the alchemist's passion for transformation—the process of the transcendent function moves in the alembic. The vessel holds space for the mundane, raw matter of life-as-it-has-been and the numinous image of unlimited creative potential. As we shall see in Varo's art, working between the two factors produces a transcendent third—neither life as it has been nor sheer unformed potential, but rather images of transformations in consciousness and the re-invention of life.

In the alembic of her painting, Varo's bull is made of more than fire and focus—it is more than masculine. Drawn to the alchemy of mixing masculine and feminine into a transcendent union or androgynous state, Varo's orange and yellow bull sprouts two sharp silver horns, the color associated with the moon, the imagination, and the feminine. The artist has complemented the bull's masculine ability to know what he wants and do what is necessary to achieve it (Jung, 1927/1970: para. 260) by giving him a small delicate face, curious eyes, and the playful hint of a woman's smile. From a Jungian perspective, Varo painted into her image of the bull flying or prancing through the sky not only a union of masculine and feminine but also of the human and divine. Looking at us with its knowing, human-like eyes, the golden bull among the stars evokes what it is like for the ego, which is usually identified with human experience and the physical body, to feel the animating presence and power of archetypal forces flickering into awareness from the unseen spaces of the unconscious. *Tauro* may have been Varo's artistic attempt to evoke the psychological movement that is possible when a person collaborates consciously with archetypes, forces Varo constellated in the painting as the star of Taurus and as the darkened alchemical sky. From a Jungian perspective, both star and sky can be seen as symbolizing the immensity of the divine powers present in the cosmos of the psyche ("Sky," 2010: 56).

What this experience may have been like for Varo brings Jung's description of the ego's encounter with instinct and archetype to mind. Jung understood the archetypal nature of the psyche to be the psychological or spiritual expression of instinctual life. "Jung," wrote Kieron LeGrice, "describes contact with the archetypal dimension of the psyche as analogous to touching a high-voltage cable: One feels positively charged with life energy and intoxicating life power" (2016: 29). In *Tauro*, Varo painted the moment when the ego encounters the archetype, the bull of instinct, flying across the sky. It is a moment when the potency of the unconscious explodes with incandescent vitality and we find ourselves sharing the heavens with a timeless being "in a field of transcendent meaning" (2016: 28). By "capturing" the bull with attributes of his opposite, the cow, Varo painted a union of opposites and the felt sense of what Hannah calls "the heroic undertaking of a god" (2006: 360). Alchemically, the artist imagined what is below, the instincts (which depth psychology locates in an imagined direction, *down* in the unconscious), with what is above, the stars, glittering in the heavens as they might have at the dawn of time, during the creation of the cosmos.

The union of the bull and the cow mark mind and spirit, attributes typically associated with the masculine, brought together with the taming and transforming feminine "power of eros," which Hannah described as "gentleness, kindness, relatedness and acceptance of others and ourselves" (385). Hannah, of course, built her reflections on the clinical work of Jung, who associated the Masculine with Logos, the principle of logic and structure. In contrast, Jung linked the Feminine with Eros, the principle of interdependence and relationship. "By Logos," Jung wrote, "I meant discrimination, judgment, insight, and by Eros I meant the capacity to relate" (1955–56/1970: para. 224). Although Jung, and the patriarchal paradigm in which he lived, assigned the Masculine and Feminine principles to the male and female genders respectively, post-Jungian thought has clarified them as fundamental qualities functioning within the world and within the psyche of all people—though our valuation of and access to them is culturally conditioned. In *Tauro* and *Emigrants,* another painting of a bull, Varo drew on the archetypal Masculine as she explored the terrain of female initiation.

In *Emigrants*, Varo cut away the bull's midsection to show not internal organs but trunk space for traveling chests and a woman who appears to be retrieving an item from one of the open boxes. The skin and fur of the bull that has been cut away gathers above the opening in the animal's body. High on the bull's back sits a woman covered in a cloak made of the fur that has been drawn back and gathered like the folds of a curtain. In this painting, Varo again brings the masculine and feminine together in an unlikely way: the head of this bull is not that of an animal, but of a man who peers ahead with pinpoint focus while pedaling two spoked wheels with his hooves.

What are we to make of this image? Is Varo the woman riding on the back of the bull? If so, where is she going? What Varo seems to have imagined with the image is the motive power of the Masculine—or perhaps the impetus given to the process of transformation by the union of opposites, for she painted the bull as a vehicle with wheels for movement and an inner compartment where the human traveler stores the things needed for her journey. The wheels bring a powerful motif into the story of the painting. The wheel, in the context of Fortune, the tenth trump card from *The Thoth Tarot*,

> is the profound symbol of wholeness, in constant movement and yet unchanging in its center... It is the wheel of the heavens that has constantly rotated around the earth for millions of years. The power behind the hub is the Eternal moving the wheel.
>
> (Akron & Banzhaf, 1995: 66)

Beyond forging a relationship with divine forces, it is the working hypothesis of this book that Varo was working to *change* things, both in herself and in the patriarchal world around her. In these pages, we work in depth psychological ground, aware that bringing separated opposites together to reconstitute them in a new synthesis is a cornerstone of alchemical psychology as described by Jung and practiced artistically by Varo. Steeped in Jung's way of working with symbols, Varo painted in a bid to bring new life to a troubled world. In painting the alchemical mechanics of transforming opposites into a third thing, Barron wrote that Varo

> reminds us that alchemy is art, even as art is alchemy. The great artists of every age create images that serve not only their own personal transformation, but bring to all humanity the fresh images that are needed to contain, compensate for, and transform the one-sided, unbalanced *zeitgeist* of the collective, and thus bring about individuation. (2006: "About the Cover Art")

Mother, father, and the making of an alchemist

Remedios Varo's struggle with the polarities in her life and in the larger world around her began as the child of parents who embodied opposing forces. Varo was born in 1908 in Anglés, a village caught on a curve of the Ter River in a valley in the Pyrenees mountains. She was raised in the Gerona region in the province of Catalonia in the northeastern corner of Spain. Her father, Don Rodrigo, was born in Andalusia, home to what Kaplan described as "flamboyant Gypsy dancers, elegant toreros, lush gardens, melancholy music, and ornately patterned Moorish buildings" (1988: 12). Andalusians, Kaplan wrote, have been described as

> gay, full of smiles and laughter in their talk, a frivolous light-hearted people. They pride themselves on verbal wit and an allusiveness so fine and constant that the mind has to work at double speed to keep up with their fancifulness, their hyperbole, their mocking and their sparkling

conceit... [They are] nervous, easily carried up and down by their feelings... [With] a weakness for the cruel or dangerous practical joke, they love horseplay at the expense of strangers. (12)

A hydraulic engineer, Don Rodrigo was "a commanding figure in Remedios's life" (Kaplan, 1988: 15). Indeed, when Rodrigo noticed his young daughter's interest in the sketches and diagrams that he made for engineering projects, he offered to teach her mechanical drawing. Rodrigo also introduced his daughter to more liberal religious values than the formal Catholic dogma followed by her mother, Doña Ignacia.

Born in Gupúzcoa, in Basque country, separated from the rest of Spain by mountains, Doña Ignacia did not share her husband's liberal fantasies of an international community where all are welcome, and everyone speaks a common language (Kaplan, 1988: 14). The Basques, Kaplan wrote, quoting from Salvador de Madariaga's modern history of Spain,

> are seen as practical and down-to-earth—"an obstinate, tenacious, reserved, and industrious people focused on independence, self-sufficiency, and a simple and strict devotion to Catholicism." Neither fanatical nor apocalyptic, "their religion is plain, their faith is unmovable and is married to a sense of tradition which rules them." (15)

Although similar in temperament to her father,

> with their shared tendency toward fantasy and their mutual interest in art, [Varo] always felt cowed by him and kept him emotionally at a distance. She was much closer to her mother, who was the mainstay of the family. Varo cared deeply about her mother's feelings and, as an adult, often worried aloud that she had shamed this good-hearted, traditionally devout woman by [her rejection of Catholicism and] the nonconformity of her [bohemian] style of living. (16)

Varo may have rejected Catholicism as an adult, but first she had to endure being raised in a "convent school run by strict nuns" (16). Spanish poet Rafael Alberti, an older contemporary of Varo's, described his upbringing as "reactionary and savage Catholicism that darkened the blueness of the sky ... covering us with layers and layers of grey ashes" (as cited in Kaplan, 1988: 16). Mary Gordon evoked the experience of the "stifling, closed, female world" of a Catholic convent:

> The complicated psychology of convent school piety ... [was a] mix of self-love, self-dramatization, ambition, deceit and competition that marks the religious lives of girls who have only one another for company... It is a world of passions, inhabited by romantic ascetics full

of loves, hatred, secrets, biting rancors, furtive, longed-for indulgences and ghastly penances.

(As cited in Kaplan, 1988: 16)

We can imagine conflicts such as these finding their painful way into the polarization of Varo's inner world—her Andalusian temperament tormented by the savagery of Catholicism's stifling oppressions and her devotion to her Catholic mother. We will look shortly at a series of paintings that suggest clearly that Varo was expressing and working out her childhood experiences in the convent in Spain. In these works, it is also clear that while Varo rejected the oppressive aspects of Catholicism, she did not turn away from the divine entirely. In fact, Varo's mature work evokes a powerful sense of what Jung described as a religious attitude, one "peculiar to a consciousness which has been changed by an experience of the *numinosum*" (1940/ 1969, para. 9). It is an attitude "informed by the careful observation of, and respect for, invisible forces and personal experience" (Sharp, 1991: 117).

Varo devoted her life and art to the alchemical transformation of darkness into light. In Part I we look in more detail at Varo's dream of the executioner. In the dream, we recall, Varo, as the dream ego, is to be executed for discovering a secret that, if told to others, will destroy the fabric of the world. What happens next in the dream is perhaps the answer to an important question: What secret knowledge did Varo discover that was so dangerous she had to be killed? Here let us foreshadow our later amplifications to say that Varo was working within her dream of the executioner, in her paintings, and in her personal life, to transmute and redeem the raw dark matter of suffering within patriarchal culture in a way that perhaps only a woman can. "All true redemption," Joseph Henderson wrote,

> resides in our ability to humanize this negative counterpart of the divine image of God. In accordance with this process there may later appear the healing power of the feminine, with its polytheistic coloring, to transform the destructive wrath into a wholesome and love-inspiring unity. (1984: 34)

Varo found the light. She found and experienced redemption. She found her way into and through the dark places in her life. From a Jungian perspective, she showed the willingness and ability to face what Henderson called a "full encounter with the shadow" (1984: 34). Such an encounter brings to light the interstices of the personal and cultural unconscious revealing its secrets. When ruled by the Feminine principle, an encounter with shadow is concerned

> with meaning rather than with facts, with an entirety rather than with causative chains of pieces... This feminine experience of immersing

oneself in one's situation as a means to becoming conscious of it means that rather than being guided by the mind, the whole personality, down to its animal and vegetable elements, is involving itself in the process. The knowledge—the consciousness—gained through this experience can never be shared directly with another person. This learning comes only from living. Attempts to share what has been gained in the feminine mode will take the form of images, metaphors, parables, paintings, poems, or stories.

(Sullivan, 1989: 23–4)

From a Jungian perspective, Varo, through the process of attending to images and fantasies in both her inner life and in her paintings, was engaging in "the spiritual cultivation of symbols—where instinct is transformed into meaning" (Šolc & Didier, 2018: 282).

In both literal and imaginal ways, the painted worlds Varo left for us look nothing like the tormented spaces of her shadow. Psychologically, the traumas of her life left a mark on her personality. Diagnostically speaking, Varo seems to have experienced trauma, along with both anxiety and depressed mood. Alchemically speaking, the artist mined these difficulties as *prima materia*, that is, the raw first matter of our life experiences. It could not have been easy for her, first to live the suffering itself, then to re-encounter the shadow in service to healing. In *Visit to the Past*, a 1957 pencil drawing on paper, the artist places her character, a cloaked version of herself, walking through the door of a room for rent. "It is a simple room," Kaplan wrote,

surely lived in by many others in the years since she had left. Yet, returning as a visitor, luggage in hand, she finds it haunted by her own presence: lurking behind the walls, peering out from the tabletop, bursting forth from the upholstery are ghosts of herself ... As this painting suggests, the weight of her memories must have stayed with her for years. It is a disturbing portrayal in which the past, like a shadow self, comes to dominate the present. (1988: 148)

Varo did not talk about being depressed. In fact, there were some experiences—such as her capture and confinement in a French prison camp early in World War II—she did not talk about at all. But the signs and symptoms of her distress can be seen in her paintings. According to Kaplan, the "feeling of the past pressing in, of the pressure of family and heritage, is ... explored in a small, undated pencil drawing that was exhibited with the title *Fear*" (149). In the drawing,

a wheeled character, crouching low under a heavy drape, pedals urgently out from a long, deep tunnel as figures reach from behind the walls to grab at her as she passes. The succession of archways leading back into deep space suggests the past out of which she comes—a corridor of memory from which she seeks to flee, menaced by the wraithlike "ancestors" lurking on either side [of the passageway]. (149, 151)

The nervous figure in Varo's drawing bicycles away from images representing people, known or unknown, who have frightened or perhaps even menaced her. From a Jungian perspective, we might also consider these frightening apparitions as projected versions of aspects of Varo's personality that are reaching out to her from behind the wall that separates material life from the unconscious spaces of the psyche. These figures may be images of her own personality that need help in some way.

The image of the bicyclist pedaling away from unknown aspects of herself evokes a question: What is Varo afraid of? From a Jungian perspective, *Fear* may capture Varo's attempt to distance herself from what Jung called the *shadow archetype*, that is, "the dangerous aspect of the unrecognized dark half of the personality" (1943/1966: para. 152) that hides "unconscious aspects of oneself, both good and bad, which the ego has either repressed or never recognized" (Sharp, 1991: 123). For Jung, facing and integrating shadow aspects of ourselves is a moral choice the ego must make if the life-long unfolding of the personality—a process he called *individuation*—is to take place. From this perspective, individuation is a psychological process of differentiation in which the ego gradually distinguishes itself from unconscious influences and the archetypal layers of the psyche. The aim of individuation, wrote Jungian analyst Daryl Sharp, "is not to overcome one's personal psychology, to become perfect, but to become familiar with it" (1991: 68).

The nature of the alchemical first matter

Jung noticed a link between the shadow and what the alchemists called the *nigredo*, an operation that breaks down the original form of the matter being worked on so that the complexed aspects of personality can soften, separate out, and then be brought back together in a new way. Jung formed the concept of the complex at the Burghölzli Mental Hospital in Zurich between 1901 and 1904 (Bair, 2004: 66). The process began when the director of the hospital Eugene Bleuler sent Franz Riklin, a young assistant like Jung, to study at Emil Kraepelin's prestigious psychiatric clinic at the University of Munich. There, "Riklin learned of a new procedure called the association experiment" (Kerr, 1993: 44). Back at the Burghölzli, Riklin and Jung collaborated on their own version of the association experiment. At first, wrote Deirdre Bair, a Jung biographer, the clinicians based their work on the Freudian technique of free association, "in which the investigator merely offered words to the subject-patient, who responded or not in any given time" (2004: 65). Soon, however, Jung and Riklin changed the procedure to one of rigorous, controlled empirical investigation in which a subject was presented with a list of one hundred words selected for the possible associations they might raise and then instructed to respond with the first word that came to mind. Their refinement was to concentrate instead on the disturbances the subject exhibited in response to certain words said by the investigator and to measure the degree of distress by the amount of time it took the subject to formulate a reply. In most cases, these disturbing words could be grouped into a related cluster that Jung called "stimulus-words," which had much to do with either something in the patient's conscious knowledge or with information unconsciously repressed. (65)

As the word association experiments continued, Bair wrote,

> Jung found that patients differed in the amount of time they took to formulate responses to the stimulus-words, usually hesitating before those that had something to do with distressing personal information. Together with Riklin, [Jung] coined the term "complex" to stand for "personal matter" that was "always a collection of various ideas, held together by an emotional tone common to all." (65)

As he refined his clinical experiences into developing theories about the nature of unconscious processes, Jung's ideas about psychological complexes crystalized to the point where he believed it was a natural "tendency of the psyche to split into basic structural units" (as cited in Wilson, 2004: 47). Blending theory and praxis Jung wrote, "The tendency [of the psyche] to split [into units of functioning] means that parts of the psyche detach themselves from consciousness to such an extent that they not only appear foreign but lead an autonomous life of their own" (1937/1969: para. 253). "Complexes," Jung added,

> are psychic fragments which have split off owing to traumatic influences or certain incompatible tendencies. As the association experiments prove, complexes interfere with the intentions of the will and disturb the conscious performance; they produce disturbances of memory and blockages in the flow of associations; they appear and disappear according to their own laws; they can temporarily obsess consciousness, or influence speech and action in an unconscious way. In a word, complexes behave like independent beings. (para. 253)

For Jung, a fundamental aspect of a complex was the unconscious nature of its presence and functioning:

> As a rule there is a marked unconsciousness of any complexes, ... since unconsciousness helps the complex to assimilate even the ego, the result

being a momentary and unconscious alteration of personality known as identification with the complex. In the Middle Ages it went by another name: it was called possession. (1948/1969: para. 204)

James Hillman put the influence of a complex in alchemical terms, writing about the psychological experience of being possessed by our complexes:

The mind in *nigredo* shows characteristics of downward and backward thinking, an intellect caught in reductive and depressive reasonings and figurings out: past history, materialized fantasies, and concretistic explanations, coupled with a bitterly stubborn protest against its condition. The [complexed] psyche knows itself as victimized, traumatized, dependent, and limited by circumstantiality and substantiality. (2010: 214)

During the blackening, Hillman concluded that complexes create a particular kind of psychological distress: "There is pain and ignorance; we suffer without the help of knowledge" (2010: 215).

Nathan Schwartz-Salant fingered a similar theoretical thread in the introduction to his compilation of Jung's writings on alchemical psychology. In alchemy, Schwartz-Salant wrote, the shadow "corresponds to the *nigredo*, which includes not only the imagery [and suffering] of the shadow and the chthonic [instinctual or somatic] side of life, but also the shadow's mysterious purpose in dissolving old structures so that new ones can be created" (1995: 15).

This might be what the figures reaching out to Varo in *Fear* want from her. As symbols, these beings might represent aspects of Varo's personality, perhaps even aspects of her soul, reaching for her because they need her to see them, understand them, embody them. These figures, seen as projected images of Varo's shadow, appear in frightful guise not because they intend to terrorize the artist, but because they are images of unresolved suffering that wish to be acknowledged and cared for. The nervous figure on the bicycle might be Varo's artistic attempt to give form to unresolved unconscious upset. The painting may be the artist's attempt to blacken, and to break down, the fearful and limiting traumas of her life. *Fear* may be Varo's attempt to capture, in the cauldron of a painting, the raw matter of psychological pain in a process of differentiation constellated in the archetypal layers of her psyche for the purpose of healing.

With Jung's researches into the theory and practice of alchemical psychology in mind, Varo's imagery shows how the artist used painting as a transformational practice in which parts of her personality that had been injured, and even traumatized, could be contained in the vessel, the image. Painting, in this way, helped Varo face her shadow, helped her contain and communicate with the demons who stalked the passageways of her soul. In *Fear*,

Varo evoked the anxiety she felt when faced with the parts of her personality that had been hurt deeply. From a Jungian perspective, the imagery may also relate to the terror she felt when faced with the moral task of engaging with her shadow and with archetypal powers that threatened to overwhelm and perhaps even possess her.

Jung quoted an alchemist, who, having come up against dark inner forces, uttered an earnest prayer that translates from the Latin as: "Purge the horrible darknesses of our mind, light a light for our senses!" (1943/1968: para. 41). "The author of this sentence," Jung added, "must have been undergoing the experience of the *nigredo*, the first stage of the work, which was felt as 'melancholia' in alchemy and corresponds to the encounter with the shadow in psychology" (para. 41).

Psychoanalyst Julia Kristeva evoked the type of despair found in the depressive depths of the *nigredo*. "Where does this black sun come from?" Kristeva asked. "Out of what eerie galaxy do its invisible, lethargic rays reach me, pinning me down to the ground, to my bed, compelling me to silence, to renunciation?" (1987/1989: 3). Using the black sun as an alchemical metaphor for the suffering a person can encounter when making a descent into the unconscious, Kristeva wrote of the way "an infinite number of misfortunes weigh us down every day" (4). For Kristeva, this inner darkness left her with

> a life that is unlivable, heavy with daily sorrows, tears held back or shed, a total despair, scorching at times, then wan and empty. In short, a devitalized existence that, although occasionally fired by the effort I make to prolong it, is ready at any moment for a plunge into death. An avenging death or a liberating death, it is henceforth the inner threshold of my despondency, the impossible meaning of a life whose burden constantly seems unbearable... I live a living death, my flesh is wounded, bleeding, cadaverized, my rhythm slowed down or interrupted, time has been erased or bloated, absorbed into sorrow. (3–4)

As a person and a painter, Varo needed to travel along the corridors into such shadowy spaces to find redemptive meaning, healing, and inspiration for her life and for her creative work.

Black and blue: Imagination and the importance of the *nigredo*

To lay the foundation for Varo's process of transformation and to find the alchemical mindset to follow her journey into the alembic of painting, we turn again to Hillman. We want to see if we can finger the threads of a new possibility: Varo's paintings, if we can decode their mysterious metaphorical messages, may support our ability to successfully address trauma and cultural complexes—experiences and qualities split off from consciousness at the group level as intolerable and dystonic to the group identity—related to patriarchal misogyny.

From the perspective of alchemical psychology, Hillman believed there is a relationship between the black of the *nigredo* and the depressed blue of melancholy. For Hillman, the black of the *nigredo* furthers a person's process of transformation through "the suppression of color and the absence of light" (2010: 109), scorching and blighting the psyche. "The appearance of blue in the coloration process," on the other hand,

> indicates that span of the spectrum where thought and image begin to coalesce, images provide the medium for thoughts while reflections take an imaginative turn away from the dark and confined frustration of the *nigredo* and toward the wider horizon of mind. (110)

"The blue shadow," Hillman concluded, "is the imaginal ground that allows the eye to see imaginatively... The shift to blue allows air so that the nigredo can meditate itself, ... recognize that this very shadow state expresses 'the essence of things.' " (111).

With Varo in mind, Hillman's perspective suggests that the blue moods of melancholy helped the artist access her imagination. Imagination, in turn, helped Varo transform what had been injured in the *nigredo* of traumatic experience into visions and ideas her waking ego could then shape with pencil and paintbrush.

With these thoughts, we begin to investigate the art and life of a painter whose images display the experience of following an alchemical path of transformation—a pattern of change that "occurs continuously in the unconscious as it strives throughout a lifetime to create a self" (Schwartz-Salant, 1998: 175). The working hypothesis here is that Varo's images on canvas and in her dream of the executioner bring vital insights to our efforts to make the world a place where everyone, including women and people of color, have what Frances Kendall called, in the context of race and white privilege, "an equitable opportunity to contribute and thrive" (2013: 1).

At a foundational level, our transit into Varo's alchemical world borrows from Jung, who believed that when we do the personal work of individuation we are contributing to the betterment of the world around us: "If the individual is not truly regenerated in spirit, society cannot be either, for society is the sum total of individuals in need of redemption" (Jung, 1957/1970: para. 536). Elsewhere in "The Undiscovered Self," Jung described the relationship between the personal work of individuation and the advancement of culture in more specific terms: "Anyone who has insight into his own actions, and has thus found access to the unconscious, involuntarily exercises an influence on his environment" (para. 583). Crystallizing Jung's thinking around the relationship between the personal work of individu-ation and transformation at the collective level, Edinger wrote,

> [People] who are aware of the operation of the opposites within them-selves have ... experienced the *coniunctio*—the subject matter of the *Mysterium*. Such people, then, are conscious carriers of the opposites. And, to the extent that such individuals exist and carry the opposites within themselves, they do not feed the exteriorization of the terrible strife between the opposites. There is a reason to believe that if society is to be redeemed, it will be done through the cumulative efforts of such individuals. And when a sufficient number of people carry the con-sciousness of wholeness, the world itself has a chance to become whole. (1995: 325–6)

The reverse is true as well—that individuals suffer trauma at the hands of a collective in need of redemption. "My practice," Hillman argued,

> tells me I can no longer distinguish clearly between neurosis of self and neurosis of world, psychopathology of self and psychopathology of world. Moreover, it tells me that to place neurosis and psychopathology solely in personal reality is a delusional repression of what is actually, realistically, being experienced. (1982: 93)

When either psychology or art criticism fail to examine the personal wound for its collective traces, these disciplines collude with the cultural and pol-itical mechanisms of power, oppression, and repression. With healing at both personal and collective levels in mind, it is important to follow Varo's work through an alchemical process that finds within personal trauma cultural pathologies inflicted by the patriarchy—a process of transform-ation that points to the redemptive power of the disavowed and abjected feminine.

Shortly, we will look in detail at a host of Varo's paintings, pieces painted during the last decade of the artist's life, which ended unexpectedly, as we have said, with a heart attack in Mexico City in the fall of 1963. We also explore the images in Varo's dream of the executioner. Our intent is to mine the images, sifting into these representations of the artist's unconscious inner life. We make the journey to fathom a message—for Varo was communi-cating with us through her images. Through her paintings, Varo wanted us to experience the surprise and wonder of divine forces. She also wanted us to know piercing truths about patriarchy, including how male domination silences female expression, annihilates a woman's ability to experience a cohesive sense of self, and deprives both men and women of wholeness.

Working with the images in Varo's paintings and with the motifs and symbols related to the imagery of her dream of the executioner, we engage in *mundificatio*, an alchemically psychological purification process that involves "the removal of the superfluities that always cling to merely natural products, and especially to the symbolic unconscious contents which the alchemist found projected into matter" (Jung, 1946/1966: para. 486). For Jung, working to "reduce the dream material to its most general principles ... is what the laboratory worker called the *extractio animae*, and what in the psychological field we would call the working-through of the idea contained in the dream" (para. 486).

In his 1936 essay "Individual Dream Symbolism in Relation to Alchemy," Jung wrote about a process he called *imaginatio*, one method for producing the alchemical *lapis*, a metaphor used to represent the successful transmutation of a base substance into a more purified one:

> The *imaginatio* is to be understood here as the real and literal power to create images ... *Imaginatio* is the active evocation of (inner) images... an authentic feat of thought or ideation, which does not spin aimless and groundless fantasies 'into the blue'—does not, that is to say, just play with its objects, but tries to grasp the inner facts and portray them in images true to their nature. This activity is an *opus*, a work. (1936/1968: para. 219)

In this alchemical work, we travel with Varo into the realm of *imaginatio*, where we find metaphorical realms of redemption, love, and wonder. Here, in these symbolic spaces of soul, we experience and reflect upon the processes of transformation at work in the artist's life and work. Through the experience of her imaginal opus, we come to understand the individuation demands that compelled Varo to paint not only so she could heal from, and even transform, the traumas of her life, but also so she could point us in the direction of a world that works for everyone, not just those with patriarchal privilege and power.

Feminist and Jungian analyst Marion Woodman saw "patriarchy as a power principle" that, consumed by exerting "control over" self and other (as cited in Hoff, 1997: para. 21), oppresses women and sacrifices the relational feminine with its "connective quality of Eros" in both women and men (Jung, 1951/1968: para. 29). Tracking in similar terrain, Sharp described the power complex as being "associated with an attitude that seeks to subordinate all influences and experience to the supremacy of the personal ego" (1991: 101). When this occurs, "where love reigns, there is no will to power; and where the will to power is paramount, love is lacking" (Jung, 1943/1966: para. 78).

Logically, Jung contended, the opposite of the connective nature of Eros is fear or *phobos*. We see in the patriarchal will to power a defense against the fear of the feminine principle of Eros, the nature of which entangles one in the vulnerabilities of embodied, relational experience and interdependence.

Moreover, as Woodman noted, the feminine principle is rooted in the cyclical nature of life in which "all change, all growth, presupposes the death of the old" (Woodman & Sieff, 2009: 194). "The terror of this unknown force" contained within the archetypal Feminine, wrote Jungian analyst Sylvia Shaindel Senensky, "is at the base of the strictures of patriarchy" and its preoccupation with control and domination (2003: 87). In this regard, Woodman differentiated the Death Mother as the feminine in service to the "need for power, control, safety, and domination" from the Apocalyptic Mother, who precipitates the death of values "rooted in fear and power" (Woodman & Sieff, 2009: 194). The Death Mother "prevents new life from coming in," turning "life into stone"; in contrast, the Apocalyptic Mother seeds death and destruction, sacrificing the old "to create space for the life we have yet to live" (194).

In her paintings and in her dream confrontation with the executioner, Varo created a generative space between phobos and Eros, holding the tension between her experience of the traumatic oppression of women and the emergent, numinous, and creative qualities of the Feminine. In this way, Varo's paintings become more than profound pieces of art—infused with the alchemical power of *imaginatio,* they become symbolic acts of resistance that protest the patriarchal sacrifice of love as a defense against loss.

All art is propaganda: Patriarchy and Varo's alchemical practice of painting

Like other artists contemporaneous to her, Varo's life and art are grounded in the Spanish and Basque culture, and in the horrors of the Spanish Civil War and World War II. Indeed, Varo was hardly the first Spanish artist to use creative expression as a form of propaganda. Picasso, for example, painted *Guernica* as a political statement—the mural-sized oil painting first exhibited at the Spanish display at the International Exposition in Paris in 1937 was the artist's way of expressing his rage at the bombing of civilians in a Basque village by the Luftwaffe during the Spanish Civil War. Salvador Dalí, like Varo a student at the Royal Academy of Fine Arts of San Fernando in Madrid during the 1920s, shocked viewers with images that conveyed a hatred of conformity and evoked "a telling vision of the world as a site of anxiety and displacement" following the losses of World War I "and the ominous shadows of annihilation that were cast by the Great War" (Stich, 1990: 91, 86). Nationalist militia assassinated poet and playwright Federico García Lorca in August 1936. Lorca's work was censored in Spain for nearly two decades, in part because homoerotic themes threatened patriarchal masculine values.

George Orwell may not have been Spanish, but Varo's country of birth nevertheless played a decisive role in the creation of *1984,* a novel about the terrors of totalitarian government that Orwell based in part on his frontline experiences fighting for the Republican army during the Spanish Civil War. In his introduction to George Packer's collection of Orwell's critical essays, Keith Gessen took readers into the trenches on the night in 1937 when Orwell was shot in the throat and almost died. Gessen wrote of the impact of the sniper's bullet on Orwell's perceptions of the world and upon the development of his voice as a writer:

> Spain gave him a jolt—not the fighting or the injury, though these had their effects, but the calculated campaign of deception he saw in the press when he got back [to London from the war] ... "Early in life I had noticed that no event is ever correctly reported in a newspaper," Orwell recalled, "but in Spain, for the first time, I saw newspaper reports which did not bear any relation to the facts, not even the relationship which is implied in an ordinary lie. I saw great battles reported where there had been no fighting, and complete silence where hundreds of men had been killed... This kind of thing is frightening to me, because it often gives me the feeling that the very concept of objective truth is fading out of the world." (2008: xxvi)

In 1942, Orwell wrote a series of three reviews on the poetry of T. S. Eliot, working to pinpoint the meaning of the poem, *Prufrock*. "It is fashionable to say," Orwell wrote,

> that in verse only the words count and the "meaning" is irrelevant, but in fact every poem contains a prose-meaning, and when the poem is any good it is meaning which the poet urgently wishes to express. All art is to some extent propaganda. (2008: 198)

Varo, of course, worked not as a poet or writer, as Orwell did, but as a painter from the lineage of Surrealism, an art movement that featured the artistic expression of unconscious processes. Yet with the pieces she painted, Varo was producing propaganda, for her images convey symbolic messages sent from the unseen spaces of the unconscious psyche, realms inhabited by archetypal forces trying to birth themselves into the material world in a bid to further the evolution of things. Moreover, what distinguishes Varo from her artistic contemporaries—such as Picasso, Lorca, and the surrealist Dalí—is that she worked from the perspective of a woman and the Feminine. Varo's paintings are peopled with figures that strike one as female and yet are abstractly drawn, as if pointing to a presence or the embodiment of that which is archetypal, more than personal. As we shall see, these figures are often engaged in activities associated with both women and the archetypal Feminine, such as weaving, an act that can be seen as symbolic of the relational, ecological Feminine in which all life is woven together (Sullivan, 1989: 20).

Working not with words, as Orwell did, but with images, Varo practiced an artistic form of alchemical psychology. Like the owl in her 1957 painting, *Creation of the Birds*, Varo is a composite creature: a hybrid blend of artist, social justice activist, and symbolic alchemist. Combining these talents, Varo works by herself, on herself. Her paintings project images of the changes taking place in her inner life and in her relationship with the oppression she experiences in the outer world. Varo worked with pigment and paintbrush to engage with unconscious personal and collective forces. She painted to breathe life into the ghosts that haunt and archetypal presences that people her inner world. In psychological and spiritual ways, art became for Varo an alchemical oven, the warmth of which produces a cold clarity of the mind. Scholar Gloria Durán quoted Ida Rodriguez Prampolini, a Mexican academic, art historian, and cultural preservationist, referring to Varo: "La imagen, antés de surgir, está detenida tan largo tiempo en la mano del pintor, que se enfría, se torna intelectual [The image, before emerging, is held so long in the painter's hand, that it cools, becomes intellectual]" (as cited in Durán, 1988: 303).

However, as Nobel Prize recipient physicist Frank Wilczek warned, in attempting to see through the mechanical to the quantum level of reality, "knowledge without imagination is barren" ("Why Science Needs Imagination and Beauty," 2013: para. 1). As a creative artist peering through the distortions of ordinary lies that so disturbed Orwell, and searching through the obfuscating assumptions of collective, patriarchal life to glimpse the trueness of the unconscious, shapes and colors bubble in the cauldron of Varo's imagination. With her mind and paintbrush, Varo stirs a dangerous brew, for imagination, wrote Carlota Caulfield, a scholar from Mills College, "subverts reality and causes the surrealist object to appear" (1999: para. 4). In this way, Varo shaped images that speak to changes and growth at intimate layers of personal life but also at the level of the collective.

For Varo, painting was an alchemical vessel, her images heated by her capacity to hold the patriarchally determined polarity between reason and the masculine principle of *Logos*, on the one hand, and the imagination and the feminine principle of Eros, on the other. In 1957, in *Creation of the Birds*, Varo painted herself as an owl seated at a desk, a violin-heart powering her paintbrush as she fashions birds from light streaming from a star through a nearby window and refracted through a prism. The painting, like her art, is a vessel containing Varo's passion for the transcendent and numinous. Hillman wrote about the importance of such a containing vessel to the transformation processes at work in alchemy:

Alchemy is a profession of marginals; those at the edge. Those who live from their own fires, sweating it out, self-sustaining their own temperatures which may be at variance with the collective climate.

Tapas: the ardor of internal heat. In India the sage sits in the Himalayan snow and with his own body heat melts a place to be, contained by his own containment. (2010: 21)

According to Hillman, the flame that fires the alchemical ardor for the divine needs to be contained, held in. To practice alchemy, an artifex needs a vessel—an instrument of keeping, as Hillman called it (2010: 38–9). "Vessels," Hillman said, "are the way we embrace events, store them, style them" (38). Working in a vessel, heat can be held "inside the head by warming the mind's reveries. Imagine, project, fantasize, think" (37). Here, Hillman tracked into the terrain of interiority: "Within? Where is that? Within the vessel, whatever the vessel may be: wherever there is a contained and separated focus, a holding zone, something cooking" (39). "Interiority," Hillman added,

> is within all things—the garden bed that is in preparation, the poem that is the focus of attentive emotions. Keep a close watch on these interiorities; by watching we are vesseling, for it is the glass vessel that allows the watching and watching provides the very separation and containment expressed concretely by the glass vessel. (39)

Varo painted, watching herself in the mirror of her images. Other selves, in turn, watch *her*, searching through canvased worlds for wonder, animation, and love. For Varo often painted herself—a woman with hair the color of fire, dark eyes in the shape of almonds, a look tinged with longing and sadness reflecting across her ambivalent face. In other painted worlds, Varo imagined women at work catching moonlight in a cage or weaving the garment of a new world. Varo's characters are always searching, devoted to exploration, determined to locate and engage with the numinous unseen forces that power human life.

Mirror of the marvelous: Art, psyche, and the experience of the numinous

Varo's way of blending art and psyche attunes her work to the alchemical affinity with the *numinous*, a term Jung borrowed from Rudolph Otto, a German theologian, philosopher, and comparative religionist. Otto described the profound psychological experience of the deep Self as a mystery that is both "daunting and ... fascinating" (1923/1958: 31). Schwartz-Salant evoked the alchemical affinity with divine presence in his introduction to *Jung on Alchemy*:

> Alchemy ... is a body of thought that requires that one be open to an Other dimension of existence in order both to understand the basic

concepts, and to operate with them in an attempt to transform material life and the human personality as well. This Other dimension, which is often referred to as God in alchemical thinking, is that domain of human experience that, in early cultures, was mediated by the shaman, or priest, and was eventually codified into dogma in later religions. This codification was always balanced or opposed by a counter-movement of mystics who were determined not to lose a more immediate link with the sacred. Many alchemists were such people, informed by their visions and by being 'killed and reborn' through their experiences of the *numinosum*. (1995: 6)

An artist, Varo grounded her practice of alchemical psychology in metaphor—in the use of images and symbols. From a Jungian perspective, Hillman wrote, "metaphors are psychological language—and all alchemy is metaphorical" (2010: 152). For Varo, images were metaphorical vessels, alchemical ovens in which the beauty and terror of the numinous could be cooked into a form—a painting—that baked the human soul into embodied material experience. "Images," Hillman added, "are not reflections of the world, but are the light by which we see the world" (153). Fired with imagination, Varo painted new selves and new worlds, the images carrying the spark of the soul, or the transpersonal Self, from the unconscious.

Why study the paintings of Remedios Varo? What meaning might be added to our own experience through symbolic exploration of the motifs that come alive in this artist's life and art? Here, at the beginning, an early answer: We follow Varo to continue the work she was about: symbolizing and embodying the sacred, the mythic, in service not only to our own processes of personal growth but also to the unmaking of patriarchal structures that oppress women and marginalize people of color. For in the amplified images in Varo's paintings, and from her dream of the executioner, we see that the recognition of a numinous cosmos infused with wonder and love is menacing to fear-based patriarchal structures.

In what follows, we explore the art and life of a woman traumatized by war and patriarchy and tormented by psychological pain. But Varo did something with her suffering: through the practice of painting, the artist devoted herself to what Jungian analyst Naomi Ruth Lowinsky calls "the mystery of becoming conscious and present to the divinity of human suffering" (2003: 331). Through a nuanced amplification of the images and symbols in the artist's paintings and her dream of the executioner, we see in Varo's experience that psychological courage cannot come into being without fear. Through the eye of trauma and affliction, we see in Varo that death (figuratively and perhaps even literally) is a necessary ingredient in the alchemical transformation of human life. We see revealed in her painted and dream images a redemptive possibility for unmaking a culture based on the will to power into one centered in love.

Robert Sardello, who writes on depth psychology, archetypal psychology, spirituality, and the development of soul life, describes the art historian's meticulous attention to imagery as "a practice manual for meditating" with an artist's paintings (2008: ix). Willing to enter into a reverie of sorts, the viewer using this approach to being with painted images can come upon "a whole new way of questioning—of *questing*—not in order to find an answer or solve a problem, but rather as a way of developing the inner capacity of letting things speak for themselves" (ix). "Working with painting as a spiritual practice," Sardello wrote,

> requires something very different than other forms of spiritual practices. This work takes place in the realm of feeling. That is, it is necessary to enter into the feeling of the paintings, not what the paintings make us feel. (ix)

How might this sensitivity to feeling inform the experience of engaging with the paintings of Remedios Varo? And would a similar sensibility work with contemplation of the imagery in her dream of the executioner? Varo's paintings, and some of the images in the artist's dream of death, evoke a world of wonder, of unseen forces. They create a subjective experience of liberation. In *What Painting Is*, James Elkins evoked the practice of spiritual alchemy. A painter-turned-art historian, Elkins approached alchemy as

> a magical language to explore what it is a painter really does in the studio—the smells, the mess, the struggle to control the uncontrollable, the special knowledge only painters hold of how colors will mix, and how they will look. (1999: back cover)

Holding in mind the image of Varo as painter and female alchemical adept, and the creative process of painting (or dreaming) as the vessel in which the projected expressions of her unconscious are being cooked, Elkins' description of the interface between art and alchemy seems to apply:

> For a "spiritual" alchemist, whatever happens in the furnace is an allegory of what takes place in the alchemist's mind or soul. The fetid water that begins the process is like the darkened spirit, confused and half-rotten. As the substances mingle and fuse, they become purer, stronger, and more valuable, just as the soul becomes more holy. The philosopher's stone is the sign of the mind's perfection, the almost transcendent state where all impurities have been killed, burned, melted away, or fused, and the soul is bright and calm. Alchemists paid close attention to their crucibles, watching substances mingle and separate, always in some degree thinking of the struggles and contaminations of

earthly life, and ultimately wondering about their own souls and minds. (1999: 4)

Writing with the value of studying Jung's work on alchemical symbolism in mind, Schwartz-Salant pinpointed the psychological purpose of paying close attention to the way the alchemists lived quiet lives devoted to participating in the psyche's mysterious method for destroying old structures in order for new ones to be created:

> The alchemists knew, from their own and from the accumulated experience of centuries of traditional cultures, that their personalities could be transformed. Through initiation rites they felt different, behaved differently, and grew in new ways. No longer bound to the compulsion of adolescent states of mind or to the flights into promiscuity that wasted their sexual energies, people in traditional cultures learned that they could "die" and be "reborn." And in their reborn form they actually did see the world differently... Their imagination could become a guide to truth instead of being a capricious trickster. And some alchemists could feel a guiding center that formed in their innermost being and which was strangely linked in feeling to experiences of their most ecstatic journeys. (1995: 5)

"Alchemy," Schwartz-Salant reflected,

> developed within this respect for a human concern for the sacred. As a consequence, its very methods were intrinsically bound to the power of illumination and the imagination, and it especially applied the ideas of death and rebirth, so central to initiation rites and mystical experience, to material and psychological change. (5)

Jung wrote that the *vas bene clausum*, the well-sealed vessel, "is a precautionary measure very frequently mentioned in alchemy, and is the equivalent of the magic circle" (1936/1968, para. 219). Both vessel and circle "protect what is within from the intrusion and admixture of what is without, as well as to prevent it from escaping" (para. 219). The equivalent of the alchemical vessel, for Varo, is a painted canvas. More than likely, in retreating into her studio and her inner life, Varo sought to differentiate from and keep out influences that would silence or criticize her and paint from the deep well of her imagination, intellect, and feeling. Yet Varo also seems committed in her imagery to gifting something from her creativity to the surrounding world. In *Creation of the Birds*, for example, the artist painted herself as an androgynous wise owl whose images pulse forth from a violin heart, transforming colors and light that enter the canvas from beyond it into birds who then fly off the canvas, through a window and into the world.

Wonder, Surrealism, and Jungian psychology

Varo's paintings often feature a person looking for wonder, for something miraculous. Emerging from the carnage of World War I, surrealist artists embarked upon a quest for the fantastic and the impossible. They did not shy away from the upheaval and confusion present as those in the post-war world confronted "new concerns about the self and society" (Stich, 1990: 11). In fact, wrote art historian Sidra Stich, the Surrealists "exalted in reclaiming the suppressed realms of human expression and in confronting contradiction, difference, disjunction, multiplicity, rupture, and incongruity" (11).

Although she was a Surrealist, Varo's work exemplifies an unswerving commitment to discovering a deeper wisdom—a woman's truth and authenticity occluded by patriarchal complexes. Devoted to evoking a woman's experience of transforming what is base in one's nature into a more conscious life, Varo's work is distinct in its feminism. Further, for Spanish scholar Durán, "the paintings of Varo ... prove that if the inspiration for feminist surrealism lies at all in modern psychology, it is not in Freud, but in Carl Gustav Jung" (1988: 302). "Even the titles of Varo's paintings," Durán noted,

> are a reminder of many of Jung's preoccupations such as the quest for wholeness. The related theme of the arduous voyage is also common, as we see in her *Explor[ation of] the Sources of the Orinoco [River]*, where the woman explorer in an egg-like vessel (which has been compared to the alchemist's egg) finally reaches the river's source where she finds a crystal goblet housed within a tree of the submerged forest. The waters pouring from the mystical goblet or chalice have produced the river itself. (302)

Durán suggested that other motifs common in Varo's work—water, numinous light, magical stones, and the quest of the explorer who seeks the treasure hard to attain—"turn out to have their counterpart in Jung's thinking" (1988: 302). In the surrealist fascination for "the chance amorous encounter," as found in Varo, who used the same title (*Encounter*) for two 1959 paintings, Durán sees something like Jung's ideas around synchronicity. One of these two works

> portrays a statue descending from a pedestal ... to meet a woman made of fire. Varo tells us humorously that this is an ideal encounter for a statue who is always cold. Fire and life, therefore, animate Varo's world, turning cold stone into living matter... The animation of matter is part and parcel of their interest, and that of Jung, in the medieval study of alchemy. (302–3)

Steeped in the Jungian belief in "the liberating effect of the unconscious" (Durán, 1988: 301), Varo's work grew from the ground of alchemical psychology's attempt to bring forth what Jung, following the sixteenth-century alchemist Gerhard Dorn, called "the fire-point, the divine centre in man" (1955–56/1970: para. 49). For alchemists, this image of the "God within us" (1928/1966, para. 399) must be liberated through alchemical operations intended to reveal the divine aspect imprisoned in matter. Although, clearly, for Varo the divine aspect that needs to be liberated—and made conscious and available so that humanity might engage and partner with it—is the Feminine.

Jung posited this divine presence as the Self, by which he meant the ego-transcendent and transpersonal entirety of the psyche, or the "archetype of wholeness" (Sharp, 1991: 119). "Varo's art," Durán wrote, "reflects her personal independence and her search for self or wholeness" (1988: 308). The artist evoked her quest by painting motifs of creation, bringing to life through metaphor a "fairy-tale world of light, music, harmony, and the tale of the quest to reach beyond the normal, daylight world and to find our place in the universe" (310). Engaged in such a quest, Durán argued, "consciously or unconsciously, Varo's work incorporates the symbols that Jung has identified with the search for self or wholeness" (305).

From a Jungian perspective, the way we engage with and understand the deep Self is through symbols, or what Jung called the "primordial image" (1921/1971: para. 746). "I call the image *primordial*" or archaic, Jung wrote, "when it possesses unmistakable mythological parallels" (para. 684). For Jung, the word *primordial* described an archetype that connects the image possessing an archaic character with the collective layer of the psyche that is older than human history (para. 747). Primordial images, he believed, emerge from the creative womb of the unconscious, as a "condensation of the living process" (para. 749). "Wisdom," Jung wrote in *Modern Man in Search of a Soul*, "is a return to these symbols" (as cited in Durán, 1988: 305).

Primordial images are ripe with meaning that points back to mysterious and numinous forces. Birthed in the collective layer of the objective psyche, primordial images relate to a feminine mode of holistic thinking that brings "together the inner experience with its outer reality" and to the nonlinear feminine that connects consciousness with the unknown and the nonpersonal forces of the Self through symbolic and literal cycles of birth, death, and rebirth (Sullivan, 1989: 23). Jung believed that alchemy—a metaphoric process for working in the psyche as a vessel that creates increased consciousness from the dead or outworn aspects of life—offered a possible "solution through compensation to the patriarchal suppression of the feminine" (Schwartz-Salant, 1995: 26).

Devoted to the search for self-discovery, Varo's inspiration for her paintings drew from a deep well that included everything from alchemy, astrology, and mysticism to magic, the occult, and science. "Deeply superstitious and strongly attuned to nature, she held a mystical belief in forces beyond the self that influence and direct events. She approached both her life and her art committed to this vision" (Kaplan, 1988: 7). "Varo," Kaplan noted, "was a sensitive, vivacious, humorous woman, intelligent and alive to the world" (7). Kaplan quoted a friend of Varo's from Mexico in a bid to reveal something of the artist's inner spirit:

> Like a vibratile insect, always alert, she lived in perpetual exploration of clues, of revelations, expanding her intelligence and her intuition to understand the hidden meanings of being and of life... She had an exceptional love for all that could be experienced through the senses: her touch passed and repassed over the warm surface of wood or the coolness and solidity of a rock. She could be absorbed for hours in the weave of a cloth or the play of light on a window pane. She saw in everything the life latent within; she observed the most diverse objects, delighting in all their details, the infinite hues, the textures, colors, and forms. (7–8)

Kaplan highlighted the autobiographical nature of Varo's mature works. "Most of Varo's personages bear the delicate heart-shaped face with large almond eyes, long sharp nose, and thick mane of lively hair that marked the artist's own appearance" (1988: 9). For Kaplan, the artistic personas Varo created for herself

> serve as self-portraits transmuted through fantasy. Despite her warning—"I do not wish to talk about myself because I hold very deeply the belief that what is important is the work, not the person"— so much of the work is metaphorically autobiographical that exploring the interplay between her life and her art is essential to understanding her significance. (9)

Although Varo, whose mature images grew from the ground of Surrealism, an art movement that featured the artistic expression of unconscious processes, and from the Western tradition we know as depth psychology, she was by no means a psychoanalyst. Varo painted to make art of her pain. She painted to breathe life into imaginal forces she could not see. Archetypally speaking, Varo painted to make change, in herself, and in the world around her.

Psychology, alchemy, and the mercurial nature of the *prima materia*

Beginning with the next chapter, we look in some detail at the connections that can be made between Varo's personal search for the numinous archetypal presences that animate human experience and her artistic practice of alchemical psychology. As with all alchemy, such a depth psychological descent into Varo's imaginal world begins with the *prima materia*, the raw experience of inner and outer life. Before engaging further with the imagery in Varo's paintings, and in her dream of death by beheading, it will help to ground our imaginal investigations in Jung's key thoughts around the nature of the *prima materia*.

"In alchemical texts," wrote Schwartz-Salant, "the term *prima materia* refers to energies and processes which are most fundamental to the transformative process" (1998: 32). Yet like a fish that shimmers for a moment below the surface of the water, then darts out of view into the shadowy depths, the *prima materia* is difficult to hold in one's mind. A concept that hints at the foundational aspects of life, the *prima materia* includes and transcends human experience. Jung tried to put his finger on the alluring but also confounding nature of the alchemical first matter:

> The *prima materia* [is] "tantalizing": it is cheap as dirt and can be had everywhere, only nobody knows it; it is as vague and evasive as the lapis that is to be produced from it; it has a "thousand names." And the worst thing is that without it the work cannot even be begun. (1942/ 1967: para. 209)

Jung added:

> It is incorrect to maintain that the alchemists never said what the *prima materia* was: on the contrary, they gave all too many definitions and so were everlastingly contradicting themselves. For one alchemist the *prima materia* was quicksilver, for others it was ore, iron, gold, lead, salt, sulphur, vinegar, water, air, fire, earth, blood, water of life, lapis, poison, spirit, cloud, sky, dew, shadow, sea, mother, moon, dragon, Venus, chaos, microcosm … Ruland's *Lexicon* gives no less than fifty synonyms, and a great many more could be added. (1937/ 1968: para. 425)

From a sea swimming with alchemical metaphors, Schwartz-Salant noted that "Johannes Fabricius, a scholar of alchemy, takes Jung to task for 'never specifying his general assumption of the *prima materia* as a symbol for the erupting unconscious psyche'" (1998: 33). Fabricius observed the *prima materia* as a "revival of those unconscious layers" that contain remnants of the turmoil and upheaval of adolescence (as cited in Schwartz-Salant, 1998: 33). Fabricius, Schwartz-Salant wrote, equated the *prima materia* with the adolescent "awakening of love in the midst of bewildering chaos, which is experienced as a process wherein the existing elements of creation dissolve while giving birth to a new cosmos" (33).

Fabricius's comments mesh nicely with the artistic intention underlying the life and work of Remedios Varo, for this is why Varo painted: Her artistic "revival of those unconscious layers" birthed a new cosmos on her canvases as she worked to make the world new again through imagination. Like the woman in *Solar Music*, Varo used image and symbol to depict the numinous experience of playing with her violin bow the streams of light that illuminate the darkness of the forest with its golden light. Varo's *prima materia*, however, went beyond the personal and even the human. With an eye that saw beyond Western science's one-sided objectification of the world, Varo's sensibilities aligned with the alchemists who "believed that any substance had its own nature … and that this nature existed not only on the concrete, material plane but on the emotional, mental and spiritual planes as well" (Schwartz-Salant, 1995: 29). Moreover, in paintings such as *Creation of the Birds,* the metaphysical and transcendent nature of Varo's images suggests contact with the numinous as first matter that propels and cooks within her creativity.

As an artist, Varo drew from a deep well of disciplines as inspiration for her work. Art historians and scholars, including Tere Arcq and Fariba Bogzaran, have commented on Varo's interest in alchemical psychology, most often in biographical surveys of the artist's life or in essays or book chapters exploring the meaning and symbolism of specific themes and paintings. In what follows we dig deeper into the alchemical soil that nurtured Varo's mysterious imagery. Along the way we discover that, for Varo, the alchemical transformation of old forms into new ones served not only as processes of personal growth but also as fuel for the growth and evolution of the world around her. The *Workshop of God* is one name the alchemists used for the laboratory in which they performed their operations. Let us now step with Varo into this numinous space.

Note

1   This is the author's translation of the words Octavio Paz imagines Varo saying in "Visiones y Desapariciones de Remedios Varo" ["Visions and Disappearances of Remedios Varo"], a poem by Paz in *Remedios Varo* (Paz & Callois, 1966: 8–10).

References

Agosin, M. (1998). Introduction. In M. Agosin (Ed.), *A woman's gaze: Latin American women artists* (9–26). Fredonia, NY: White Pine Press.

Akron, & Banzhaf, H. (1995). *The Crowley tarot: The handbook to the cards by Aleister Crowley and Lady Frieda Harris* (C. Grimm, Trans.). Stamford, CT: U.S. Games Systems.

Bair, D. (2004). *Jung: A biography.* New York, NY: Back Bay Books.

Barron, M. W. (2006). About the cover art: *Useless science, or the alchemist* by Remedios Varo. *Spring: A Journal of Archetype and Culture, 74.*

Caulfield, C. (1999, Spring). Textual and visual strategies in the world of Remedios Varo. *Corner*, 2. Retrieved from www.cornermag.net/corner02/page04.htm

Crucifixion. (2010). In A. Ronnberg & K. Martin (Eds.), *The book of symbols: Reflections on archetypal images* (744–5). Cologne, Germany: Taschen.

Durán, G. (1988). The antipodes of Surrealism: Salvador Dalí and Remedios Varo. *Symposium: A Quarterly Journal in Modern Literatures*, 42(4), 297–311.

Edinger, E. (1985). *Anatomy of the psyche: Alchemical symbolism in psychotherapy.* La Salle, IL: Open Court.

Edinger, E. (1995). *The Mysterium lectures: A journey through C. G. Jung's Mysterium Coniunctionis.* Toronto, Canada: Inner City Books.

Elkins, J. (1999). *What painting is.* New York, NY: Routledge.

Engel, P. (1986). *Remedios Varo: Science into art.* New York, NY: New York Academy of Science.

Gessen, K. (2008). Introduction. In G. Packer (Ed.), *George Orwell: All art is propaganda* (xvii–xxxii). New York, NY: Houghton, Mifflin, Harcourt.

Hannah, B. (2006). *The archetypal symbolism of animals: Lectures given at the C. G. Jung Institute, Zurich, 1954–1958.* Wilmette, IL: Chiron.

Hauck, D. W. (1999). *The emerald tablet: Alchemy for personal transformation.* New York, NY: Penguin Press.

Henderson, J. (1984). *Cultural attitudes in psychological perspective.* Toronto, Canada: Inner City Books.

Hillman, J. (1982). *The thought of the heart and the soul of the world.* Woodstock, CT: Spring Publications.

Hillman, J. (2005). *Senex & puer.* Putnam, CT: Spring Publications.

Hillman, J. (2010). *Alchemical psychology.* Putman, CT: Spring Publications.

Hoff, B. (1997). Inner man, inner woman: An interview with Marion Woodman. *M.E.N. Magazine* (1993, December). menweb.org/woodman.htm

Hollis, J. (1995). *Tracking the gods: The place of myth in modern life.* Toronto, Canada: Inner City Books.

Hollis, J. (2004). *Mythologems: Incarnations of the invisible world.* Toronto, Canada: Inner City Books.

Jung, C. G. (1928/1966). The relations between the ego and the unconscious (R. F. C. Hull, Trans.). In H. Read et al. (Eds.), *The collected works of C. G. Jung* (Vol. 7, 2nd ed., 121–241). Princeton, NJ: Princeton University Press.

Jung, C. G. (1943/1966). On the psychology of the unconscious (R. F. C. Hull, Trans.). In H. Read et al. (Eds.), *The collected works of C. G. Jung* (Vol. 7, 2nd ed., 1–119). Princeton, NJ: Princeton University Press.

Jung, C. G. (1946/1966). The psychology of the transference (R. F. C. Hull, Trans.). In H. Read et al. (Eds.), *The collected works of C. G. Jung* (Vol. 16, 2nd ed., 163–323). Princeton, NJ: Princeton University Press.

Jung, C. G. (1942/1967). Paracelsus as a spiritual phenomenon (R. F. C,. Hull,, Trans.). In H. Read et al. (Eds.), *The collected works of C. G. Jung* (Vol. 13, 109–89). Princeton, NJ: Princeton University Press.

Jung, C. G. (1936/1968). Individual dream symbolism in relation to alchemy (R. F. C. Hull, Trans.). In H. Read et al. (Eds.), *The collected works of C. G. Jung* (Vol. 12, 2nd ed., 39–224). Princeton, NJ: Princeton University Press.

Jung, C. G. (1937/1968). Religious ideas in alchemy (R. F. C. Hull, Trans.). In H. Read et al. (Eds.), *The collected works of C. G. Jung* (Vol. 12, 2nd ed., 225–483). Princeton, NJ: Princeton University Press.

Jung, C. G. (1943/1968). Introduction to the religious and psychological problems of alchemy (R. F. C. Hull, Trans.). In H. Read et al. (Eds.), *The collected works of C. G. Jung* (Vol. 12, 2nd ed., 1–38). Princeton, NJ: Princeton University Press.

Jung, C. G. (1951/1968). The self (R. F. C. Hull, Trans.). In (H. Read et al., Eds.). *The collected works of C. G. Jung* (Vol. 9ii, 2nd ed., 23–35). Princeton, NJ: Princeton University Press.

Jung, C. G. (1937/1969). Psychological factors determining human behavior (R. F. C. Hull, Trans.). In H. Read et al. (Eds.), *The collected works of C. G. Jung* (Vol. 8, 2nd ed., 114–25). Princeton, NJ: Princeton University Press.

Jung, C. G. (1940/1969). Psychology and religion. In H. Read et al. (Eds.), *The collected works of C. G. Jung* (Vol. 11, 2nd ed., 3–107). Princeton, NJ: Princeton University Press.

Jung, C. G. (1948/1969). A review of the complex theory (R. F. C. Hull, Trans.). In H. Read et al. (Eds.), *The collected works of C. G. Jung* (Vol. 8, 2nd ed., 92–104). Princeton, NJ: Princeton University Press.

Jung, C. G. (1927/1970). Woman in Europe (R. F. C. Hull, Trans.). In H. Read et al. (Eds.), *The collected works of C. G. Jung* (Vol. 10, 2nd ed., 113–33). Princeton, NJ: Princeton University Press.

Jung, C. G. (1955–56/1970). *Mysterium coniunctionis* (R. F. C. Hull, Trans.) (H. Read et al., Eds.), *The collected works of C. G. Jung* (Vol. 14, 2nd ed.). Princeton, NJ: Princeton University Press.

Jung, C. G. (1957/1970). The undiscovered self (present and future) (R. F. C. Hull, Trans.). In H. Read et al. (Eds.), *The collected works of C. G. Jung* (Vol. 10, 2nd ed., 245–305). Princeton, NJ: Princeton University Press.

Jung, C. G. (1921/1971). Definitions (R. F. C. Hull, Trans.). In H. Read et al. (Eds.), *The collected works of C. G. Jung* (Vol. 6, 408–86). Princeton, NJ: Princeton University Press.

Kaplan, J. (1988). *Unexpected journeys: The art and life of Remedios Varo.* New York, NY: Abbeville Press.

Kendall, F. (2013). *Understanding white privilege: Creating pathways to authentic relationships across race* (2nd ed.). New York, NY: Routledge.

Kerr, J. (1993). *A most dangerous method: The story of Jung, Freud, and Sabina Spielrein.* New York, NY: Vintage Books.

Kristeva, J. (1987/1989). *The black sun: Depression and melancholia* (L. Roudiez, Trans.). New York, NY: Oxford University Press.

LeGrice, K. (2016). *Archetypal reflections: Insights and ideas from Jungian psychology.* London, UK: Muswell Hill Press.

Lowinsky, R. (2003). Wrestling with God: From the Book of Job to the poets of the Shoah. In J. Beebe (Ed.), *Terror, violence, and the impulse to destroy* (307–34). Einsiedeln, Switzerland: Daiman Verlag.

Orwell, G. (2008). T. S. Eliot. In G. Packer (Ed.), *George Orwell: All art is propaganda* (194–201). New York, NY: Houghton, Mifflin, Harcourt.

Otto, R. (1923/1958). *The idea of the holy* (J. Harvey, Trans.). New York, NY: Oxford University Press.

Paz, O., & Callois, R. (1966). *Remedios Varo*. Mexico City, Mexico: Ediciones ERA.

Sardello, R. (2008). Introduction. In K. Falk, *The unknown Hieronymus Bosch* (ix–xvi). Benson, NC: Goldenstone Press.

Schwartz-Salant, N. (1995). Introduction. In N. Schwartz-Salant (Ed.), *Jung on alchemy* (1–43). Princeton, NJ: Princeton University Press.

Schwartz-Salant, N. (1998). *The mystery of human relationship: Alchemy and the transformation of the self*. New York, NY: Routledge.

Senensky, S. S. (2003). *Healing and empowering the feminine: A labyrinth journey*. Wilmette, IL: Chiron.

Sharp, D. (1991). *C. G. Jung lexicon: A primer of terms & concepts*. Toronto, Canada: Inner City Books.

Sky. (2010). In A. Ronnberg & K. Martin (Eds.), *The book of symbols: Reflections on archetypal images* (56–7). Cologne, Germany: Taschen.

Šolc, V., & Didier, G. (2018). *Dark religion: Fundamentalism from the perspective of Jungian psychology*. Asheville, NC: Chiron.

Stich, S. (1990). *Anxious visions: Surrealist art*. Berkeley, CA: University Art Museum.

Sullivan, B. S. (1989). *Psychotherapy grounded in the feminine principle*. Asheville, NC: Chiron.

Varo, R. (1997/2018). *Letters, dreams & other writings* (M. Carson, Trans.). Cambridge, MA: Wakefield Press.

Why Science Needs Imagination and Beauty. (2013). *BBC Future*. Retrieved from www.bbc.com/future/article/20131127-secret-to-thinking-like-a-genius

Wilkerson, S. (2019). *A most mysterious union: The role of alchemy in Goethe's Faust*. Asheville, NC: Chiron.

Wilson, J. (2004). The abyss experience and the trauma complex: A Jungian perspective of posttraumatic stress disorder and dissociation. *Journal of Trauma & Dissociation, 5*(3), 43–67.

Woodman, M., & Sieff, D. (2009). Confronting Death Mother: An interview with Marion Woodman. *Spring: A Journal of Archetype and Culture (The Psychology of Violence), 81*, 177–200.

Chapter 2

The fructifying bonfire of trauma and death

As an individual and as an artist, Remedios Varo worked, as each of us does, with the unfiltered experiences of her life. As we have seen, *prima materia* is a term the alchemists used to refer to the basic components of one's life. From a Jungian perspective, the first matter of a person's life draws from instincts as well as from dream images and other fantasies, emotions, conflicts, and feeling-toned complexes, as we engage in the psychological work of individuation.

Remedios as remedy: The replacement child and a search for identity

For Varo, the first matter of her personal life includes a psychological challenge that may have begun the moment she was born. Remedios was so named by her mother, Doña Ignacia, "in dedication to the Virgen de los Remedios as a 'remedy' to forget an older daughter who had died" (Kaplan, 1988: 11). Did Remedios Varo know she was a replacement child— "a living child who comes to take the place of a dead one?" (Abramovitch, as cited in Schellinski, 2020: 21).

We do not know the dynamics of the family system into which Varo was born. Something we *do* know, however, is that when a child dies, parents can become overcome with grief. Replacement children are often conceived in an unconscious attempt by parents to assuage the grief they feel at the loss of a child who has died. "Rather than seeing the unique new being," Kristina Schellinski wrote, quoting John Bowlby, "parents may ... 'mislocate' a lost person and seek it in the presence of another" (2020: 51). Were these dynamics involved in, or related to, Varo's lifelong experience of loneliness and alienation, and her restless existential search for self-discovery? In addition, was the experience of being a substitute for a missing sister related to Varo's prominent fear of death, an image featured in the artist's dream of the executioner?

Our study of Varo's paintings offers evidence that the artist may, in fact, have used art as a way of working out identity issues related to her deceased older sister, for Varo's imagined worlds often include ghosts, hidden beings who reach out from behind walls or peer at her from below the floor. Are these figures expressions of a lost sister? Perhaps they are. "In an adult replacement child," Schellinski wrote, "the unconscious can be contaminated, even poisoned by the vestiges of the missing other" (2020: 157).

Remembering that images are multifaceted in their symbolism, it is also possible that the hidden beings in many of Varo's paintings could be symbolic depictions of the artist's search for self-discovery. "The challenge for [an adult] replacement child," Schellinski argued, "is the healing of its *inner image* of *other*: moving from *a representation of missing inner other* towards a representation of an *alive-and-present inner other* that can then allow for fulfilling relationship[s] with other human beings" (2020: 153, emphasis in original). Psychologically, effecting such a shift "requires becoming conscious of projections and ceasing compensatory attempts of finding *other* on the outside rather than within. Finding an inner image of the *inner animus/ anima, alive and well*, is necessary for connecting with the true self" (153). Perhaps these dynamics are one way of accounting for the importance, in Varo's dream of the executioner, of weaving her destiny with the man to whom she wished to be connected "for all eternity" (Varo, 1997/2018: 96). According to Schellinski, adult replacement children feel compelled to discover images of the contrasexual other (as Jung referred to the *anima* and *animus*) within their own soul.

Many, if not most, of Varo's painted characters are explorers; they are searching for something. From a Jungian perspective, we can consider Varo's imaginal explorers as projected expressions of the artist's "true self" in the process of coming "*back to life*" (Schellinski, 2020: 11, emphasis in original). In other words, through painting Varo may have been working to reconstruct her identity. She may have been working to shape an authentic and embodied sense of self that had been overshadowed, perhaps even occluded, by the specter of the missing other, that is, the dead, and therefore lost, sister. On a personal level, there is a powerful transformation at work in Varo's art. From a Jungian perspective, painting, for Varo, becomes a path of individuation, an artistic practice she engages in to express the voice—the music—of her soul. With the dynamics of the replacement child in mind, for Varo, painting helped the artist image a journey of transformation, a transit in which she traveled from the emptiness of non-being into a living sense of herself as a person in her own right.

At the risk of making too much of psychological dynamics that may or may not have impacted Varo's well-being, there is another aspect of the experience of the replacement child that is worth looking at briefly in the context of the artist's dream of the executioner and of her death by heart attack in the fall of 1963. When a living child substitutes for a dead one, the replacement child is forced to deal with "two archetypal forces, the most profound pair of opposites, of life and death ... *mingled* at the beginning of life" (Schellinski, 2020: 135, emphasis in original). "To reckon with images of the archetype of death," Schellinski observed, "is a difficult, if not impossible task for a child; it is often later, as an adult, that a replacement child will see a need to consciously enter into a dialogue with images of these archetypal forces" (135). Through painting, Varo seemed to face and integrate aspects of the shadow archetype. "An adult replacement child," Schellinski wrote, "needs to find the *positive shadow*, the unknown parts of its identity in those cases when its life force was overshadowed when parts of ego consciousness and unconscious parts of self were contaminated by elements of a disappeared person" (136, emphasis in original).

From a teleological perspective, could the psychological dynamics of the adult replacement child have uniquely positioned Varo in her unfolding and deepening exploration of the numinous Feminine to take us, as we continue to follow the artist through her painted images and dream of the executioner, into a relationship with life and death, not as opposites but as spiraling, creative partners?

Tension of opposites: Masculine and Feminine in the theater of war

In her paintings, Varo also expressed the distress she experienced when her mother forced her to attend school at a Catholic convent that stifled her self-expression and possibly harmed her ability to form a cohesive sense of self. From our look in Chapter Five at a series of three Varo paintings, it is clear that the middle-aged artist was working out feelings of confinement related to the distress she felt as a young girl at the convent in Spain.

Following the arc of Varo's life beyond her family of origin, the young artist's experience of the world became even more upsetting as she emerged into young adulthood. Varo was traumatized by war on two occasions, first by the violence in Madrid that preceded the Spanish Civil War in the 1930s, and later by the experience of being arrested and detained at a French prison camp during the winter of 1940.

Born in 1908, Varo grew up in a country in which liberals and conservatives had been fighting one another for political control for much of the nineteenth century. The conflict between those who wished to reform the Spanish government and conservatives determined to keep things the way they were boiled over in the fall of 1934, when coal miners armed with guns and explosives attacked and seized several towns. Conservatives called on the monarchist general Francisco Franco, who hired Moroccan mercenaries to suppress the rebellion. "The Moroccans," wrote Richard Rhodes, "were enthusiastic and inventive killers: castrating the wounded was a favorite sport, robbing the dead a recreation" (2015: 7). Then, in 1936, Spain voted a democratic government into office and banished Franco. With the taste of blood in their mouths, generals led by Franco commanded fighting forces hellbent "in the name of Christian Spain to overthrow the legitimate Spanish government and hack their way to power" (7).

According to Rhodes, Franco turned the overthrow of the secular Spanish state into a violent "religious crusade," burning churches and destroying statues of figures who carried the numinosity of religious and inspirational meaning (2015: 16). The people's militia targeted religious iconography and was only slightly less brutal. Pieces of liturgical vestments were cut from cassocks and stoles, then sewn onto military uniforms. "More radical anti-clericals," Rhodes wrote, "went beyond slapping idols," exhuming "the desiccated bodies of priests and nuns from church crypts and putting them on public display to expose their fetid mortality" (16). "With bullets flying in both directions and artillery shattering buildings," Rhodes added, anarchist militias even began executing priests, "the living idols of a church that had conspired with their class enemies to oppress them" (16).

Varo's personal experience of the Spanish Civil War came in 1935, a year before the conflict formally broke out. At the time, she was living in Barcelona with her first husband, artist Gerardo Lizarraga. In 1935, in the buildup to war, Barcelona was "a volatile city with sporadic street fighting, political murders, and a rhythm of growing violence foreshadowing the chaos to come" (Kaplan, 1988: 45). The simmering conflict later became the most violent and terrible war in Spain's history, "with blood running in the gutters" (45). According to Kaplan, a unique feature of the war was that "civilian massacre was far more common than death on the front line" (45). In such a climate, Varo's biographer added, "violence and fear ruled the streets. No one was safe, no one immune, not Varo, not her family, who helplessly watched as their younger son, Luis, took up arms in Franco's army and soon lost his life" (45, 47).

In this atmosphere, which was "increasingly hostile to creative pursuits," Varo continued to paint (Kaplan, 1988: 47). Two of her works from 1936 were later shown in surrealist exhibitions. One of these pieces, *Painting*, features what Kaplan called "curious mannequinlike half-figures with hairless heads and staring eyes [who] stand in rows, separated by walls with high spikes" (47). For Kaplan, these distorted and dismembered painted bodies are Varo's "intentional ... or unconscious" attempt to give voice to the "wounded and dazed" victims of war "who could be seen on the streets of her city" (48).

Varo left no written reflections about what she saw, felt, or experienced in Barcelona during the buildup to the Spanish Civil War. The artist did, however, produce a second painting in 1936, an image she called *Double Agent*. According to Kaplan, the image is the first in a long line of later works in which Varo painted herself into a story of her own making (1988: 48). In *Double Agent*, Varo's projected self appears as a woman whose head rises warily through a crack in the floor of a small, closed room. Pressed up against one wall of the room is an androgynous figure with a huge bumblebee on its back. The figure looks trapped, its avenues for escape, Kaplan noted, "are either inaccessible or distinctly unappealing" (48).

For Kaplan, the woman peering up from the crack in the floor "raises a question fundamental to civil war—who is the double agent? Is it this figure or the one with its nose pressed against the wall?" (1988: 48). The only thing a viewer of the painting knows with any certainty is that

> Varo has surely given her self-portrait character an excellent vantage point from which to spy. But has she trapped the half-man, half-woman? Or has it trapped her? Or have they both been trapped by that larger creature [with a red hand] reaching in from outside? Fears of entrapment and of the treachery of double agents become prudent in a civil war in which enemy and ally are indistinguishable. (48)

Double Agent also exhibits Varo's consciousness that extended beyond her own fear and pain to social and political forces as part of her *prima materia*, the psychological ground in which she worked to become herself. The hand entering through the window holds a sperm—an image of the inseminating masculine entering the container—and the room's back wall is covered with breasts above a tree. Life seems held in the blood-red hand and sperm, with the sustaining feminine drained of vitality, pinned to the colorless wall. The larger-than-life bumblebee, as an archetypal force, perhaps works to gather the pollen of possibilities from the androgynous figure pressed against the other wall as if paralyzed. Varo moves up into the scene through a crack in its foundation, the idea of the need to spy suggesting that danger is associated with seeing what she has painted: a diorama of what happens to the feminine and to androgyny—a symbol of wholeness—in a scene dominated by a hand that inseminates the picture with the intruding will to power.

Prison: Varo in the underworld

Varo met the surrealist poet Benjamin Péret in Barcelona in the fall of 1936. At the time, Varo was still married to Lizarraga. She was also in a relationship with Esteban Francés, a Spanish surrealist painter. Varo spent much of the Spanish Civil War with Péret, who had arrived in Barcelona in the summer of 1936 "as one of the early group[s] of foreigners who volunteered to defend the Spanish Republic against destruction by Nationalist rebels" (Kaplan, 1988: 49–50). Kaplan wrote that Péret had for years been one of the more active French Surrealists, "having been jailed, then expelled from Brazil five years earlier for Communist political activity" (50).

By March 1937, Péret was fighting in the Spanish Civil War in an anarchist division on the Aragon front, an area known to the readers of

Orwell's memoir, *Homage to Catalonia* (Kaplan, 1988: 52). Like Orwell, Péret saw little serious combat. Also like Orwell, he joined the Partido Obrero de Unificación Marxista (Worker's Party of Marxist Unification), or POUM, "a renegade working-class" faction opposed to the Stalinist form of Communism (Lynskey, 2019: 9–10). As the surrealist closest to André Breton, the movement's founder, Péret was serious about more than Surrealism and poetry—this was an artist willing to put his life on the line to blend art with what we would today call social justice: "The real poet," Péret declared, "cannot be recognized as such if he does not oppose the world in which he lives by total nonconformism" (as cited in Kaplan, 1988: 50). "Péret," Kaplan added,

> was seen as a man who was true to his principles regardless of the consequences. Although his poetry is filled with violent and scatological images, he is remembered as a most gentle man, aroused to violence only when confronted with injustice, particularly as perpetrated by the church and the police. (55)

While the frontline may have been relatively safe, "there was greater danger in Barcelona itself, where association with the POUM was becoming increasingly dangerous" (Kaplan, 1988: 53). Membership in the POUM was declared illegal in June 1937 (53). Secret police began arresting anyone with proven ties. Péret was at risk, but so was Varo. To say that Varo and Péret fell in love that first autumn of the Spanish Civil War may not be correct. But there was attraction—enough that Varo followed Péret back to Paris in 1937. According to Kaplan, Varo's choice

> was a move based on passion—the passion of a young woman for a romantic older figure, a poet central to Surrealism, and a Frenchman with whom she could participate in the Parisian artistic milieu. It was also a move that offered Varo escape from her war-torn country and welcome relief from its terrors. The man, the return to Paris, the surrealist movement, the relief from fear—all combined to make it a move that she eagerly undertook. But it was to have unanticipated ramifications that would exact a heavy psychological toll. (53)

There were two main consequences Varo faced as a result of her decision to move to Paris with Péret in 1937. The first came when the Nationalists won the Spanish Civil War in 1939 and Franco closed the border to anyone connected with Republican opposition. By moving with Péret to Paris, Varo unknowingly made it impossible for her to ever return to Spain. She had orphaned herself. According to Kaplan, the "abrupt and painful break" with her family distressed Varo "throughout the rest of her life" (1988: 53). For Varo, the second consequence—her capture and confinement in a

French prison camp and flight from the Germans during World War II—also involved upset she would never fully recover from.

When Varo and Péret "arrived in Paris in the spring of 1937, the streets were still safe, remote from bombs, machine guns, food lines, and fear" (Kaplan, 1988: 55). But the next year, when German forces captured Austria and annexed the Sudetenland, Paris began bracing for war. In 1939, France and England declared war on Germany. That summer, the Louvre and other state museums closed, the art shipped to outlying provinces for safekeeping. When Germany swept through Austria, Czechoslovakia, and Poland, life for foreign nationals like Varo became increasingly dangerous. Things got truly dicey for Varo when those holding a foreign passport were required to carry identity cards. Any infraction of the rules meant deportation to Spain, a country now ruled by the dictator Franco, and "where summary executions of Republican sympathizers [was] common" (69). Varo's association with Péret, an outspoken Communist, only added to her anxiety.

According to Kaplan, Péret was recalled for military duty in February 1940. In May, the poet was "arrested for political activism and incarcerated in a military prison in Rennes, a city west of Paris in the province of Brittany" (69). In prison, Péret described a vision of a "charming sprite" who, according to Kaplan, appeared "to him on the painted panes of his cell windows" (69). Péret wrote that in his vision the sprite "tossed butterflies over her head with a light, graceful gesture" (as cited in Kaplan, 1988: 69). The sprite reminded Péret of Varo. He wrote:

> I had not any news of her and her fate worried me much more than my own. I knew she was menaced both by internment in a French camp and by expulsion—which would have meant a concentration camp. I could not forget the expression of terrified distress which I had seen on her face when I had left her, eight or ten days before in Paris.
>
> (As cited in Kaplan, 1988: 69)

The timing of Péret's mention of Varo is odd. If the incarcerated poet was writing from prison in May 1940, having left Varo "eight or ten days" before in Paris (Kaplan, 1988: 69), how is it that he can highlight Varo's capture and confinement in a French concentration camp—a traumatizing experience that, according to Kaplan, did not take place until the winter of 1940? (71). We know little of Varo's experience, for she never talked about where she was taken, how long she was held, or what happened to her in the camp while she was there (71).

What we do know is that Varo "was arrested, merely for being Péret's companion" (Kaplan, 1988: 71). Walter Gruen, Varo's partner in her later years in Mexico City, speculated that her imprisonment may have had to do with "having hidden a deserter from the French army" (as cited in

Lozano, 2000: 144). This claim is unproven. Kaplan cited Varo's "friends," who speculated that the artist was held in the camp for "several months" (1988: 71). Upon her release, Varo stayed several weeks with a friend, Georgette Dupin, in Paris. "Dupin," Kaplan wrote, "vividly recalls that [the] devastating effect [of internment] had left Varo terribly traumatized and shaken" (71).

We hear a similar refrain from Walter Gruen, who, after her death, related that, in her early years in Mexico City, beginning in 1941, Varo "suffered frequent nightmares and would wake up feeling virtually destroyed" (Lozano, 2000: 53 fn 35). We also have pencil drawings by Varo's first husband, Gerardo Lizarraga, who, like many other Spanish refugees, fled Barcelona for what he hoped was safer ground across the border in France—only to be captured and confined in a French concentration camp (Kaplan, 1988: 70–1). Lizarraga called one piece *Mother Earth Fenced with Barbed Wire* (70). The image evokes the particular intensity of anguish and unmistakable suffering by a person whose feeling nature has been bludgeoned by bombs and bloodshed. In the presence of Lizarraga's soldier and woman, we wonder if the image of suffering expresses the terror Varo felt during her own confinement.

A short time after Varo's release from prison, German forces invaded Paris. It was June 1940. Soon, France was divided. Varo wanted to stay in Paris until she could find out where Péret was incarcerated. But with the German occupation, Varo realized that her time had run out. "Taking what little she could carry, Varo joined the millions who fled Paris in the face of the Nazi invasion" (Kaplan, 1988: 72).

Varo, only recently at the very epicenter of Surrealism with Péret in Paris, now found herself traumatized and in terror—again. The unknown upsets of her time in the concentration camp still a burden to her, Varo fled "in utter panic toward the unoccupied zone" in southern France (Kaplan, 1988: 72). One of more than eight million refugees, Varo caught a break. Faced with the prospect of walking across France to reach the unoccupied zone, Varo met up instead with Oscar Dominguez, a friend and Spanish surrealist painter, who had a seat in a car heading for the unoccupied zone. Dominguez offered Varo his seat. Varo refused. Dominguez offered again. Varo refused—repeatedly. Dominguez insisted and Varo finally accepted the ride. The trip south was not without incident. German planes strafed the roads clogged with cars, soldiers, and refugees. People were starving and terrified. Black smoke and bullets from machine guns fired from Luftwaffe planes filled the air.

But there was beauty as well. Kaplan cited friends who recalled hearing from Varo how she and the Americans who helped her to safety would stop "in front of each cathedral to admire it," and how touched they all were "at encountering, almost unreal, an almond tree in flower" (1988: 72). Varo eventually found her way to a fishing village on the Mediterranean coast. Here she paired up for a time with Victor Brauner, a Romanian Jewish surrealist painter hiding from authorities. Varo and Brauner moved in together. They spent their days helping local fishermen haul in their catch. The artists cooked, ate fish, and painted. According to both Kaplan and Renée Riese Hubert, the relationship was clearly an intimate and probably sexual one (Kaplan, 1988: 66; Hubert, 1994: 256). "Despite the political tensions and constant threats of surveillance," Kaplan wrote, "their time together [was] apparently quite tender" (1988: 72). Brauner evoked the sweet sensuous depth of his feeling for Varo in a letter:

> My very dear Remedios, ... Your walk is like a subtle wind and like that of birds or butterflies high in the sky... Your hair is the roots of invisible stars... Is your hair liquid or rather liquid flame which licks the air that surrounds the objects that I wish to be... The color of the odor of your skin [is] perfumed by a distant Oriental flavor... Your body in movement has the sound of the light wind they call a Zephyr or the lightness of a little cascade full of trout.
>
> (As cited in Kaplan, 1988: 73)

Varo left the fishing village for Marseilles in August 1940. A year or so later, Brauner gifted his departed paramour with a watercolor in which a woman, probably Varo, walks confident and naked, large eyes looking ahead, a mane of hair flying wild. "To my very dear Remedios," Brauner wrote, "with the memory of an indelible period of my life" (as cited in Kaplan, 1988: 73). Varo kept both the letter and the painting for the rest of her life.

In Marseilles, Varo waited for Péret, who had bribed his way out of prison and was making his way across France to her, riding long distances hiding in the back of a horse-drawn wagon covered by straw (Kaplan, 1988: 74). A port city, Marseilles, in the summer of 1940—the time Varo and Péret were there—linked the North African colonies of Algeria, Morocco, and Tunisia with metropolitan France. While Germany prepared to invade Britain and Mussolini was sending Italian forces into North Africa, Varo and Péret tried to get enough money together to pay for the ocean crossing to Mexico. The artist couple chose Mexico as their place of refuge for several reasons. First, and most importantly, Mexico's leftist government instituted an open-door policy for European refugees. "One of the reasons Mexico became such a popular sanctuary for artists," wrote Susan Aberth, a biographer of Leonora Carrington, Varo's close friend in Mexico, "was that the government did not pry into their previous political backgrounds" (2010: 57). A second reason drawing Varo to Mexico had to do with language, Spanish being both Varo's native language and that spoken in Mexico. Third, Varo and Péret had heard glowing reports of Mexico from André Breton. Breton had visited Mexico in 1938. He "found a land where powerful beliefs in the interconnectedness of all life had already mediated the polarities of Western thought that Surrealism sought to resolve into a new reality—a 'surreality'" (Chadwick, 1991: 10).

It took six months for Varo and Péret to get the money together to pay for the ocean crossing. Their political asylum had been worked out by the Emergency Rescue Committee, an organization hiding refugees in Marseilles in 1940. According to Kaplan, the "goal of the committee, organized in New York three days after the Nazi occupation of Paris, was to save as many of Europe's leading intellectuals and artists as possible by expediting their escape from France" (1988: 74). Kaplan quoted Victor Serge, "a Russian Marxist journalist and friend of Péret," who described the impact of the Emergency Rescue Committee's efforts: "In our ranks are enough doctors, psychologists, engineers, educationists, poets, painters, writers, musicians, economists, and public men to vitalize a whole great country" (as cited in Kaplan, 1988: 75).

With their travel visas in the works, there was still the matter of how the artists were going to get from Marseilles to Casablanca—and how they were going to pay for the trip of nearly one thousand miles. Kaplan wrote that Varo liked to tell the story of this leg of her journey to exile in Mexico: A thief stole their cash—but may have saved their lives. The thief who took their money worked for the black-market owner of a boat. Soon after they were unable to catch their boat, having lost their fare, Varo and Péret learned from newspaper accounts that the boat's owner was "a psychopathic killer who had murdered the previous refugees he had offered to help—a charge verified by the mute testimony of twelve bodies found buried in his backyard" (Kaplan, 1988: 82). In Casablanca, Varo worked to make up at least some of the money stolen in Marseilles. As told by Kaplan, "Remembering that Moslems used white shrouds to bury their dead, Varo, ever resourceful, went to a local mosque and arranged to sell the few white bed sheets she had managed to pack to get money for food" (82).

Varo and Péret left the port at Casablanca late in November 1941 aboard a Portuguese vessel, the *Serpa Pinto*. They arrived in Mexico City a few weeks later. Varo was relieved but shaken from multiple traumas. Outwardly, the artist expressed her inner torment as anxiety, fear of aging, and insects, and through the nervous habit of chain-smoking. Engel wrote:

> She is described by friends and acquaintances as a woman of great sensitivity and charm—intelligent, well-read, refined, good-natured, but also, by turns, nervous, fearful, morose. At such times she would become intensely introspective, retreating inside her studio, seeing no one. (1986: 13)

The trauma complex, art, and the healing capacity of imagination

Given her withdrawal and shift into behavior that Engel described as sullen and ill-tempered, it seems clear that Varo was struggling to recover from what modern psychotherapy would call posttraumatic stress. Emmett Early, a Jungian-oriented clinical psychologist who has worked with veterans of the Vietnam War, found that healing from trauma often includes "isolation, alienation, bouts of depression and anger" (1993: 51). Early, following Jung, linked the experience of trauma with the constellation of psychological complexes. Citing the work of C. A. Meier, a Jungian-oriented psychiatrist, Early wrote, "Jung took the term *complex* from the Latin verb *complector*, meaning 'to encircle, envelope, embrace, take possession of,' and the Latin noun *complexus*, which means 'mutual entwinement'" (4). As Jung defined them,

> Complexes are psychic fragments which have split off owing to traumatic influences or certain incompatible tendencies. As the association experiments prove, complexes interfere with the intentions of the will and disturb the conscious performance; they produce disturbances of memory and blockages in the flow of associations; they appear and disappear according to their own laws; they can temporarily obsess consciousness, or influence speech and action in an unconscious way. In a word, complexes behave like independent beings. (1937/ 1969: para. 253)

Jung used the word *dissociation* to refer to the formation of complexes, explaining that "trauma as a complex [has] a high emotional charge" and "brings about the dissociation of the psyche" (1946/1966, paras. 262, 266). Wilson described how a person experiencing trauma can feel a host of distressing emotions, including "fear, helplessness, terror, annihilation, [and] anxiety" (2004: 56). Jung linked the intensity of the trauma to the severity of the complex that develops as a person tries to cope with the fact that the devastating experience has destroyed his or her previous approach to life (1948/1969: para. 594). Psychologically, the formation of and dissociation from a complex is a move the psyche makes to prevent overwhelming and intolerable emotions from eclipsing the functioning of the ego. However, evoking the shattering experience of psychological trauma in a 1928 essay, "The Therapeutic Value of Abreaction," Jung also observed that the complex acts autonomously from the conscious will. It "forces itself tyrannically upon the conscious mind. The explosion of affect is a complete invasion of the individual, it pounces upon him like an enemy or wild animal" (1928/ 1966: para. 267). Therapeutically, Jung believed the work of healing has less to do with abreaction, that is, the release of the emotions associated with the overwhelming experience, and more to do with integrating the upsetting material that has been split off, or dissociated, from the conscious mind (para. 266).

In this work, we are less interested in labeling any condition or illness Varo might have experienced than we are in the role psychological trauma played in the production of her paintings. We are especially interested in the insight, healing, and transformation that the practice of painting brought to Varo's life and, through her work, to ours. In this regard, Jungian psychology approaches traumatic experience as a potential resource with healing value. "Psychological trauma," wrote Early, "puts the psyche at odds with itself by injecting unwanted emotions and images into consciousness" (1993: 57). Early described trauma to the psyche as an experience in which a person is "made helpless and overwhelmed, often with the threat of death" (37).

From a Jungian perspective, Early emphasized that psychological trauma can bring more to an individual than torment and the threat of annihilation—it can break one's heart and mind open to ways of thinking, feeling, and being that would not have been possible were it not for the trauma. With Varo's paintings in mind, we wonder: Did the terror of war, the distressing dislocation of exile, imprisonment, and the pain of patriarchal misogyny, actually *help* Varo produce paintings that evoke an intimate and numinous connection with the beautiful but also terrifying forces of the archetypal world?

We see imaginal evidence that Varo was trying to heal from being deeply hurt in one of the paintings she exhibited at the Galería Diana in Mexico City in the mid-1950s. In *Caravan*, Varo painted a tower-shaped house on wheels. "In this image," Kaplan wrote,

> a house on wheels, with pulleys and propellers, is [pedaled] by a mys-
> terious cloaked man who steers the curious vehicle through a lushly
> wooded landscape. Inside the house—which is filled with doorways and
> windows, each oriented toward a different direction—sits a woman at
> a piano. (1988: 120)

"This caravan," Varo wrote of her house on wheels, "represents a true and harmonious home, inside of which there are all perspectives, and happily it goes from here to there, the man guiding it, the woman tranquilly making music" (as cited in Kaplan, 1988: 120)

The image of the caravan traveling through a dark and mist-filled forest may be a metaphor for the "new-found security" Varo experienced living in Mexico City with Péret and a group of artist friends that included Leonora Carrington (Kaplan, 1988: 120). In the caravan, Kaplan wrote,

> the woman, a musician, is safely inside an interior that radiates warmth,
> freed to concentrate on her art by the man who is outside, bundled

up against the elements, guiding the process of their home. The house travels "happily," the woman works "tranquilly," all expressions of the ease that Varo was now enjoying. (120, 122)

Kaplan connected the emotional warmth and safety of the woman in the caravan to the artist's use of color:

> The caravan interior is painted in golden tones that glow from the center of the canvas. Using the technical skills she had developed through her academic and engineering training, Varo precisely rendered the interior from a variety of perspectives so that hallways and stairwells create a maze of spaces changing direction as they recede. She created sky effects in rich blue-green-grays by blowing thinned paint onto the canvas and letting it pool, then blotting these pools to produce a texture of dots and splotches that evokes a dense and watery mist. For the forest floor she used a related technique in which viscous paint was sandwiched between two pieces of paper or canvas that were then pulled apart, creating accidental textures that suggest a mossy landscape. (1988: 122)

Looking closely at *Caravan*, we see that Varo was also representing darker and more troubling emotions beyond the warmth and safety that characterized her life in Mexico City and her "almost conspiratorial" friendship with Carrington (Moorhead, 2017: 177). Kaplan pinpointed the aspects of shadow Varo was in the process of transforming through the practice of painting: "The muffled mouth and suspicious glance of the driver, the fierce concentration of the pianist, the isolation of this house and its inhabitants all suggest the lonely rootlessness that was at the core of Varo's personal experience" (1988: 122). Kaplan added that the "use of fantastic vehicles as emblems for her personal dislocation" formed into a persistent theme of Varo's mature work over the last ten years of her life (122). The isolation of the tower on wheels, Kaplan reflected,

> alone in a deep and misty woods, is reinforced by the isolation of the figures themselves—she inside, he out, facing away from each other and totally absorbed in separate activities. This theme of human isolation is one that Varo continued to explore: it is rare to find people in direct contact with one another in her work. (122)

One of the features of trauma, especially in combination with a cultural environment that suppresses the relational feminine and vulnerability, is the tendency to produce isolation. Did Varo's isolation foster her turn inward to the imaginal figures that often accompany her in her paintings? In *Sympathy*, another image exhibited at the Galería Diana in Mexico City in 1955 or 1956, Varo explored the relationship between a troubled woman and a magical cat. Varo explained the image:

> This lady's cat jumps onto the table, producing the sort of disorder that one must learn to tolerate if one likes cats (as I do). Upon caressing [the cat,] so many sparks fly that they form a very complicated electrical gadget. Some sparks and electricity go to her head and rapidly make a permanent wave.
>
> (As cited in Kaplan, 1988: 122–3).

Varo had originally called *Sympathy* by another name: *Madness of the Cat*. For Kaplan this suggested the underlying shadow of psychological trauma:

> The anger, ferocity, and madness… as well as the rabies that infects the cat and that it may now be transmitting to the woman. The cat has leapt upon the table and spilled a glass of milk all over the floor; when stroked, it emits potent sparks. This cat seems to have an alter ego: another cat, only partially visible, lurks at the woman's feet, hiding in the folds of the tablecloth. The most mundane domestic accident has been transformed into an exchange laden with both sympathy and madness, communication and confrontation. (123–4)

Kaplan did not use the word *trauma*, but Varo's biographer put her finger on the destructive impact of psychological splitting when she wrote of the tension in the artist's work between moments of meaningful contact and isolation and alienation. "Varo," Kaplan wrote, "was a woman for whom direct contact and deep, lasting friendships had always been essential. Perhaps the tone of isolation and dislocation that recurs in her paintings was the unavoidable aftermath of so many years of insecurity" (1988: 122).

Sympathy offers, in comparison to the isolation and coldness in *Caravan*, "strongly contrasting emotional tones" in the "sympathetic bond between the woman and her cat, the eye contact, the touch, and the electrical force set up by the emotional vibration between them" (Kaplan, 1988: 123). "Varo," Kaplan added,

> had always surrounded herself with cats; her niece remembers with fondness the many strays that her aunt took in from the street. Intrigued by their elegant mystery, she saw them as personal allies… Surely that is why, in the Gabino Barreda group portrait [artist and friend Gunther] Gerzso had posed her in a feline position, surrounded by cats, and disguised with a cat's-eye mask. (123)

The emergence of Varo's feline-like nature can be seen in her painted depictions of her search for identity and selfhood. As we imagine further into Varo's works in the coming chapters, we see in these images the development of qualities archetypally associated with cats, in whom "the tame and the tiger dwell ... in sinuous, if paradoxical accord" ("Cat," 2010: 300). "Cats," wrote an essayist in *The Book of Symbols*, "traverse the liminal and the nighttime, gazing out from their darknesses with full-moon eyes and secret smiles" (300). The essayist added, "Padding proprietarily through the spaces of our mutual habitation, cats travel light, but bring whole other worlds in tow" (300). One finds that "in fairy tales, a cat may assume the role of a psychopomp whose nervy instinctual vitality compensates the over-refinement and 'sublimated' instincts of the human hero or heroine" (300). With these thoughts and Varo's affinity for feline sensibilities in mind, *Sympathy* foreshadows Varo's relationship with aspects of her psyche split off by trauma and childhood conditioning as a daughter of Catholicism and the patriarchy as that relationship becomes not just troubling and disruptive but also vitalizing and transformative.

References

Aberth, S. (2010). *Leonora Carrington: Surrealism, alchemy and art.* Burlington, VT: Lund Humphries.

Cat. (2010). In A. Ronnberg & K. Martin (Eds.), *The book of symbols: Reflections on archetypal images* (300–3). Cologne, Germany: Taschen.

Chadwick, W. (1991). *Leonora Carrington: The Mexican years.* Albuquerque, NM: University of New Mexico Press.

Early, E. (1993). *The raven's return: The influence of psychological trauma on individuals and cultures.* Wilmette, IL: Chiron.

Engel, P. (1986). *Remedios Varo: Science into art.* New York, NY: New York Academy of Science.

Hubert, R. R. (1994). *Magnifying mirrors: Women, surrealism, & Partnership.* Lincoln, NE: University of Nebraska Press.

Jung, C. G. (1928/1966). The therapeutic value of abreaction. In H. Read et al. (Eds.), *The collected works of C. G. Jung* (Vol. 16, 2nd ed., 129–38). Princeton, NJ: Princeton University Press.

Jung, C. G. (1946/1966). The psychology of the transference (R. F. C. Hull, Trans.). In H. Read et al. (Eds.), *The collected works of C. G. Jung* (Vol. 16, 2nd ed., 163–323). Princeton, NJ: Princeton University Press.

Jung, C. G. (1937/1969). Psychological factors determining human behavior (R. F. C. Hull, Trans.). In H. Read et al. (Eds.), *The collected works of C. G. Jung* (Vol. 8, 2nd ed., 114–25). Princeton, NJ: Princeton University Press.

Jung, C. G. (1948/1969). The psychological foundations of belief in spirits (R. F. C. Hull, Trans.). In H. Read et al. (Eds.), *The collected works of C. G. Jung* (Vol. 8, 2nd ed., 301–18). Princeton, NJ: Princeton University Press.

Kaplan, J. (1988). *Unexpected journeys: The art and life of Remedios Varo.* New York, NY: Abbeville Press.

Lozano, L-M. (2000). *The magic of Remedios Varo* (E. Goldson & L. Valenzuela, Trans.). Washington, DC: National Museum of Women in the Arts.

Lynskey, D. (2019). *The ministry of truth: The biography of Orwell's 1984.* New York, NY: Doubleday.

Moorhead, J. (2017). *The surreal life of Leonora Carrington.* London, UK: Virago.

Rhodes, R. (2015). *Hell and good company: The Spanish civil war and the world it made.* New York, NY: Simon & Schuster.

Schellinski, K. (2020). *Individuation for adult replacement children: Ways of coming into being.* New York, NY: Routledge.

Varo, R. (1997/2018). *Letters, dreams & other writings* (M. Carson, Trans.). Cambridge, MA: Wakefield Press.

Wilson, J. (2004). The abyss experience and the trauma complex: A Jungian perspective of posttraumatic stress disorder and dissociation. *Journal of Trauma & Dissociation, 5*(3), 43–67.

Chapter 3

Putting the canvas on the easel
Surrealism, alchemy, and the unconscious

Varo's painted images engage the viewer in an alchemical movement of misty swirls and eerie distortions of perspective. Her figures are isolated and often confined in secluded spaces—a tower or forest—and held captive by unknown forces. Engaged in spiritual practices dedicated to self-knowledge, in her paintings Varo often depicted a relationship between human figures and a mysterious force from which an essence is being extracted, woven, or generated. A Varo painting creates strong feeling. "Varo's canvases," Kaplan writes,

> were intimate, often humorous, depicting personal narrative and scaled to private response. It is this private quality that is so striking in her paintings. They are quite small, very quiet, and invite the kind of personal contemplation evoked by an illuminated prayer book. Her painstakingly slow technique (a small painting might require months to complete) demands slow and deliberate viewing. The work is not bright or flashy or broad in any way. It is intimate, both technically and thematically, and it elicits an intimate response. (1988: 133–4)

Thomas Pynchon evoked the intimate quality of Varo's imagery in *The Crying of Lot 49*. Early in Pynchon's novel, heroine Oedipa Maas weeps as she lingers in the presence of Varo's painting, *Embroidering the Earth's Mantle*, a work we look at in some detail in Chapter Five. Oedipa weeps because the image Varo painted of a girl trapped in a tower highlights the isolation and fear Oedipa experiences in her own life.

Weeping is one reaction that comes up for viewers in the presence of a Varo painting. Others have vocalized different experiences of the numinous nature of Varo's imagery: "Varo is much more than a painter," wrote art historian and curator Luis-Martín Lozano, "she is an illusionist opening the door to a visually fascinating and unimagined world" (2000: 43). Varo's friend, poet Octavio Paz, wrote, "With the same invisible violence of the wind to disperse the clouds but with greater delicacy, as if she were painting with her eyes and not with her hands, Remedios clears the fabric and on its transparent surface accumulates clarities" (1967/2011: 45). For art historian Tere Arcq, Varo's

> painting has a magical, mysterious quality. Her canvases reveal worlds that are marvelous, timeless, governed by laws that escape our own systems of logic. Her works betray a constant spiritual quest, a desire to capture the harmonious unity and interconnection between all things, to conjure up before our eyes the invisible realms that inhabit her soul, to find that "magic key" that opens the doors to a hidden universe. (2008: 21)

Varo created nearly 400 paintings, drawings, and sketches in what Peter Engel described as her "short, traumatic life" (1986:1). Compelled by "desire and action to capture a truth that is fugitive in essence" (Sánchez, 2008: 14), Varo's mature work, created in Mexico City between 1954 and 1963, features "more than 100 intricate works in oil on canvas or masonite" (Lauter, 2013: 1). Engel evoked the wonder of Varo's painted imaginal realms in which

> vicarious adventurers travel through forests and fields, up above the clouds, along rivers, and down the streets of abandoned cities—nearly always solitary, and often bearing the almond-shaped eyes and androgynous features of Varo's self-portraits. They are propelled by the unlikeliest contraptions, jerry-built constructions of pulleys and gears, sprockets and cogs, wheels and wings, vehicles that are scientific in appearance but magical in operation. They run on such insubstantial fuel as stardust, music, sunlight, and heavenly ether. (1986: 2)

André Breton, founder of Surrealism, once described Varo as "femininity itself, here in hieroglyphics the game and the fire in the eye of the bird" (as cited in Engel, 1986: 8). "Less cryptically," Engel added, Breton wrote of Varo's work: " 'Surrealism claims it entirely' " (8). Engel believed Breton "was partly correct: Varo's [paintings are] indeed [of] a hieroglyphic nature, for her work abounds in hieroglyphs, literally sacred writings" (8). Observing that "the symbolism employed by the male Surrealists was primarily Freudian and profane," Engel wrote, "Varo's, and that of other women painters associated with the Surrealists, was mythic and sacred, with much of it culled from a medieval lexicon" (8). "Varo's paintings," Engel reflected,

> recall the Middle Ages and early Renaissance not only in her use of symbolism but also in her subject matter, style, and atmosphere. Her settings are defined by heavy Gothic or Romanesque buildings, the architecture of her childhood, painted in somber grays and browns

and lit by a low-sitting, late afternoon sun... The figures who roam her enchanted woods and pace the parapets of her monasteries and castles are the stylized, sometimes caricatured inhabitants of medieval life and legend: magicians in robes, nuns in habits, an itinerant juggler with a face the shape of a pentagram, a medieval symbol of the occult. (8)

What fascinated Varo about the Middle Ages? Engel, an architect who devoted a decade to the study of the artist's imagery, suggested that the answer has to do with an alchemical blending of opposites. The Middle Ages was

> perhaps the last period in history when the rational and the irrational, the scientific and the spiritual, meshed so thoroughly. This was a time when the *harmonices mundi*, the harmonies of the world, could be seen in all objects, however mundane; when science was not considered antithetical to religion; and when the diversity and plenitude of nature was evidence not of a ruthless struggle for survival but of a great chain of being, set in place by a benevolent Creator. To the medieval mind, understanding the world was a matter of explicating an icono-graphic code in which each material object was not merely a thing in itself, but the symbolic emissary of a profound and otherworldly power. (1986: 8)

"Seen against a medieval backdrop of universal order," Engel concluded, "Varo's work can be understood as striving to restore to the modern world the harmony that by all appearances it has lost" (8–9).

Surrealism and alchemy: Re-enchanting the world

If the Middle Ages pinpoints Varo's philosophical and scientific bearings, art-istically her paintings grew from the ground of Surrealism, a movement that originated formally in Paris in 1924 with the publication of *Manifeste du Surrealism*, or the *First Surrealist Manifesto*, by Breton, a French poet with anti-fascist beliefs (Suleiman, 1990: 28). Breton also founded and published the debut issue of *La Révolution Surréaliste*, a journal that featured articles on violence, death, and suicide in a bid to start work on "a new declaration of the rights of man" (1990: 21, 28–9). Inspired by Freud's exploration of the unconscious and committed to revolution against bourgeois rationalism, Breton published a dozen issues of *La Révolution Surréaliste* between 1924 and 1929 (1990: 28–9). Fueled by a contempt for established tradition, Surrealism mushroomed into an avant-garde cultural movement, the intel-lectual and artistic proclamations of which could be heard through a host of creative methods, from literature and philosophy to painting, photography, and film.

Art historian David Lomas wrote *The Haunted Self: Surrealism, Psychoanalysis, Subjectivity* to explore a question vital to both the practice of Western depth psychology and to artistic, intellectual, and social attempts by surrealists "to reject the notion of a unified, indivisible self by revealing the subject to be haunted by otherness and instability" (2000: dust jacket). His question: How did the roots of Freudian psychoanalysis and Surrealism become entwined with each other?

André Breton came across the writings of the pioneer psychoanalysts in the summer of 1917 (Polizzotti, 1995). Breton was a medical student at the time, working at the psychiatric center in Saint-Dizier, a township located east of Paris, in northeastern France. Breton's path to Freud started with the writings of Jean-Martin Charcot, a French neurologist, and Emil Kraepelin, one of the more influential psychiatrists in Germany. The trail led further, to Constanza Pascal, the author "of an important work on schizophrenia" (Polizzotti, 1995: 51). According to Mark Polizzotti, Freud's theories about the unconscious and the importance of dreams came into view for Breton through *Précis de psychiatrie*, a textbook on the specifics of psychiatry by Emmanuel Régis, and *La Psychoanalyse des névroses et des psychoses*, or *Psychoanalysis of Neuroses and Psychoses*, by Régis and Angélo Hesnard (1995: 51).

Breton was electrified by Freud's efforts to unearth the uncharted terrain of the unconscious mind. Whereas Freud and other psychiatrists worked to help suffering patients release repressed emotions and to bring previously unconscious thoughts and motivations into awareness, Breton was more interested in tapping into "the roots of artistic creation" (Polizzotti, 1995: 52). As a poet, Breton found in psychoanalysis a method that could help him track into the uncharted terrain of the unconscious mind to answer

> the questions that had been preoccupying him for several years: Toward what ends did one create poetry? What were the boundaries between "poetry" and "life," and must they be maintained? Above all, what was the veritable source of poetic imagery? (1995: 103)

As a medical student, Breton searched for the unconscious source of artistic creation in the speech of his patients on the neurological ward at Saint-Dizier, and later in advertising's "hijacking of stock phrases" and "in the chance juxtapositions" that appear in the art of collage (Polizzotti, 1995: 103). While these and other methods

> had so far produced inconclusive results, their convergence suggested [to Breton] that the most fertile images derived not from a deliberate, individual process of creation, but from a connection with more universal mental substrata—were not, in other words, dictated by the voice

of reason, but whispered by what Victor Hugo called the "mouth of shadows." (103)

Breton finally found what he was looking for—access to experience uncontaminated by rationality—in the practice of automatic writing, a creative process in which the artist surrenders conscious control over the poem or painting in a bid to touch into "the immense but hidden influence of the unconscious in human lives" (Ades, 2011: 23).

For Breton, Surrealism derived its name from the integration of two states—dream and reality. From an artistic point of view, "the principal image of the dream," wrote Mary Ann Caws, functioned "as the enabling 'capillary tissue' between the exterior world of facts and the interior world of emotions, between reality and, let us say, the imagination" (1990: ix). One of the more memorable passages in the *First Surrealist Manifesto* "is Breton's famous definition of Surrealism itself:

> SURREALISM, *n.* Psychic automatism in its pure state, by which one proposes to express—verbally, by means of the written word, or in any other manner—the actual functioning of thought. Dictation of thought, in the absence of any control exercised by reason, exempt from any aesthetic or moral concern.
>
> (Breton, as cited in Polizzotti, 1995: 209)

Breton "explicitly characterized Surrealism as a philosophical, not aesthetic, undertaking" (Polizzotti, 1995: 209). According to Maurice Nadeau, who wrote what is considered its definitive history, the surrealist

> movement was envisaged by its founders not as a new artistic school, but as a means of knowledge, a discovery of continents which had not yet been systematically explored: the unconscious, the marvelous, the dream, madness, hallucinatory states—in short, if we add the fantastic and the marvelous as they occurred throughout the world, the other side of the logical decor. The final goal remained the reconciliation of two hitherto warring realms: man and the world. (1944/ 1965: 80)

As Surrealism's "intellectual and reflective conscience" (Lepetit, 2012/ 2014: 433), how did Breton hope to bring about "the future resolution of the states of dream and reality, in appearance so contradictory, in a sort of absolute reality, or surréalité" (Breton, as cited in Jones, 1995: para. 4)? According to Patrick Lepetit, a French author who explored the link between Surrealism and a host of esoteric traditions, including alchemy, Breton rooted the movement's artistic foundation in alchemical soil:

Descent into the self, illumination of hidden places, light cast on symbols, awakening—we are unquestionably in the presence here of an initiatory kind of language, one that can be compared with these quotes of Paracelsus from *The Seven Books of the Archidoxes of Magic*: "He who wishes to work on the Great Work should visit his soul, penetrate the deepest part of his being, and carry out a concealed and mysterious labor." (2012/2014: 307–8)

Influenced by alchemy and other esoteric practices, the surrealists—poets, essayists, painters, and artists in other media, including automatic writing and performance art—used creative methods to engage unconscious forces in a bid to unlock imagination and increase consciousness.

These artists were working with unconscious forces not only from an aesthetic perspective, but from a philosophical point of view dedicated to creating "unprecedented moral and psychological upheaval" (Polizzotti, 1995: 105). Devoted to exploring dreams as unfiltered expressions of the unconscious psyche, surrealist artists, including Varo, blended art, depth psychology, and esoteric disciplines, including alchemy, in a bid to "remake human understanding" (Roger, 2012/2014: xiii). What does it mean to remake human understanding? Although surrealists were irresistibly attracted to magic, observed Michel Löwy, a French sociologist, philosopher, and member of the surrealist movement since around 1970, "it was not because they desired—like traditional magicians—to control the forces of nature with ritual acts or secret words. Their—immense—ambition is of an entirely different quality: *to change life*." (as cited in Lepetit, 2012/2014: 299, emphasis in original).

With Surrealism's revolutionary philosophical and political mission in mind, it is critical to ask a creative question: How, precisely, did surrealist artists—including Varo, who was influenced by the movement—intend to instigate cultural change? In *The Esoteric Secrets of Surrealism*, quoting Breton from a 1953 essay, Lepetit wrote:

The definition of surrealism in the First Manifesto merely "retouches" a great traditional saying concerning the necessity of "breaking through the drumhead of reasoning reason and looking at the hole," a procedure that will cause symbols that were once mysterious to light up. (2012/2014: 306–7)

Thus, it was the "immense poetic charge" carried by "magical practices with language, in the kabbalah, alchemy, and other hermetic arts," that interested the surrealists (Löwy, as cited in Lepetit, 2012/2014: 299). Löwy concluded:

This charge—in the explosive sense of the word—would serve them to dynamite the established cultural order and its sensible positivist conformism. Sparks flying from the different forms of magic could set fire to the powder and thereby help surrealism in its eminently subversive enterprise of poetically re-enchanting the world.

(As cited in Lepetit, 2012/2014: 299)

As an artist working in the surrealist lineage, Varo's devotion to changing the world around her—to poetically re-enchanting the world, as Löwy put it—is a thread we follow throughout this work.

Elsewhere, other scholars have linked the personal transformation Varo experienced through the process of painting with the impactful symbolic power her themes and images convey. In *Creation of the Birds*, Varo painted the transformation that occurs when, aspiring "to bring something new into the world," we collaborate with numinous "forces beyond ourselves" (Lauter, 1984: 97).

In these pages we look at the transformation that painting brought to the suffering Varo experienced in her life. Our intention is to look from Jungian, archetypal, and feminist perspectives at the disabling experience of misogyny, institutionalized through the violent system of male domination called patriarchy. With the imagery in her paintings and dream of the executioner as our guide, we follow Varo into an imagined world in which women see with divine eyes, looking within for what is needed to make themselves and the culture around them more conscious, more caring, more alive.

Our sensitivity to suffering is crucial as we work, as Varo did, to highlight female empowerment. But we must also cultivate psychological courage as we reach into the problems of patriarchy for solutions that sound unreal to the literal mind. Jungian psychology excels at touching into trouble for the purpose of liberating the healing already present in the wound. By painting women who lived in concert with forces they could not see, Varo practiced a similarly subversive form of healing art.

Patriarchy blinds men to shame they cannot bear to feel. "If a man feels shame," wrote psychoanalyst Mary Ayers, "he feels disrespected, powerless" (2011: xv). For a man this is "a feeling worse than death" (xv). In distress, the patriarchal male disavows feeling in a bid to armor himself against the unbearable vulnerability his shame conceals. In patriarchy, a man projects shame onto a woman—and then punishes the body and being of the woman whose presence reminds him that he is not invincible, as his attempts to dominate would have him believe. Caught in the machinery of male domination, a woman loses her experience of being. Unseen for who she is, she ceases to exist. She feels unreal, unmade.

Remedios Varo sat before an easel and tried to paint a way out of the problem of patriarchy. Varo died with the project of remaking the world still unfinished. There is much work left to do. Even today, in Western cultures, women's issues with depression, anxiety, body image, sexuality, and psychosomatic symptoms are seen as the problem—and sometimes the fault—of the individual girl or woman. Post-Jungian cultural complex theory broadens the understanding of self and the unconscious to include a framework that recognizes these symptoms as more than personal. Devoted, as Varo was, to a homeopathic search for the liberating essence held in the archetypal image, we find these symptoms are the internalization of a male-dominated cultural paradigm that objectifies and oppresses women and the feminine. Such a post-Jungian approach shifts the psychoanalytic perspective and lifts the burden of psychosocial and somatic symptoms from the individual alone to one of seeing "a continuum in the content and structure of complexes that ranges from the personal to the cultural to the archetypal" (Singer, 2004: 22).

This is where the practice of alchemical psychology comes in.

Jung himself studied alchemy for more than three decades. Some critics thought Jung a fool for spending so much time on such an obscure and esoteric subject. But Jung knew he had found a way to illuminate the processes of transformation taking place in the unconscious. Varo took Jung's alchemical approach to heart. With mysterious and arresting imagery, Varo used painting as a cauldron in which ideas and images cooked, the pain and possibility of her life (and maybe of human life itself) brewing together in an artistic and alchemical effort to engineer a new world.

Conveyed into our hearts and hands, as if by one of Varo's fantastic machines, the artist's alchemical project, and ours, arrives bearing a sense of urgency, for the system of male domination called patriarchy has been happening now for several thousand years. At times in her life, Varo found herself as the meat caught in the grinder. Fascist male violence tore open the world she knew. But the artist did not give up. She dreamed and painted. She refused to be a thing deadened by the male gaze. In these pages, we work, as Varo did, with the bigger picture in mind: making something new and more sustainable at the levels of community and culture through imagination.

For Varo, painting was a devotional, spiritual, and imaginal practice of engaging with and responding to images and symbols arising from the unconscious. Importantly, the impetus behind her practice of painting and the motive force powering this artist's lifelong search for self-discovery lies not in personal growth but in metaphysical inquiry: Varo's paintings probe the universe from a philosophical perspective that is interested in delving deeply into the nature of initial conditions, such as being, knowing, substance, cause, identity, time, and space.

The heroine's quest: Symbolic alchemy and the transformation of deep suffering

From a personal standpoint, Varo painted because from an early age she had an innate gift for the craft. She studied art as a young woman because painting offered a way into a life of her own—a life free, to some extent, from the limits her family and culture imposed upon her. Varo's mature work makes it clear that for her, painting marked a path to profound personal growth. However, painting was more than a technique Varo employed to externalize her inner life and become more aware of her own experience. Painting, for Varo, constituted a symbolic search for self-discovery, a female quest to touch and hold the wonder, meaning, and love that can be extracted from deep suffering.

From an archetypal perspective, we can say that in her search, Varo painted not from the ego but from the soul. This transforms the figures in her paintings into archetypal presences who are trying to be seen and known in a bid to bring something needed to the established order of things. A gifted artist, Varo's practice of painting included meticulous study and disciplined experimentation over many years as she honed her ability to engage with the numinous power of symbols and to channel and express living archetypal energy. Following Varo, through our researches we continue the work she was about—symbolizing and embodying the sacred in service not only to our own processes of personal growth but at a cultural level, to the reshaping of patriarchal structures that blind men to their humanity and objectify women and the feminine.

Varo was searching for what was missing in herself and in the world around her. Painting, for Varo, was a path she followed, an experience she needed to change and grow personally, but also, through her imagery, to suggest solutions to the harm she saw happening in the world around her. For Varo, images marked the way into the wilderness of her own dreams and nightmares. Her paintings are singularly appealing; they arrest us. In their presence, we stop. If we are patient and devoted, Varo's imagery helps us finger the pulsebeat of a right and good way to live. In search of this world, this way, her paintings tell us where to go—and why.

To follow the symbolic clues this artist left behind, we orient ourselves to image and metaphor, to a nonliteral style of paying attention to what lies below conscious awareness. In surrendering our need to know, to control, to impose our meaning on things, we hope to invite new aspects of ourselves into being. From a Jungian perspective, this is the way archetypal forces enlarge our waking experience. It is the way images and symbols come alive, bringing insight and meaning. Our work here is to engage with the images in Varo's paintings on their terms, not ours, and then to try to embody our experience of the image. What we are hoping for—what Varo was hoping for—is not perfection or enlightenment but the alchemical "production of a kind of stability following a great deal of turmoil" (Pinkus, 2010: 21).

References

Ades, D. (2011). *The colour of my dreams: The surrealist revolution in art.* Vancouver, Canada: Vancouver Art Gallery.

Arcq, T. (2008). In search of the miraculous. In M. Orellano (Ed.), *Five keys to the secret world of Remedios Varo* (19–90). Mexico City, Mexico: Artes de Mexico.

Ayers, M. (2011). *Masculine shame: From succubus to the eternal feminine.* New York, NY: Routledge.

Caws, M. A. (1990). Introduction: Linkings and reflections. In A. Breton, *Communicating vessels* (vii–xxiii). Lincoln, NE: University of Nebraska Press.

Engel, P. (1986). *Remedios Varo: Science into art.* New York, NY: New York Academy of Science.

Jones, R. (1995). Rodney Graham. *Frieze.* Retrieved from frieze.com/article/rodney-graham-1

Kaplan, J. (1988). *Unexpected journeys: The art and life of Remedios Varo.* New York, NY: Abbeville Press.

Lauter, E. (1984). *Women as mythmakers: Poetry and visual art by twentieth-century women.* Bloomington, IN: Indiana University Press.

Lauter, E. (2013). *Transfiguration: Re-Imagining Remedios Varo.* Georgetown, KY: Finishing Line Press.

Lepetit, P. (2012/2014). *The esoteric secrets of Surrealism: Origins, magic, and secret societies* (J. Graham, Trans.). Rochester, VT: Inner Traditions.

Lomas, D. (2000). *The haunted self: Surrealism, psychoanalysis, subjectivity.* New Haven, CT: Yale University Press.

Lozano, L-M. (2000). *The magic of Remedios Varo* (E. Goldson & L. Valenzuela), Trans. Washington, DC: National Museum of Women in the Arts.

Nadeau, M. (1944/1965). *The history of Surrealism* (R. Howard, Trans.). New York, NY: Macmillan.

Paz, O. (1967/2011). *Alternating current* (H. Lane, Trans.). New York, NY: Arcade.

Pinkus, K. (2010). *Alchemical mercury: A theory of ambivalence.* Stanford, CA; Stanford University Press.

Polizzotti, M. (1995). *Revolution of the mind: The life of André Breton.* New York, NY: Farrar, Straus and Giroux.

Pynchon, T. (1966). *The crying of lot 49.* New York, NY: Harper & Row.

Roger, B. (2012/2014). Foreword. In P. Lepetit, *The esoteric secrets of Surrealism: Origins, magic, and secret societies* (J. Graham, Trans.) (xi–xiv). Rochester, VT: Inner Traditions.

Sánchez, A. R. (2008). Five birds emerge from the ice. In M. Orellano (Ed.), *Five keys to the secret world of Remedios Varo* (14–8). Mexico City, Mexico: Artes de Mexico.

Singer, T. (2004). The cultural complex and archetypal defenses of the group spirit: Baby Zeus, Elian Gonzales, Constantine's Sword, and other holy wars (with special attention to "the axis of evil"). In T. Singer & S. Kimbles (Eds.), *The cultural complex: Contemporary Jungian perspectives on psyche and society.* New York, NY: Routledge.

Suleiman, S. R. (1990). *Subversive intent: Gender, politics, and the avant-garde.* Cambridge, MA: Harvard University Press.

Chapter 4

The end as beginning

Varo's dream of the executioner, last painting, and death

Working with images and symbols, pigments, paintbrush, and colors, and steeped in the alchemical process of transformation aimed at making something new from the destruction of the original form, Varo engaged in a psychological and metaphysical search for what classical Jungian psychology calls the deep Self. "The symbol," wrote Jeffrey Miller, in the context of the transcendent function, "is the quintessential example of something that is neither rational nor irrational, neither conscious nor unconscious, neither purely reason nor instinct" (2004: 50). Standing with a foot in both the conscious and unconscious, the symbol "allows us to move between and create dialogue among these territories that do not otherwise touch one another" (50). These are the symbolic spaces Remedios Varo traveled in, the numinous archetypal ground she painted from.

We begin at the end, with the artist's death from a heart attack in Mexico City in the fall of 1963. Our intention: to track back through the artist's work the thread of her dream of the executioner. We start with Varo's dream of death because the imagery invites the questions that guide this work: What was the dangerous secret Varo discovered? Who was the man Varo wanted to weave her destiny with? What is the symbolic meaning of the figure of the executioner? What is the alchemical symbolism of the egg? How might the imagery represent the presence of unconscious complexes at work in Varo's psyche and patriarchal culture? And perhaps most importantly, how might the imagery in Varo's dream link the psychological experience of imagination and the feminine with personal and cultural transformation?

We finger now and then the threads of the dream of the executioner throughout the rest of our look at alchemical psychology in Varo's art and life. As we hold this thread here, it is colored black, for in the practice of alchemical psychology, the death of what is commences the needed destruction of the original form of the substance being worked on. In the cyclical, ouroboric nature of life, the alchemical psyche makes something new from the remnants of once useful but now outworn attitudes and ways of being.

In this chapter, and at other points throughout the rest of this work, we sift into the symbolism layered into Varo's dream of the executioner. The intention behind our devotion to the imagery is to explore the link between the dream and the making of art as a subversive practice that furthers the lifelong process of individuation and the unfolding of the personality. Our archetypal approach to the art and life of Varo borrows from the work of Jung, who "observed that even the most upsetting and difficult manifestations of the psyche were part of a life-affirming purpose" (McNiff, 2004: 97). With Varo's dream of the executioner in mind, such a perspective prompts a question: Are Jung's words true about death dreams—are these images imaginal premonitions that may portend the final move in a person's process of personal growth?

As we follow Varo into a hidden world where owls paint and women weave the garment of a new world, we calibrate our compass not to a destination but to the enlivening experience of the archetypal terrain of image and symbol. Our travels together are devoted to a psychological experience of the images in more than three dozen Varo paintings, along with symbolic amplification of the imagery in the artist's dream of the executioner. Beyond art as a mode of self-inquiry, we consider another possibility: Varo was working not only to accomplish personal growth, but through painted images to birth archetypal forces into the material world in a bid to bring vitality and transformation to human experience at a collective level.

Later in this chapter, we look at *Still Life Reviving*, the last painting Varo completed before her heart attack, because this piece suggests the larger-than-personal context her life, work, and transformation entailed. We travel with Varo into the symbolic spaces of this painting and the imaginal connections between the painting and her death. Nestled alongside our look at *Still Life Reviving* are hints of a nuanced, symbolic amplification of Varo's dream of an encounter with an executioner ordered to kill her for discovering "an extremely important secret, something like a part of the 'absolute truth'" (Varo, 1997/2018: 94). As we look in later chapters at other paintings, and finally at the dream itself, we will begin to unravel what Varo knew that was so subversive it would destroy the "social structure" of the world if others knew it (94).

The dream of the executioner and the renewing aspect of the dangerous secret

In the dream of the executioner, Varo has a secret. As we begin to consider such a symbol, a thought or two from a Jungian perspective may help us touch into the imaginal bedrock of things. In *Psyche and Death*, German psychotherapist Edgar Herzog wrote,

The ability to endure the presence of death in life is of decisive importance for human living. To open oneself to death is to accept the aspect of "becoming," that is, of transformation, which is the very stuff of life. (1948/2000: 9)

"Death-dreams," Herzog added, "are associated with an ever-increasing courage and an increasing readiness to face crises involving the transformation of the personality" (138).

In an essay on the alchemical aspects of Varo's work, Fariba Bogzaran, an artist and scientist, wrote,

> Similar to shamanic initiation, death is the symbolic demise of the old self. In shamanic dream traditions, the dreamer going through the initiation to become a shaman might experience his or her "dream body" being dismembered, burnt or beheaded. "All flesh that is derived from the earth must be decomposed and again reduced to earth ... then the earthy salt produces a new generation by celestial resuscitation ... For in earth is found the balm of nature and salt of those who have found the science of all things." (2008: 174)

With the image of death in the form of the executioner, and with the symbolic demise of the old self in mind, we wonder: How might the images in the dream be commenting upon or communicating about the process of transformation at work in Varo's life and in her art? On the subject of dream images, we might consider, as Jung did, "that as a rule the peculiar character of a dream-symbol depends upon the fact that it combines polar opposites in a single image" (Herzog, 1948/2000: 70). Symbolically speaking, from within the dream, the death of the old self suggests the death of the ego; however, we might also look at the death of the collective ego—after all, the knowledge Varo possesses in the dream threatens to destroy the fabric of the world.

Applied to the image of the executioner, Varo's encounter with death might also be seen not only as termination of a life (real or imagined) but as death in service to "transformation by new birth" (Herzog, 1948/2000: 70). "Inner crises of transformation," Herzog wrote,

> are often foreshadowed by dreams in which the patient is confronted by death, either directly or in the form of an archaic image. Such an experience of dying is potentially an expression of the full reality of life in that it symbolizes transformation, but it only bears fruit if the dreamer can go beyond the purely negative aspect of the death-image which does no more than create panic; and this "going beyond" is not a question of intellectual insight, but of sufficient maturity to accept death within life as it is actually lived. (136)

Still Life Reviving: **Varo's last painting and preparation for death**

"If each dream is a step into the underworld," Hillman wrote, "then remembering a dream is a recollection of death and opens a frightening crevice under our feet" (1979: 131). "Each dream," Hillman added, "is practice in entering the underworld, a preparation of the psyche for death" (133).[1] With the imagery in Varo's dream of the executioner in mind, we wonder: Did Varo's actions within the dream mean that, at least on an unconscious level, she had accepted the possibility that her physical life was (or might be) coming to an end?

According to Tere Arcq, Varo "had a presentiment of her passing" (2008: 84). Arcq described the process as conscious enough that, in the months leading up to her death, the artist "made up some packages with some of her more precious belongings, such as her collection of crystals and stones, and gave them to her closest friends" (84). Margaret Carson, translator of a recent volume of Varo's letters, dreams, and other writings, added in a footnote that Walter Gruen, the artist's companion during her later years in Mexico City, believed that imaginal death at the hands of the executioner was, indeed, evidence that an unconscious part of Varo's psyche was trying to signal the end of her human life (see Varo, 1997/2018, "Translator's Notes": 120).

Following these thoughts and turning inward toward the archetypal imperatives at work in Varo's life, the imagery in the artist's dream of the executioner suggests psychologically that the teleological arc of her physical life was in the process of arriving at a place of completion. We see metaphorical possibilities of this process of transformation both in the dream of the executioner and in her final work, an oil on canvas Varo called *Still Life Reviving*.

The painting, Engel wrote, "works on many levels. On a literal level, with its energized depiction of a common domestic scene, it is a sardonic comment on the inertness of the typical still life" (1986: 14). Metaphorically, the painting depicts fruit revolving like "planets circling the sun"; philosophically it

> is a powerful affirmation of the concept of reincarnation, of the birth, death, and rebirth of all things. For here, in the real or scientific world, the harmony is not perfect: the fruits, representing planets that have swerved out of orbit (to a medieval mind like Varo's, a sure sign of the apocalypse), have collided and scattered their seeds to the ground. But from this portent of chaos and destruction, comes instead a cycle of regeneration, the creation of new matter to replace the old, for the seeds have taken root and sprouted as plants that will bear fruit. And the universe can go on. Neither simple harmony nor uncontrolled chaos, *Still Life Reviving* is Varo's boldest and most hopeful statement of a world in mythic and scientific balance. (14)

Figure 4.1 Study for *Still Life Reviving*, Remedios Varo, pencil tracing on paper, 1963. © Artists Rights Society (ARS), NY. Photo Credit: Schalkwijk/Art Resource, NY.

Engel closed his essay, "Remedios Varo: Science into Art," written to introduce Varo at 1986 exhibitions of the artist's work in New York and Washington, D.C., by noting that two years after Varo finished *Still Life Reviving*, "astronomers ... discovered cosmic background radiation, a remnant of the original cosmic fireball" (1986: 14). The discovery, he added, "effectively laid the steady-state theory to rest" (14). Cosmologically speaking, steady-state theory holds that the universe is

> always expanding, but maintains a constant average density, with matter being continuously created to form new stars and galaxies at the same rate that old ones become unobservable as a consequence of their increasing distance and velocity of recession.
>
> ("Steady-State Theory," 2020: para. 1)

Steady-state theory, popular in the 1950s, became obsolete after astronomers discovered that the cosmos is continually evolving.

In his essay, Engel wondered what Varo would have made of the astronomers' discovery. Engel added that the artist's heart attack fixed things so that Varo did not have the opportunity to reflect on it: "Around the time of *Still Life Reviving*, she became obsessed with disease and death to the point of near-paralysis, like the fruit in the painting that remain frozen in mid-air" (1986: 14). If, however, we imagine Varo's planetary fruit in movement, "swerving out of orbit" as they rise, her image reflects a process of dynamic evolution.

In the fall of 1963, Varo "confided to her close friend Gunther Gerzso that she no longer wanted to live" (Engel, 1986: 14). Based on Engel's timeline, Varo was dead within a month. The cause of death was listed as a heart attack, brought on, it seems, by the stress to her nervous system of multiple unresolved traumas, and her habit of drinking "endless cups of coffee" and smoking as many as three packs of cigarettes a day (Kaplan, 1988: 223).

Still Life Reviving, as we have said, proved to be Varo's last finished work. "Strangely enough," Engel wrote, the artist's final canvas

> is her only major painting without a human figure. It is as if she saw her life winding down and could keep it going only on a higher plane, transmuted from flesh to spirit, from mass to pure energy. *Still Life Reviving* is thus a self-portrait, after all. Varo cannot be seen, and yet her presence lingers, like the cosmic background radiation, long after the substance has vanished. (1986: 14)

Varo's images in *Still Life Reviving* link the nature of human life with the cyclical and creative nature of the cosmos. If George Orwell was right, and "all art is to some extent propaganda" (2008: 198), Varo, in *Still Life Reviving*, seems to want to protest as deadening the unmediated archetypal Masculine drive for control, perfection, and self-preservation. The enlivening evolution that sustains life requires, values, and makes creative use of imperfection, chaos, and death. As a self-portrait, *Still Life Reviving* depicts Varo at the end of her life as having integrated these archetypal forces to obtain both an abstract understanding and an embodied experience of herself as fecund and alive.

Threads of change: Death, rebirth, and the dream of the executioner

Varo's dream of the executioner includes a host of images that are important if we are to engage with and understand the alchemical process of transformation at work in her art and life. There is the egg. There is weaving. There is the executioner. There is the man with whom she wove her destiny for all eternity. And there is the secret—the knowledge so dangerous she had to be killed. From a Jungian perspective, we can consider these related images as symbolic threads. In the chapters that follow we weave the threads of the dream through the artist's paintings to blend them into a gestalt that reveals the essence of who Varo was and the social change her images are trying to help us create.

In what follows, we work with Varo's dream and paintings not to unravel them, as Freud said, but, following Hillman, to restore to the images their "capacity to perturb the soul to excess that, by bringing an image close to death," makes it live again (1979: 130). For Varo, a painting was like a mirror: She was looking at herself in the images. Or perhaps she was looking at personified figures who were dreaming her life toward—or into—death for the purpose of initiating the rebirth of life on a more conscious, and more ensouled, plane.

With Varo, there is a powerful alchemy at work in which the ego responds to the soul's need to come alive through intimate proximity with death. Varo's images transport us into a realm of night and death where the soul shows us *its* experience of death and dying—thus bringing itself to life. Varo's paintings evoke the beauty and terror of soul living its trueness in and through its familiarity with and closeness to death. Lingering in the underworld and engaging with Varo in the alchemical process of *imaginatio,* we see that the soul knows how to engage with death, not only for the betterment of one person but for community and culture as well.

Note

1 In *The Dream and the Underworld,* Hillman wrote that "the idea that dreams are a preparation for death appears both among the romantics and the Greeks ... We may understand this now less literally and more as the removal of elements (*Tagesreste*) out of life and giving them soul values" (fn 55, 223).

References

Arcq, T. (2008). In search of the miraculous. In M. Orellano (Ed.), *Five keys to the secret world of Remedios Varo* (19–90). Mexico City, Mexico: Artes de Mexico.

Bogzaran, F. (2008). Dreams of alchemy. In M. Orellano (Ed.), *Five keys to the secret world of Remedios Varo* (159–86). Mexico City, Mexico: Artes de Mexico.

Engel, P. (1986). *Remedios Varo: Science into art.* New York, NY: New York Academy of Science.

Herzog, E. (1948/2000). *Psyche and death: Death-demons in folklore, myths, and modern dreams* (E. Cox & E. Rolfe, Trans.). Woodstock, CT: Spring Publications.

Hillman, J. (1979). *The dream and the underworld.* New York, NY: Harper & Row.

Kaplan, J. (1988). *Unexpected journeys: The art and life of Remedios Varo.* New York, NY: Abbeville Press.

McNiff, S. (2004). *Art heals: How creativity cures the soul.* Boston, MA: Shambhala.

Miller, J. (2004). *The transcendent function.* Albany, NY: State University of New York Press.

Orwell, G. (2008). T. S. Eliot. In G. Packer (Ed.), *George Orwell: All art is propaganda* (194–201). New York, NY: Houghton, Mifflin, Harcourt.

Steady-State Theory. (2020). In *Encyclopedia Britannica*. Retrieved from www.britannica.com/science/steady-state-theory

Varo, R. (1997/2018). *Letters, dreams & other writings* (M. Carson, Trans.). Cambridge, MA: Wakefield Press.

Chapter 5

Embroidering the Earth's Mantle

Psychology, alchemy, and weaving the garment of a new world

Embroidering the Earth's Mantle is one of Varo's more recognizable images. The painting is the center panel in a triptych, a series of three oil paintings Varo made on masonite in 1960–61. To understand the story told by and the symbolic threads woven through the three paintings, it is important to look at each piece.

Before we engage with the first painting in the triptych, *Toward the Tower*, it is necessary to finger briefly the threads of sewing, weaving, and painting as experiences that offered Varo a connection to women in her female lineage and an outlet through which she could channel her prodigious creative energies. "Varo," Kaplan wrote,

> had such a consuming interest in costumes and sewing that her sewing machine was accorded a position of honor at the 1983 retrospective of her work in Mexico City. She had made her own clothes since childhood, saying that tailors had no idea of a woman's anatomy, and as her cousins remember excitedly, she even designed her own shoes. (1988: 101)

Kaplan discovered a family photograph showing Varo as a girl, at work on a drawing (28). Her grandmother, Doña Maria Josefa Cejalvo, sits to her left, bent over a sewing machine. Sewing and weaving were skills the young girl would continue to perfect for the rest of her life, even in her paintings.

Kaplan explored the imagery in *Tailleur pour dames* (*Women's Tailor*), a 1957 piece that displayed "the breadth of imagination that Varo invested in costume design" (1988: 100).

The scene Varo painted takes place in "a fashion showroom in which a tailor has his models parade his latest creations before a potential client" (100). At the center of the image, a woman models a garment that is practical, and therefore ideal,

> for traveling, the back being in the shape of a boat. Upon reaching a body of water one falls over backwards. Behind the head is a rudder

Figure 5.1 Women's Tailor, Remedios Varo, oil on masonite, 1957. © Artists Rights Society (ARS), NY. Photo credit: Private Collection, Christie's Images/Bridgeman Images.

which one guides by pulling ribbons which go to the breast and from which hangs a compass ... On firm ground it rolls along and the lapels serve as miniature sails, as well as the walking stick in which there is a sail rolled up that unfolds.

(Varo, as cited in Kaplan, 1988: 100)

Another model sits on a chair made of a "miraculous cloth that hardens at will and can serve as a seat" (Varo, as cited in Kaplan, 1988: 101). Varo described a third model as "a widow" whose stylish garment is fashioned from "an effervescent cloth, like champagne" (101). The garment, Varo added, "has a little pocket for carrying a vial of poison and ends in a very becoming reptile's tail" (101). Not to be outdone (or left out), Varo noted that she painted the face of the tailor "in the shape of scissors," with a shadow "so rebellious that he has to pin it to the ceiling" (101). Last, but not least, is the tailor's client, a woman seated in the center of a bench at the viewer's left edge of the scene. The woman appears in triplicate, with a figure identical to her on either side of her. As described by Varo, these two figures appear as ghostlike outlines of a woman "who is contemplating the models," but "doesn't know which of the three styles to choose" from (101). The two "transparent repetitions," Varo said of the woman with her two shadow selves, "represent the state of doubt in which she finds herself" (101).

Varo's affinity with the craft of sewing and the painted figures in *Women's Tailor* reveal something of the artist's psychological life. Through their apparel, Varo hinted at the occupations of the figures in the painting. At the center is the adventurer, who falls metaphorically back into the waters of the unconscious, guided by her heart as compass. Behind her, Varo painted a model who seems to exemplify a woman trapped: She wears a scarf "of a miraculous cloth that hardens at will" designed "for going to those cocktail parties where you cannot move" (Varo, as cited in Kaplan, 1988: 101). In contrast, Varo wrote, the widow, no longer bound to a husband, is dressed in "an effervescent cloth, like champagne," a drink associated with celebration, and with the experience of release (thinking of the bubbles that rush forth when the cork of the bottle is removed) (101). With her vial of poison and reptile tail, in a garment that crisscrosses, the widow in the tailor's shop reminds us, perhaps, of the caduceus, the symbol of two intertwining snakes representing both venom and antivenom and thus an alchemical idea: The healing is in the wound. The undecided woman on the bench suggests the importance of contemplating what one may be preparing to do and how one may be best suited to it.

In a fundamental way, Varo learned to paint as she learned to sew. For Varo, an engineer's daughter, before sewing there was getting ready to sew—thinking about the type of garment she wanted to make, what kind of fabric to use, what colors would be best. The preparation that went into designing and sewing a garment brought Varo into an intimate and repeating rhythm she learned to love: the in-and-back-out of needle and thread, the binding of one thing with another, making scraps into a finished dress. The in-and-back-out motion of sewing resonates with the rhythm of contemplative psychological life—a scrap of soul, a projected piece of complexed emotion that Varo could catch on a thread of imagination and then sew, with paintbrush as needle, into tableaus of the real—alchemical scenes of transformation that deftly image new possibilities for herself and the world.

Later in her life, Varo brought the same meticulous precision to painting. "Conceiving whole scenes in her head," the artist began a painting "with meticulous drawings, working from live models for details of pose and gesture and from illustrated encyclopedias and objects she collected for furniture and prop details" (Kaplan, 1988: 125). Next, Varo

> transferred her completed drawings using a technique adapted from the methods of early Renaissance panel painters, pressing detail by detail through tracing paper onto the stiff fiberboard that she had carefully prepared with a white gesso ground. [Gesso is a primer made from a combination of paint pigment, chalk, and a binding agent, and is applied to help oil paint adhere to the surface of a canvas]. Painting

with thin glazes of oil and layers of varnish, she built up luminous color surfaces to which she added minute details, using a single-hair brush for precision. She also blew and blotted paint and added further details and highlights by scratching into the surface to reveal the white of the gesso beneath. The resulting combination of exquisitely controlled details and loosely flowing surfaces became a hallmark of Varo's style. (125)

For Varo, then, the paintbrush was also a knitting needle, the practice and process of painting a loom upon which she wove her soul's expressions of its inner life. With weaving, Varo was working metaphorically with a motif of great mythological power:

> Considered to be a woman's activity in many cultures, "weaving is an attribute of the fate-spinners ... the woven item, fabric or basketry is thought to impact the power of resurrection. The matter woven can produce the world of creation, of matter, vegetation or life. A woven garment was often given to the King-hero prior to his sacrifice; it guaranteed his resurrection." In some of [Varo's] best-known paintings, she used the act of weaving as a mode of creating a new reality.
>
> (Bogzaran, 2008: 177)

According to Arcq, a curator with expertise in surrealist art, Varo "often portrayed women weaving or embroidering in her paintings in order to address a fundamental theme: the transformation of the human being as a result of a conscious will" (2008: 40). In her essay, "In Search of the Miraculous," Arcq drew on insights on spiritual development from Rodney Collin, a British writer who trained with G. I. Gurdjieff's most prominent disciple, P. D. Ouspensky. Quoting from Collin's 1954 work, *The Theory of Celestial Influence: Man, the Universe and Cosmic Mystery,* and referencing Varo's use of weaving as a metaphor, Arcq wrote:

> Collin points out that there are four processes in a [human] being's inner evolution, and to illustrate this he uses the metaphor of processing and dying wool. First, the wool must be cleaned, passing through a purification process; second, it must be bleached, as the false personality is destroyed in order to recover its essence; third, it is dyed the desired color, in other words, the soul is implanted; finally, the color is fixed, which is the equivalent of the process of fixing the soul. The wool "is [now] ready to be woven into some material and to receive upon it designs or embroideries according to the requirements of a higher intelligence." (56–7)

With Collin's interpretation of the symbolism of weaving in mind, Arcq considered Varo's 1956 painting, *The Red Weaver.* In the painting, a dark woman patiently knits the figure of another woman who appears ready to take flight through the window. Yarn and scraps of fabric hang from the ceiling; two figures that look to be made of rags hang from the wall, useless. A small cat plays with a skein of black yarn, which is the very material the cat is made of. Where did the yarn that created the red woman come from? It is nowhere to be seen. (56–7)

Next to these thoughts, Arcq wondered,

Why did Varo entitle the painting *The Red Weaver*, when the knitting woman is black, not red? It seems to refer to the same process of purification: she knits the other woman from herself; she is "awake;" her eyes are not looking at the needles; she is not knitting with her senses but with her consciousness; she is creating her own soul and by giving it life, she begins to disappear, melding with her own shadow. (56–7)

Premonition: Weaving a woman's mystery

Varo first worked with the motifs of weaving and spinning in *Premonition*, a 1953 painting that features four women in white cloaks made from thread being spun on a loom powered by two orbs floating in the sky. Lauralie Marie Navolio, a scholar from Pacifica Graduate Institute, associated the white garments worn by the women with birth and with the swaddling clothes of infants or children (2004: 52). Navolio, who studied *Premonition* as part of a doctoral work focusing on the alchemical symbolism in a dozen Varo paintings, placed *Premonition* at a pivotal point in Varo's personal life and in her development as an artist.

The year was 1953. Varo had lived in Mexico City for more than a decade. By this time, the artist's relationship with surrealist Benjamin Perét, her second husband, had ended. So had a romance with Jean Nicolle, a French pilot who had accompanied Varo to Venezuela, where her brother, Rodrigo, got her a job making technical drawings of insects and parasites for an epidemiological study. Back in Mexico City, in 1949, Varo took up with Walter Gruen, the man she would spend the remainder of her life with.

Remedios and Walter had met in Mexico City in the early 1940s. Both had fled the European theater of war, where they had each suffered incarceration in French concentration camps (in Gruen's case he had also been held, as an Austrian, in a prisoner of war facility operated by the Germans). Walter Gruen's devotion to Varo included something the artist prized nearly as much as life itself: security. Gruen owned a prestigious record store in Mexico City. Before her work began to sell, Gruen supported Varo financially. Relieved of the burden of having to line up commercial work to pay her bills, Varo, safe in the embrace of Gruen's attentiveness and constancy, could "devote herself fully to her own artistic vision" (Kaplan, 1988: 119).

By 1953, when she painted *Premonition*, Varo had re-stitched the threads of her life into a new configuration. She was thriving, both as a person and as an artist. In *Premonition*, Varo invites us to peek behind the veil at the process of transformation taking place within her. Linger with the image and one feels a numinous ritual quality to her painting. Even with the implied movement of the pulleys, wheels, and belts, one does not hear the whirring of machinery. Instead, we step noiselessly into the silence of sacred space. "Silence," wrote Jay Ramsay, in the context of alchemy as the art of transformation, "leaves us open to pure experience. Silence means we can listen and be guided. Silence means we … have space inside us to receive what we don't yet know" (1997: 148).

Spiritually speaking, *Premonition* exposes the hopeful tenderness Varo felt as she opened into the experience of learning to live her life shaped by the unseen forces that are powering the loom. Each of Varo's paintings tells a story. As a visual narration, *Premonition* portrays Varo's birth as a sacred seamstress on a mythic scale. For on a checkerboard floor under a dark desert sky, Varo shows us the spiritual birth of four women—figures who are being robed in divine essence and spun into a new way of being.

Premonition overflows with symbolism. Looking at the wheels that power the loom as a type of circle, from a classical Jungian perspective they may be seen as representing the driving influence of the archetypal Self. The wheels in Varo's painting turn on power produced by belts that wrap around the two spheres orbiting in the sky above. As circles, the spheres also may be considered symbolic representations of the mysterious presence and wisdom of the Self. Navolio linked the orbs in Varo's painting to an image featured in one of Jung's reflections on Mercurius: "the sphere girdled in quick-silver," an alchemical symbol for the raw matter being worked on in the opus (as cited in Navolio, 2004: 53). With these symbols in mind, "Varo's image invokes Mercurius as the animating figure of a transformational process which is energized by forces 'beyond' in the sky, but which takes place on earth, in the physical form of weaving on a loom powered by wheels" (Navolio, 2004: 53). We might also say that in its dual representation—as cosmic orbs and wheels—the spiritual and instinctual aspects of the Self combine to spin the fabric that clothes the female figures.

Moved by the motion of the wheels, we come symbolically to the loom itself. "Weaving," Navolio wrote, "has long been identified with feminine activity," and "looms are associated with feminine industry" (2004: 54). What is Varo trying to tell us through the image of women being threaded into a new reality by the unseen presence that energizes the loom? Through the imagery in the painting, the artist

is revealing that she has discovered something new and mysterious in her psyche, and also that she has come to realize that a power far beyond her personal capacities is, in fact, responsible for her artistic achievements, just as it is responsible in the painting for the construction of the clothing. (56)

From a Jungian perspective, *Premonition* "depicts the mechanism of ... creation as being powered by forces far outside daily human experience—essentially by Mercurius as a manifestation of the Self" (Navolio, 2004: 56). In the painting, Varo "has taken a personal symbol—dressmaking—and reworked it into [a narrative depiction of] how transcendent influences can fuel and shape an artistic endeavor" (56).

Before leaving the ritual birth in *Premonition*, and before looking at the Varo triptych that includes *Embroidering the Earth's Mantle*, there is a detail that adds nuance to our engagement with the artist's imagery. In the original painting, Varo chose silver and white for the color of the spheres that power the loom. In some reproductions of the painting, however, there is a hint of blue to the spheres and to the machinery, including the wheels. In some reproductions even the cloaks worn by the women have a tint of blue to them. Blue, as we noted earlier, is a color the alchemists associated with imagination and with the mood of melancholy.

This blue thread leads back into the scene Varo painted in *The Red Weaver*, a work we looked at earlier. In this painting, a woman weaves in a tower. With the knitting needles in her lap, the "garment" the weaver produces is another woman. Nearing completion, the red woman, knitted from thread that gathers from a source in the clouds, rises toward an open window. Here Varo again uses weaving as a metaphor to depict and express the inner experience of a woman's birth into her own female nature.

Varo's use of the color blue in *The Red Weaver* is psychologically meaningful. The weaver appears blue, or black as Arcq observed, or a combination of both. The thread being used to knit the red woman is also blue, as are the clouds and sky from which the thread appears to gather beyond the window. Even the color of the fur of the cat playing with the ball of yarn is a black that shines with a hint of blue. Symbolically, Varo may want the viewer of the painting to know that imagination, symbolized by the color blue, can be used to weave a new experience from the remnants of the blackened first matter. The artist may also be trying to tell us that melancholy can be transformed from the density of depressed mood into the emotional fullness and vitality symbolized by the color red and by the coming to life of the woman whose potential has been woven into a new form from the black and blue matter of difficult experience.

Wholeness, from a Jungian perspective, is not about perfection; it is about the fullness brought about through a relationship with the Self. The blue moods of melancholy and the subtractions of suffering are needed for our personality to ripen into its fullness. Varo used weaving in the paintings we have looked at to evoke the experience needed for a woman to come home to herself. Eight years after painting *Premonition*, in 1961, Varo's work with the metaphor of weaving reached a new level of clarity in *Embroidering the Earth's Mantle*. With this image, Arcq said, Varo granted a group of young women in a tower "the power to transform the cosmos, the universe, or perhaps even fate" (2008: 40).

Toward the Tower: Varo, the beehive, and the retelling of a traitorous truth

The first painting in Varo's triptych, *Toward the Tower*, shows a group of uniformed girls bicycling away from a tower. The girls all look the same: white collar, gray cloak, red hair. The girls follow a "Mother Superior" figure and a bearded man who carries a bag on his back. Birds emerge from the bag, flying in what appears to be a formation guarding the girls. The painting, rendered in blue-grays and brown-golds, recreates the *prima materia* of the "restrictive atmosphere of [Varo's] early years in Spain," and can be seen, Kaplan believes, as a self-reflection on a "rebellious schoolgirl yearning for escape" (1988: 18). Commenting further on the painting, Juliana Gonzáles, a friend of Varo's, saw the tower as a metaphor, a

> beehive structure created by thousands of enthusiastic souls, working hard to prolong traditions, to perpetuate the work of the ancestors. An old and austere world enclosed by walls of virtue, lined with great chests filled with virtue; sentiments firm and inflexible without possibility of deviation. The Spanish child in a world of shadows, of fears, of narrow corridors, of musty furniture ... a world in which improvisation has no place, for all is prearranged.
>
> (As cited in Kaplan, 1988: 18)

In a note, Varo reflected on the plot and meaning of her painting:

> The girls are leaving their beehive-house to go to their job. They're being guarded by the birds so that none can escape. Their eyes are as if hypnotized, they hold their knitting needles like handlebars. Only the girl in front resists the hypnosis. (1997/2018: 109)

In this first of the three related paintings, Varo sets up a tension. As an imagined self-reflection and symbolic self-portrait, Varo has portrayed the world of a girl trapped in soul-stifling convention. In this unconscious space, black birds guard the girls. Perhaps they act like Jungian psychoanalyst Donald Kalsched's intrapsychic Protector/Persecutor, a representative of "an archaic ... internal self-care system" determined "to preserve, protect, and persecute the vulnerable personal spirit of the individual in an effort to keep it 'inside' and out of reality" (1996: 115). The birds fly with the girls to signify the new ideas and potentials that are hidden in shadow and the oppressive forces that prevent them from being birthed into the conscious experience of the young woman who resists the hypnosis.

Varo's note reveals an important symbolic detail: The girls are fleeing a *beehive* house. Working imagistically toward transformation from an image of austere, inflexible structure, Varo engaged with the enlivening psychological potency of the symbol. With an understanding of alchemical psychology in mind, we can consider the beehive tower as a painted projection—an experience of the artist's unconscious inner life communicated in the form of an image. According to Sandra Thomson, the alchemists noticed profound changes taking place within themselves in working with both matter and the projected contents of their own souls: In alchemical work, "the emerging knowledge and self-awareness results in revitalization of the inner spirit and eventually the union of the conscious mind with the unconscious to form a 'new being' who understands him or herself in a different way" (2003: 18).

From a Jungian perspective, the beehive house becomes a way for Varo to engage with her own soul, as well as a way for viewers of her work to sift into the metaphoric messages coded into the imagery. "Archetypal images," Thomson wrote, "serve to help us confront the unknown, without and within... Attending to archetypal images and associations helps us to enhance our inner perspective, and especially to awaken to unrealized possibilities" (2003: 9). Was this way of attending to her inner life and to archetypal presences an aspect of the secret knowledge Varo discovered that was dangerous to the executioner?

Cued by Varo's note about the beehive tower, we can sift deeper into the symbolism of bees. "An exploration and amplification of the symbolism of bees, the honey and the hive leads into concepts of balance in nature, of the Great Mother, and of the embodied spirit—that is, spirit embodied in matter or in the natural world" (Luton, 2011: 46). Johann Bachofen, a Swiss anthropologist and sociologist known for his theory of matriarchy and his work on the role of women in ancient societies, observed that the bee was "looked upon as a symbol of the feminine potency of nature ... It ... symbolised the earth, its motherliness, its never-resting, artfully formative busy-ness" (as cited in Luton, 2011: 51). Frith Luton, a Jungian analyst and former beekeeper, linked the symbolism of the honeybee with the theory and practice of alchemical psychology:

> Honey, the miraculous sweet golden substance or healing elixir that is produced by the bees, can be seen as one form of the alchemical lapis (the living, flowing stone) ... Symbolically, the bees' honey making, and their regulation of the hive (that is, of the whole colony) and dedication to their queen have much in common with the *chrysopoeia* (the gold-making) of alchemy and with the entire alchemical opus, and thus with the psychological individuation process described by C. G. Jung. (9–10)

"Bees," Luton wrote, "are associated with hardworking, communal activity in the service of the future of the hive. This activity focuses on the queen, the only egg-laying female" (2011: 18). Luton added: "The whole energy of the bees is directed to serving this centre, a ruling principle around which the entire life of the hive is focused" (19–20).

Amplifying the symbolism and psychology of bees, honey, and the hive, Luton looked briefly at "The Queen Bee," a fairytale from the Grimms' collection. In the story, the queen is drawn to pure honey, found only on the lips of the true princess. A symbolic tutelage in how to tell the difference between real royalty from false authority, the fairy tale, according to Luton, "suggests that the queen of the hive points the way to or symbolizes the life-preserving, inspiring and nourishing eternal value of what, in depth psychological terms, is called the Self" (20). In the process of individuation, the Self is the governing center of the generative hive of the psyche, from which images like bees are sent with creative potential into the light of consciousness and the world. Luton wrote,

> In the symbolism of divine inspiration we often see the image of a bee settling on the honeyed lips of the gifted mortal. In this way the honeybee is connected with the descent of the gifts of the spirit to humankind and then, in return, with the potential offering-up (the ascent) by humankind of creative work with eternal value. (20)

With the girls fleeing the beehive house in a hypnotic state, we see the implication that in the Catholic education of young women, creative work and its relationship with spirituality has been subsumed by patriarchal forces. Yet, for the one fleeing girl who, as Varo indicated, resists hypnosis, the fecund symbiotic interaction between bees and flowers suggests a fertilization process is at work in Varo's psyche. When a bee collects nectar and pollen from a flower, some pollen from the male reproductive part of the flower, which is called the stamen, sticks to the hairs of the bee's body and legs. When the bee visits the next flower, some of the pollen rubs off, and is transferred, onto the stigma, the tip of the pistil or the female reproductive organ of the flower. If we move from botany and entomology to the nonliteral realm of symbol and metaphor, given that each member in a colony of bees is dedicated to serving the community and the queen, the beehive-house also suggests symbolically that the imagery is not only about Varo but on another level it is about the important service one member provides to the group—one person in service to the evolution and well-being of the collective.

With *Toward the Tower*, Varo painted a potent piece of symbolic alchemy. For in this composition, Varo, an artist committed to questioning authority, images a cataclysmic moment of transformation in the girl who "resists the hypnosis," that is, refuses to ride along passively with the other girls who are following the Mother Superior and the man to their job (Varo,

1997/2018: 109). Psychologically, with the word *hypnosis*, Varo could be referring to the soporific effect on women of the internalization of cultural complexes related to misogyny and the patriarchal projection of the feminine and its devaluation onto women. In this state of hypnosis, it is as if they are functioning from a culturally imposed self that disavows their creative potential. "The group," wrote Thomas Singer, "may develop a defensive system akin to the individual," such as the projection of unwanted experiences and qualities onto nonmembers, "but in this case its goal is to protect the group or collective spirit rather than the individual spirit" (2004: 19). The group or cultural unconscious, as part of the individual psyche, informs its members' identity development, determining what self-concepts, values, and behaviors allow one to have belonging and security. The overriding will to power in the culture of patriarchy and its rugged, competitive individualism have engendered a hypnotic normalcy in which the nonrational, creative, and inclusive feminine principle has been split off from consciousness. The relational, nurturing energies have been recruited to support the status quo. In these cultures, the qualities Woodman associated with the Apocalyptic Mother, which would threaten patriarchal values, creating nonhierarchical and non-exclusionary contexts, are, unfortunately, depotentiated (Woodman & Sieff, 2015).

Thomas Singer posited that "a traumatized group presents only a 'false self' to the world, and the world cannot 'see' the group in its more authentic and vulnerable identity... The group complexes create bipolar fields," activating "in external reality the very splits that have splintered the inner world" (2004: 19). Thus, the misogynistic complex that lurks in the patriarchal cultural unconscious can be detected in the privileging of men over women, who bear the projection of a feminine construed to serve the interests of men. Singer added, "Like personal complexes, cultural complexes provide a simplistic certainty about the group's place in the world in the face of otherwise conflicting and ambiguous uncertainties" (21). This security is extended to individuals through the conformity that assures one's membership in the group. Singer highlighted how difficult it can be for a person to resist the unconscious dynamics of a complex at work on a group level:

> One can easily imagine how the individual's ego can identify with a cultural complex as a defense against a more painful and isolating personal complex. It is far easier to split off one's individual suffering ... and get caught up in a mass movement than it is to carry the burden of one's individual pain. (21)

From a Jungian perspective, this is precisely what Varo has the girl in her painting do: She stays present to her own suffering. The difficulty of doing this is compounded when one's individual pain is a consequence of oppressive and repressive factors in one's culture—when one finds oneself the only one among one's peers bicycling with eyes open. Psychologically, experiences that are unrecognizable within one's outer world

> are then unrecognizable to one's internal regime. The traumatized individual is holding what others wish to repel, that which has no place in collective reality and which is situated outside the symbolic order... Events that threaten the taboos of social order (such as incest) or that make large demands on people's fragile compassion resources ... are easier to disavow than to ingest.
>
> (Guralnik & Simeon, 2010: 405–6)

Because "one's sense of personhood [is] carved out" of the recognition and belonging received within one's social context (408), it requires moral courage to individuate, differentiating from collective unconscious influences and embodying one's authentic values and creative potential (Jung, 1921/1971: paras. 757–62).

For Varo, who felt stifled and conflicted, perhaps even traumatized, by family and cultural values related to religion and gender, and who then experienced the trauma of war and imprisonment, lingering in the distress of personal complexes is one way to begin the psychological work of separating what is personal from that which is cultural and archetypal. "Differentiating the personal, cultural and archetypal levels of complexes," Thomas Singer wrote, "requires careful attention to each of these realms, without condensing or telescoping one into the other, as if one were more real or true than the other" (2004: 21).

In *Toward the Tower*, Varo spoke a traitorous truth: In a patriarchy, women are in servitude to male authority. With the image of a group of girls following a man to their job, Varo symbolized the way girls are inculcated to hypnotically follow men and patriarchal women from the beehive of creative potential into the world. In a patriarchy, a woman's job is to go along with the subordination of her talents, the silencing of her voice, the governing of her agency—all subtle coercions in service to the muting of feminine potential and the perpetuation of male authority. With female empowerment in mind, the critical plot point in *Toward the Tower* takes place when one of the girls awakens to what is happening—and she resists.

From a Jungian perspective, the bee, the process of pollination, and the purpose of the project of pollination (service to the collective, the ongoing life of the hive) points to psychological potentials awakening below the surface of conscious awareness. Caught on canvas, aspects of Varo's personality, symbolized by honeybees, buzz away from confinement. Some cycle away as if still hypnotized, following the man with the bag on his back as if in a dream, but one of the girls is awake and resists, looking away from the road ahead. Through amplification of its scenery, Varo's image of the bicycling girls—some unaware but one with eyes alert—buzzes with vitality and possibility beyond bettering her own well-being. For this artist, devoted to the practice of re-enchanting the world through imagination, the personal work of individuation creates meaning and value for the collective as bees become metaphoric messengers carrying the secrets of life and service into the world beyond the hive.

Viewed psychologically, *Toward the Tower* captures Varo in projected form—a girl with red hair and almond eyes riding to her job from her bee-hive house, the convent where she lived in enforced uniformity with other girls. Varo's mother sent her to the nuns to learn "to fear the Devil" (Engel, 1986: 1). But for the girl whose life was supposed to remedy the death of an older sister, there was more than religious dogma to the indoctrination. The convent was where Remedios was supposed to fulfill her mother's desire that she grow into a "cheerful, supportive, self-sacrificing" Spanish wife, devoted to "traditional domestic chores such as sewing, cooking, and childrearing" (White, 2014: 16). The convent was where she was supposed to learn to submit to a life of limitation. Varo, the girl in the convent, would be expected to grow into a woman who knew her place in a patriarchal world that did not allow females to find their own job or open a bank account without her husband's permission. But in the moment caught in the painting, the girl looks away from the road she has been traveling. In her note on the painting, Varo left a symbolic clue that hints at how the story of the girl on the bicycle might continue in the next piece. The girl rides a bicycle with a knitting needle for a handlebar. With the knitting needle we finger a thread pulling us into the central painting in Varo's triptych, *Embroidering the Earth's Mantle*.

Women at work: *Embroidering the Earth's Mantle* and the alchemical Feminine

In *Embroidering the Earth's Mantle*, Varo further evoked the distress she experienced as a student in a Catholic convent.

In this middle panel of her triptych, the girls from *Toward the Tower* are now at work in a tall tower weaving the garment of the world. Under the supervision of a spiritual mistress or alchemist, the girls use their needle-work skills to weave "a landscape with houses, ponds, streams, boats, animals, and humans, all nestled within the folds of the fabric" (Kaplan, 1988: 21). With the cultural context of patriarchy in mind, the image of women confined to a tower and following instructions to weave the garment of the world suggests how stifled Varo felt, born and bred into a society in which women were considered property, a possession owned first by their father, later by a husband (White, 2014: 16).

The sadness and unexpressed anger Varo felt can be seen on the faces of the young women working in the tower, a phallic enclosure of male

Figure 5.2 Embroidering the Earth's Mantle, Remedios Varo, oil on masonite, 1961. © Artists Rights Society (ARS), NY. Image courtesy of Gallery Wendi Norris, San Francisco.

dominance. Yet in this painting, Varo held a tension of opposites for there is something else: Notice in the center of the tower, a broth boiling in a vessel stirred by the medieval figure dressed in a wine-colored cloak. Notice, too, that the threads the women are using to embroider the earth's mantle emerge from this vessel—as if the hooded alchemist is brewing the fabric into being, a birth brought about through the act of stirring and through the attentiveness to what Kaplan called the "catechism of instructions" contained in the book the spiritual leader reads from (1988: 19). Follow further the flow of the narrative Varo is weaving: Billowing clouds of fabric spill down from the battlements around the facets of the tower. Held together here is the imprisonment in conformity and the creative potential of the feminine. What Varo is imaging here is a creation myth, but one that raises the question: Is the fabric made from threads brought to life in a boiling broth used for the purpose of birthing a new cosmos or, under the direction of the androgynous alchemist, sustaining the old?

It is, perhaps, the conflict between the familiar and the birth of something new that draws Oedipa Maas in Pynchon's *The Crying of Lot 49* to

Varo's painting. Oedipa Maas is an "ordinary young housewife" who has been named the executor of the will of a wealthy former lover (Colvile, 1988: 12). Faced with a new task, Oedipa, wrote Pynchon, "felt exposed, finessed, put down. She had never executed a will in her life, didn't know where to begin, didn't know how to tell the law firm in L.A. that she didn't know where to begin" (1966: 12). Early in the story, Oedipa remembers wandering into an art gallery in Mexico City with her now-dead lover. On the wall at the gallery is Varo's painting of girls trapped in a tower embroidering the garment of a new world. Why, before she knows what is happening, does Oedipa weep? The girls in the tower remind Oedipa of herself: a "captive maiden" trapped in a man's world "seeking hopelessly to fill the void" inside herself (Pynchon, 1966: 21). Oedipa realizes that Varo's "tower, its height and architecture, are like her ego only incidental: that what really keeps her where she is is magic, anonymous and malignant, visited on her from outside and for no reason at all" (21).

In her book on the symbolic importance of Varo's painting to *The Crying of Lot 49,* Georgiana Colvile noted that Oedipa's last name, Maas, "constitutes part of the Dutch word *Maaswerk* ... which means the woof or background threads through which the warp is woven and which forms the hidden part of the tapestry" (1988: 12). Pynchon, Colvile wrote, used Varo's painting to represent "the weaving and/or embroidering of a tapestry, itself a metaphor for Oedipa's quest" to execute the will and discover herself in the process (12).

Colvile pinpointed the symbolic complexity of the title Varo chose for *Embroidering the Earth's Mantle*: "The girls are embroidering a mantle to cover the earth. The earth's 'mantle,' in a geological sense, means its crust or surface layer, which is very thin and hides its true substance" (1988: 52). Reflecting on Oedipa's desperate efforts "to fill her own inner void," Colvile wrote that Pynchon's heroine discovers that "probing deeper" into her own pain proves "dangerous, it is easier to stick to the crust or mantle of one's world," as doing otherwise threatens both one's established sense of self and social norms (52). Oedipa weeps in the presence of Varo's painting because the image evokes unconscious ambivalence: "The girls are kept busy by their work, which is cloaking their world in redundant stereotyped respectability" (52). Oedipa is drawn to the safe confines of conformity, on the one hand, while on the other hand she longs to discover deeper meaning and a sense of her own agency.

We have been looking at the first two paintings in Varo's triptych. In a narrative sense, the hypnotic feeling portrayed in *Toward the Tower* continues in the second painting as the girls work with no windows through which to see what they are weaving. The thread of the new world comes into being through their efforts but without agency or ownership. In essence, the young women are weaving a world for others to live in, a world that does not belong to them.

Self-representation and the transformative concept of the double

With all of this going on—with a static creative process perpetually bringing the world as it is into being—it's possible to overlook the aspect of the image where Varo wove a transformative element into the garment of the world. Varo's "rebellious heroine" working at the table in the front left corner of the tower weaves "a ruse" into the garment through which she escapes the tower to meet her lover (Kaplan, 1988: 21; Varo, 1997/2018: 109). The rendezvous of the lovers, Kaplan wrote, is

> subtly visible in a rendering hidden upside-down within the folds that flow from her table. In a masterful variant on the myth of creation, she has used this most genteel of domestic handicrafts to create her own hoped-for escape. Unlike Rapunzel and the Lady of Shalott, Varo's young heroine imprisoned in the tower is not merely a metaphor for confinement, but also an agent of her own liberation. To free herself from the strict academic tradition of faithfully recreating nature according to preordained rules and from the anonymity of being one among an indistinguishable many (all the girls have the same face) she connives to flee the tower that isolates her from the very life she is expected to create. (1988: 21)

The girl's image of herself with her lover, concealed by trees in a fold of cloak, evokes the motif of the doppelgänger, or double. "The Double is a complex, even riddling concept," wrote Marina Warner (2002: 163).

> It can mean a second self, or a second existence, usually coexisting in time, but sometimes sequentially, as in soul migration plots ... It can mean a lookalike who is a false twin, or, more commonly, someone who does not resemble oneself outwardly but embodies some inner truth. In this sense, the double, while wholly dissimilar, unnervingly embodies a true self... To be doubled can entail ... that you are shadowed by another, and that someone else is living with your identity, and that that identity has been stolen; in this way the doppelgänger derives its being from the nexus of ideas about soul theft and multiple, wandering spirits that structure the living dead. (163–4)

In *Embroidering the Earth's Mantle*, it might be considered that the double hidden in the fold of fabric is the authentic self—an emerging, but still unconscious, aspect of Varo's personality escaping imprisonment, symbolized by the tower. This doubling works alchemically with the *prima materia* of the patriarchal forces and expectations surrounding Varo's early life. In the painting, the artist uses imagination to distill the essence trapped in the *nigredo* and send it into the world in a rendezvous with love. In pondering "possible states of personal identity," Warner reflected that

> the copy—the you who is not you but is yet another you—challenges the premiss of individual integrity; it also performs, it seems, a daemonic act of metamorphosis from inanimate to animate that in mythology often discloses divine operation. (2002: 202)

Varo worked with the motif of doubling again in *The Lovers*, a 1963 mixed-media painting on bristol board. In this piece, Varo seats a couple on a bench. She has replaced, or refashioned, their heads into antique mirrors framed in gold. Mirrors of gold suggest symbolically that what is being reflected back to each person is connected with alchemical practices "leading to transmutation of base metal into gold as well as to a mystical union [of opposing elements] transcending space, time, and sexual differentiation" (Hubert, 1994: 269). And indeed, the faces of the lovers are identical, suggesting perhaps such a merging or union that transcends their genders.

Yet, the mirrors in *The Lovers* have troubled more than one critic. For Renée Riese Hubert, "mirrors encircling captive likenesses" suggest "a state of imprisonment" (1994: 269). Hubert suggested that the image of "lovers with their identical mirrors" might also "satirize the myth of Narcissus, who fell in love with his own drowned reflection" (269). Janet Kaplan traveled in this same symbolic direction: "Having deferred her artistic development to the demands of several love affairs," Varo "had reason to understand that such relationships could block personal fulfillment" (1988: 151). Lost in each other's mirrored gaze and threatened by clouds of vaporizing steam and a rising tide of emotion, unless the lovers can "break out of their stuporous adoration, they will surely drown. Although this is a rare instance in Varo's work of loving contact between two people, she mocks such personal attachments as a potential source of doom" (151). Yet it is very much like Varo that this image may have a double meaning. Linked with the problem the two people in the painting are having with water, it seems possible that Varo was also saying something about dissolution, the alchemical operation that liquifies aspects of the personality—such as that in which the woman finds her identity in the man she is with. In dissolution, Varo's painting suggests that fixed forms can be reconfigured.

Symbolically, Varo's image of relationship in *The Lovers* suggests the loss of Eros and true relationality, which requires the presence of an authentic other. This loss was perhaps connected to the sense of doom she felt in contemplating the type of marriage for which the convent would groom her. This contrasts with the image of lovers in *Embroidering the Earth's Mantle*. Here the lovers are hidden in the folds of the garment as if to imply the subversive nature of their meeting and the need to keep it a secret. Painting a secret into the garment, and an opening for her double into a new space, Varo re-imagines confinement in despair and hopelessness.

Sifting further into the symbolism of *Embroidering the Earth's Mantle*, look behind and to the left of the hooded alchemist at a veiled figure playing a flute, who appears to be the girls' guardian or chaperone. With this figure, Varo adds to weaving and the double a third metaphor: music. Varo, according to Navolio, "had an abiding interest in music and repeatedly looked to it as a symbol of the wholeness and harmony she sought all her life" (2004: 83). Navolio suggested that Varo's metaphorical use of music evokes Boethius, the Roman philosopher, who "distinguished three types of symbolical music," including "the music of humanity," an inner harmony that each individual hears from within (81). Virginia Woolf plucked these same harp strings in *Moments of Being*:

> We, I mean all human beings—are connected with this; that the whole world is a work of art; that we are parts of the work of art. *Hamlet* or a Beethoven quartet is the truth about this vast mass that we call the world. But there is no Shakespeare; there is no Beethoven; certainly and emphatically there is no God; we are the words; we are the music, we are the thing itself.
>
> (As cited in Marcus, 1987: epigraph)

We can see this sentiment in *Solar Music*, in which Varo depicted making music in a forest on strings of light, and in *Creation of the Birds*, where with a violin heart a figure paints birds into life.

In looking at *Embroidering the Earth's Mantle* as Varo's externalization in images of an intrapsychic dynamic responding to her sociocultural situation, the flute-playing guardian can be imagined, like the birds in the triptych's first panel, *Toward the Tower*, as both imprisoning the girls and with Boethius's inner harmony playing through the room, protecting and remembering their wholeness.

In *Embroidering the Earth's Mantle*, the hooded medieval master reads from an open book. Symbolically, wrote Navolio, a book suggests

> divine or secret knowledge... In alchemy, the *opus* was expressed symbolically by a book. At times the book was open, sometimes closed, according to whether the *prima materia* had been worked on or only extracted from the mine. (2004: 81)

With the book in Varo's painting in mind, we might think of the difference between instruction and education. If the medieval master is instructing, from the Latin *instructare*, she is packing in, imparting, or imposing, a structure, upon the girls weaving the garment of the world. If, instead, the hooded figure reads from the book of secrets in service to their *education*, from the Latin, *educare*, she is leading out that which is found within. Here the painting holds a tension between opposites: Depicted in most of the garment being woven by the girls the world appears as it is, yet the hidden image of a girl's double secreted out of the tower to meet a lover suggests the discovery of something more than instruction and the leading out of that which is within. This suggests that Varo may have been working in the space between instruction that leads to the weaving of a mantle, or superficial covering, and a deeper, more nuanced, education that involves seeking knowledge about the essence of things. What knowledge, or meaning, might the women in the tower be weaving into the garment of the new world?

In depicting a blindered use of the creative potential of the girls to hypnotically weave the world-as-it-is, Varo suggests that the edifice of unconscious obedience to instruction contains the possibility of education. Alchemically speaking, the image of the book, the vessel, and the weaving of the lovers into the garment, may also have to do with imparting knowledge of the "secret place" where "the spark of the light of nature" can be found; where the opposites of spirit and matter, conscious and unconscious, masculine and feminine, work together in a creative harmony (Jung, 1955–56/1970: para. 344). For the alchemists, this secret place was one's inner life. Through the opus, the alchemical practitioner worked to free "the spirit imprisoned in matter" (Jung, 1937/1968: para. 376). Beyond the transformation of the individual, the alchemists believed that "the divine world-soul could be liberated from imprisonment in matter" (1954/1969: para. 448). Through the depiction of her doubled self—weaving and in the weaving—Varo seems to suggest that new life can be found as long as one hopes for and has the courage to seek something essential and transcendent.

In this way, the story unfolding in the tower is doubled, from one of instruction to one of education. In this latter story, a hooded alchemist, reading from an open book, stirs a broth that brews in a silver vessel. Young women, with the guidance of a wise teacher of alchemical practices, are weaving the garment of a new world. With the book, and the broth brewing in a cauldron, Varo imagines a creation myth, a symbolic narrative designed to impart the essence of what needs to happen in the new world being woven into existence by the girls in the tower.

In the tower, the essence of things and the cloth that flows from it is a yellow gold, which speaks symbolically to changing or coloring the world in a new way. Hillman spoke to this aspect of the alchemistic attitude in a passage on the yellowing of the work: "The alchemical mind perceived changes in color in the material at hand to be changes of an essential nature" (2010: 204–5). This yellowing is a third stage in the alchemical process. It follows both the *nigredo*, an awakening to the depressing awareness of one's wounded potential, and the *albedo*, a whitening of the matter under the silver light of the moon. From the suffering of the *nigredo*, "during *albedo* the pain lifts, having been blessed by reflection and understanding. The yellow brings the pain of knowledge itself. The soul suffers its own understanding" (215). Perhaps suggested by the silver nature of the vessel the alchemist stirs, the moon illuminates that which can only be seen and extracted in darkness, stirred in a vessel that heats it while protecting it from the day world of ego consciousness. In Varo's painting, one finds the tower windowless to save the project from the day world and from an egoic logic that would co-opt what is being brewed to protect the known from the unknown.

In *Embroidering the Earth's Mantle*, Varo used weaving as an alchemical metaphor, a symbol for changes being threaded into the essential nature of the world. How does one learn such lessons? How does a person come into a vital relationship with the deep Self, and with other archetypal presences in the psyche? The alchemists believed that books and knowledge were important. But at some point, for transformation to occur, the books and teachings must be set aside for the value of lived experience. For self-knowledge, according to Jung, following alchemical teachings, "is not a one-sided intellectual pastime but a journey through the four continents, where one is exposed to all the dangers of land, sea, air, and fire" (1955–56/1970: para. 283). This means, Jung wrote, "in psychology one possesses nothing unless one has experienced it in reality. Hence a purely intellectual insight is not enough, because one knows only the words and not the substance of the thing from inside" (1951/ 1968: para. 61). With Varo's image of the open book, and the alchemical activities taking place in the tower where the girls are weaving the garment of a new world, in mind, we might ask, as Jung did in *Mysterium Coniunctionis*: "What is the psychological meaning of the procedure?" (1955–56/1970: para. 693). From a Jungian perspective, the imagery suggests that Varo's personal work of individuation has progressed to the point where she has begun to experience something new being cooked in the cauldron of her psyche.

Feeding the caged moon: Patriarchy, the Feminine, and Jung's theory of complexes

Psychologically, from a Jungian perspective, the imagery in *Embroidering the Earth's Mantle*, which was painted two years before the artist's death in 1963, suggests that Varo has worked on her complexes (or the complexes have worked on her) to the point where she has gained understanding into the ways that these "splinter psyches" are impacting her behavior and emotional reactions (Jung, 1948/1969: para. 204). For Jung, a complex is not negative or destructive in and of itself. From a Jungian perspective, creativity and split-off numinous, ego-transcendent forces in the world and the Self are part of the raw matter of life. Varo's mature work often features heroines in search of self-discovery, women who are determined to work in alchemical collaboration with the unseen forces that animate material life to free the golden aspects of the personality from the darkness of the unconscious. The forest waif who plays a sunbeam in *Solar Music*, painted in 1955, is one example of a figure who can be considered a projected form of a positive complex at work in the artist's psyche.

In her 1956 painting *Star Catcher*, Varo projected a sense of self that is fashioned as a woman dressed in what Kaplan called "an exquisite costume with delicately marked butterfly-wing sleeves" (1988: 161). Kaplan associated the *Star Catcher* with Diana, a goddess the Greeks linked with hunting, women, and the moon, a symbol of divine Feminine wisdom. From a Jungian perspective, the image suggests Varo's contact with an inner archetypal Feminine presence. With her right hand, Varo's huntress holds a butterfly net. In the cage, the huntress has imprisoned a moon. Kaplan is disturbed by the capture and confinement of the caged moon. "The image," Varo's biographer wrote, "reinforces the feelings of constraint and enclosure that fill so many of Varo's works" (161–2). For Kaplan, the "tension between the strength of the butterfly huntress and the weakness of the caged moon exemplifies the subtle interplay between powerlessness and power that was a recurring theme for Varo" (162).

But there may be another possibility. In *Star Catcher*, perhaps, Varo imagined an empowering capacity to capture and retain the moon's light—the light that illuminates the dark of the deep psyche without dispelling it as happens with daylight, the light in which one sees only the world as it is and not what lurks within and beyond it. As portrayed in the voluminous yellow-gold capes in which the huntress is dressed, this capacity to contain the light of the moon makes her a larger-than-personal Self and colors her in the hues of the *citrinitas*. Nigel Hamilton, a British psychotherapist and lecturer on Sufism and alchemy, explained that in the alchemical yellowing, or *citrinitas*, "the consciousness is transformed into 'solar light.' This 'solar light' awakens the sense of revelation and revelatory knowledge" (1985, "Stage Three: *Citrinitas* or 'Yellowing'": para. 3). With *Star Catcher* in mind, this connects to the possibility of revelation brought about by the silvering light of the moon and seeing in the dark.

In her painting, *Celestial Pablum*, created in 1958, two years after *Star Catcher*, Varo's return to the image of the caged moon hints at her process of individuation in which, in her progression toward the revelation of a world-changing secret, Varo must first struggle to find what has been secreted—split off from consciousness—within herself. In *Celestial Pablum*, in a tower floating in the clouds, the artist imaged a woman whose universe is a spire floating by itself in space, with room only for the work of feeding the moon.

Inside the tower, the woman feeds matter from stars she has ground up into food for a crescent moon that is trapped like a bird in a steel cage or contained like a child in a crib. In the painting, Varo juxtaposed a mother's devotion to nourish her baby with the isolation a mother can feel when confined in domestic space. This can be seen as an exquisite portrayal of the need to keep safe and nurture creative potential—that which emerges from the dark of the unconscious under the subtle feminine light of the moon

Figure 5.3 Celestial Pablum, Remedios Varo, oil on masonite, 1958. ©Artists Rights Society (ARS), NY. Private Collection: G. Dagli Orti/De Agostini Picture Library/ Bridgeman Images.

that blurs edges and evokes mystery—within the context of the imprisoning domestication of the archetypal Feminine. Seen in this light, the woman in the tower in the sky presents a positive aspect of an ego that, despite its sociocultural context, is devoted to nourishing the Feminine principle, symbolized by the moon.

In *Celestial Pablum*, Varo painted a poignant image of the ambivalence within a complex between the personal, culturally contextualized material it contains and the numinous, archetypal core around which that material has been organized. Varo seems to have discovered that the archetypal power of the Feminine in its relationship with Eros, birth, and death was hidden at the core of the traumatogenic complex that formed from her lived experience of the devaluation of females and domestication of the relational feminine.

In *Celestial Pablum*, we see another holding of a tension of opposites in Varo's work: The imprisonment of the moon as symbolic of the feminine suggests its depotentiation within the patriarchy. In Varo's imagination the moon is a heavenly body that is unable to lift into the sky and illuminate that which is hidden in the cosmos. The moon's survival is dependent on the woman's solitary nurturance of it, with the woman herself in a tower, sequestered from the surrounding world. In this regard, with *Celestial Pablum* and *Star Catcher*, Varo may be symbolizing what Jungian psychology might call a *power complex*.

The power complex, and Varo's struggle with powerlessness, is more than personal, as the trauma associated with it is cast off into the shadow of the patriarchal fear of powerlessness and resulting pursuit of power, which the German Third Reich exemplified in extremity. World War II made indelible marks upon Varo's well-being when she was captured and confined in a French prison camp and forced to flee France from the Germans in the winter of 1940. Earlier, we looked at *Fear*, a signed and undated pencil drawing exhibited in a 1971 retrospective of Varo's work in Mexico City. Look again at the nervous woman who bicycles through a narrow corridor, pedaling away, it seems, from faces that peer at her through openings in walls, from arms that reach out to hinder or even halt her movement. Could the white faces, arms, and hands be Varo's attempt to depict the ghostlike presence of the patriarchal power complex that haunted her life, undermined her sense of self-worth, and caused her to withdraw from relationships and isolate herself within the well-sealed alchemical vessel of her paintings? In the context of *Star Catcher* and *Celestial Pablum*, two paintings that feature caged moons, we open into the possibility that her imagery is Varo's symbolic attempt to externalize and mediate the distress and debilitating impact of powerlessness associated with this unresolved trauma.

Keeping in mind that what makes a complex harmful is the way associated ideas or images can occlude, or even eclipse, the will and agency of the ego, Marie-Louise von Franz compared the behavior of an autonomous complex with the effect of the rabies virus:

> If such a virus gets into a nerve of a person bitten by a rabid animal, it is known that the virus wanders to exactly that place in the brain of the person bitten from which it can rule the entire person. [The virus] causes [a person] to refuse water so that the virus cannot be washed out of the mouth, to wander around so that he [or she] can come into contact with the greatest number of other beings, and finally to have a biting frenzy so that the virus can be transplanted to a new carrier... Autonomous complexes behave in exactly the same manner; they can distort or destroy the entire personality.
>
> (As cited in Akron & Banzhaf, 1995: 91)

The power complex operating at the level of the cultural unconscious wreaks similar havoc, enacted in individual, collective, and systemic acts of sexism, racism, and imperialism. Jungian analyst and scholar Ann Ulanov explored the relationship between repressed contents in the psyche of individuals and the development of cultural complexes. Ulanov opened an extended passage by tracing the "defined sequence" in which repression at the level of the individual leads to "social oppression" when unconscious personal complexes are left unattended (2005: 57–8). The sequence, Ulanov wrote,

> begins when we repress contents we dislike and dread... Our ego recoils from connection to contents we feel are destructive to our ego position and from the disordered chaos from which such contents spring... We either throw such contents out of consciousness into unconsciousness or we leave them blocked in unconsciousness, refusing them admittance to our awareness. Such refusal brings relief to our egos; we get rid, we think, of disturbing contents.
>
> But such contents do not go away. They go unconscious. They remain in us as live bits of being, as volatile forces out of reach of our ego and its restraining, civilizing effects. These contents regress and achieve still more powerful form, as a hungry dog we locked in a closet becomes a savage beast bent on killing to satisfy its hunger. (58)

Next, Ulanov linked the way in which repressed personal material that remains unconscious leads to the formation of a cultural complex:

> A repressed content is like a tiny alligator we bring back from a Florida vacation that becomes increasingly inconvenient as it keeps on growing. We flush it down the toilet into our sewers. There it not only continues to grow but now, out of sight and out of reach, it joins all the other alligators flushed away by our neighbors. What we repress accumulates more life to itself, growing stronger, bigger, contaminating whatever else is in the unconscious. Pressure builds up that demands release into conscious life. Such contents burst out finally in projections onto others— usually those different from us, alien, because of physical appearance or sex or background, or distant from us because we deem them inferior or superior to us. All that our egos judge unacceptable hurls itself in projection onto our alien or distant neighbor. We identify our neighbors with that bit of ourselves we put onto and into them. Thus we inaugurate a relationship of projective identification with our neighbors. We feel we must control them because they carry a feared bit of ourselves and fear them because we cannot control them. They carry the package of unconscious contents we dread in ourselves. (58)

The contents of these cultural complexes get projected onto those who are considered "other" and those who are an integral, yet marginalized or oppressed, part of the social order, such as women and people of color.

A guiding thread of this look at alchemical psychology in the art and life of Varo is that this artist painted not only to heal personal suffering but also to highlight the presence and destructive influence on women and the feminine of cultural complexes related to misogyny and patriarchy. The relationship between repressed personal content and the formation of cultural complexes is contained within the sweeping social change brewing in Varo's alchemically attuned work. Patriarchy scapegoats the feminine, projecting onto women the unbearably vulnerable qualities it has disowned or disavowed. In sociocultural expectations of them, women are assigned the relational feminine and then devalued and oppressed for carrying it. Varo's images of authority figures as both male and female—such as the bearded man and Mother Superior leading the girls on bicycles to their work in *Toward the Tower*—suggests her awareness that females raised in patriarchy internalize its values as self-definitions and unconsciously collude with their own oppression. The figures who linger in the shadows of Varo's paintings might well represent scapegoated aspects of the feminine that the artist is bringing back into a place of value from her own psyche and for the collective.

Given the disruptive functioning and invasive presence of the complex, how might Varo have been working to soften the impact of a power complex related to, or perhaps even caused by, misogyny? With the psychological impact of an emotionally charged group of ideas or images in mind, Jung was clear: Softening a complex means taking in some of the hair of the dog that has bitten us. "A complex," Jung wrote,

> can be really overcome only if it is lived out to the full. In other words, if we are to develop further we have to draw to us and drink down to the very dregs what, because of our complexes, we have held at a distance. (1954/1968: para. 184)

For Jung, every complex contains two parts. The first part he called the *shell*. Inside the shell of the complex is an archetypal core. The shell of a complex, wrote Edward Whitmont, is

> largely shaped by childhood events, childhood traumas, difficulties and repressions and so can always be reductively traced to one's personal past and explained in terms of cause and effect. In fact they should always be experienced in this light first, for these associational patterns are the concrete manifestations of the complex in the here and now. (1991: 66)

From a Jungian perspective, a complex is disruptive when energy-charged ideas and emotions are compulsive—that is to say, when they are unconsciously projected onto other people and objects. Psychologically speaking, for the transformation of a complex to occur, a person's unconscious identity with the strong feeling that accompanies the complex needs to be brought more under the control of the ego. Whitmont evoked the ability of a complex to overwhelm the ego: "When we are identical with a drive [or complex] we never question why we are moving or where we are going: there is only automatic response to an impulse" (59). When the ego is overwhelmed by charged emotions, Whitmont added,

> this state of compulsiveness … gives us the feeling of being carried by a tremendous force of energy, in much the same way that an automobile going at the speed of eighty miles an hour may give us a feeling of exhilaration. (59)

The ego possessed by strong affect in the unconscious complex cannot contain the psychic pressure and becomes inflated. From a Jungian perspective, Whitmont explained, inflation "describes a feeling of power in which we are blown up by an unknown force that is not our own, not of our own judging and choosing" (59). We "are at our most harmful" when in "this inflated, compulsive state of identity" because the complex "will act out its extreme, inappropriate and destructive side" (59). To differentiate and transform the complex, the inflated state of identity must be dissolved. "This requires a confrontation of the drive as a *Thou*, as something that is not *I*, as something separate from ourselves. Only at this point can the inner dialogue begin" (59). From this juncture, the renewing qualities wired into the archetypal core of the complex become available to the conscious functioning of the ego.

Raveling: Varo and the transformation of cultural complexes powered by patriarchy

With these depth psychological dynamics in mind, increasingly nuanced reflections on the alchemical transformation Varo painted into *Embroidering the Earth's Mantle* can be made. Consciously or unconsciously, the artist paints a moment of transformation: on the stone floor in the center of the tower, a cauldron bubbles, the broth being brewed an alchemical image of a complex, or complexes, suffering dissolution. We cannot know the precise nature of Varo's psychological makeup. What we can surmise, if we follow the artist into the story that unfolds in the image of the young women at work in the tower, is that Varo has painted the very moment when the suffering and trance-like condition imposed by an unconscious complex dies from a disidentification with the complex and an awakening to its destructiveness and the possibility held within its archetypal core. Boiling in the cauldron in the tower is a broth bringing both the end of what has been and the beginning of what can be. From a Jungian perspective, the tension of opposites Varo imagines in *Embroidering the Earth's Mantle* is easy to see, but more difficult to put in perspective.

Varo, a master miniaturist, has embroidered into the world's mantle a new possibility, perhaps even an emerging cosmos. In her essay on Varo in an anthology on Latin American women artists, Janet Kaplan highlighted the host of factors that combined to create Varo's singular style. "Not only are her images rich with echoes of El Greco, Bosch, Goya, medieval Spanish architecture, and North African costume," Kaplan wrote, "but her style is that of the illuminated manuscript, that document of obsessive belief in the transformative power of seeing the whole world in the finest moment of detail" (1998: 124).

> Throughout her jewel-like compositions, there is a meticulous, even obsessive attention to the elaboration of fine detail that marks Varo's as a miniaturist's hand ... There is ... an essential theatricality to such miniaturist vision, in which tableaux become dollhouse-like stage sets framing an enclosed world. (124–5)

Concealed in the fold of the garment that spills from the tower in *Embroidering the Earth's Mantle* are the tiny forms of the young woman and her lover. Here, in the finest of detail, Varo may have imagined the move beyond servitude—to parents, to patriarchy, to destructive unconscious complexes. With attention to the minutest, most difficult to detect detail, while also imagining an expansive and emerging cosmos, Varo depicted the depth and intensity of deep suffering as well as the spacious flexibility of increased awareness and expanded possibilities. Once trapped, like Persephone, in an underworld of despair and deadness, the young woman sewn into the fold of the fabric of the emerging world can now leave the tower to weave the threads of new experience.

As a woman exiled and uprooted first from Spain, during her country's Civil War in the 1930s, and later from France as Germany occupied Paris during World War II, in her mature work Varo

> found a way to create a world over which she could exercise total control. In carefully constructed narrative tableaux, rich with obsessive detail, she set her often solitary characters into a world of timeless interiority. It is a transcendent time in which she could negate the flux of lived reality.
>
> (Kaplan, 1998: 125)

Poet and literary critic Susan Stewart explored the miniature as a metaphor for interiority. "The miniature," Stewart wrote, "linked to nostalgic versions of childhood and history, presents a diminutive, and thereby manipulatable, version of experience, a version which is domesticated and protected from contamination" (1984: 69). Metaphorically exploring the dollhouse as an example, Stewart commented on how the miniature transforms the time and space of everyday experience "into the infinite time of reverie" (65).

> Occupying a space within an enclosed space, the dollhouse's aptest analogy is the locket or the secret recesses of the heart: center within center, within within within. The dollhouse is a materialized secret; what we look for is the dollhouse within the dollhouse and its promise of an infinitely profound interiority. (61)

Stewart marveled at the ability of the miniature to bring microcosm and macrocosm into such a small space. "Worlds of inversion," she wrote,

> of contamination and crudeness, are controlled within the dollhouse by an absolute manipulation and control of the boundaries of time and space... Unlike the single miniature object, the miniature universe of the dollhouse cannot be known sensually; it is inaccessible to the languages of the body and thus is the most abstract of all miniature forms. Yet cognitively the dollhouse is gigantic. (63)

Varo's depiction of containment in enclosed or isolated spaces—a tower, cages, a tiny house in the clouds—reflects the alchemical vessel as

> a symbol for the attitude which prevents anything escaping outside; it is a basic attitude of introversion which, on principle, does not let anything escape into the outside world. The illusion that the whole trouble lies outside oneself has come to an end.
>
> (von Franz, 1980: 87)

Within the vessel of a painting, Varo enacted a concentrated psychological treatment; projections onto the outer world are withdrawn and contained within, which intensifies the process of coming into increased awareness. Fingering these same threads, Kaplan wrote,

> in so much of Varo's work, a dollhouse effect of cut-away architecture establishes a frontal framing and a shallow theatrical stage on which dramas of personal and cosmic discovery are enacted. Small in size but monumental in scale, Varo's miniaturized visions project an intensity of power and rigorous focus that is both highly intellectual and magically charged. (1998: 125)

Through her introverted projection of unconscious content into the microcosm of her paintings, Varo's miniature worlds engage the personal, cultural, and archetypal layers of her psyche, each of which, while contained with the individual, implies that the psyche is always relational and inter-actional. Depth psychologically, then, the alchemical vessel relates to the transitional space envisioned by pediatrician and psychoanalyst D. W. Winnicott as the

> "in-between space" … a meeting-ground of potentiality and authen-ticity, located neither within the self nor in the world of political and economic affairs. In this space, one finds the most authentic and creative aspects of our personal and communal existence.
>
> (Praglin, 2006: 1)

In her work on women's psychology in the 1970s, psychiatrist and fem-inist Jean Baker Miller challenged the patriarchal paradigm that has infected Western psychology with a definition of a healthy self as one that is inde-pendent and nonrelational, stable and unchanging across domains (1986). More recently, "in multiple contexts of research and theory, older ideas about independence and separation-individuation are giving way to a view of the person in more relational, interdependent terms" (Fishbane, 1998: 41). This underscores psychologically the feminist refrain, "The personal is political," popularized by Carol Hanisch, who argued that women's experiences are traceable to their position within the patriarchal hegemony (1969: title).

Secret recipes: Alchemy, creation, and the art of political weaving

We know that Varo read and applied the concepts and methods of Jungian psychology to her personal life and to her creative work as an artist. With painting, dreams, and the psychology of the unconscious in mind, we can consider *Embroidering the Earth's Mantle* an artistic and alchemical depic-tion of a moment in Varo's evolution: the joining together of the experience of suffering and entrapment within psychological complexes and the healing and transformative potentialities originating in the archetypal layers of the psyche.

In classical Jungian psychology, there is a close connection between personal experience, the inherent limitations of the ego, and the inexpress-ible and unknowable archetypal forces that bring insight, healing, and transformation to the personality. In *Embroidering the Earth's Mantle*, Varo hinted at the growth taking place in her own psyche through the figure of the flute player and in the image of the lovers who have escaped the tower. This internal dynamic, driven by the archetypal desire of one thing for another, an inner movement that is arcing toward the alchemical union of feminine and masculine, matures in *The Escape*, the third painting in Varo's triptych. We look in more detail at the imagery in *The Escape* toward the end of Part I, in the context of psychological reflections on the man with whom Varo weaves her destiny for eternity in the dream of the executioner. Here it is important to note that in the escape from the tower, Varo portrayed herself accompanied by a man in a seed pod that she is steering. The tableau of gold clouds amid mountain peaks conveys a longing and a quest beyond the personal. As an escape from convention and imprisonment, the image of Varo and her lover traveling on the seed pod of her imagination suggests the release into the world the possibility of a partnership in which the relational feminine and her creative Eros—the will to love rather than the will to power—is the guiding force.

Here, if we linger a little longer in the metaphoric space Varo painted, we can consider *Embroidering the Earth's Mantle* as the artist's imaginal attempt to envision a world where women are no longer objects for the sexual gratification of men or muses who must sacrifice their own voice and potential in service to the patriarchal male's need for authority. As someone who felt marginalized because of her gender, Varo painted a journey into a new possibility not just for herself but for other women who long for more agency and choice.

The motif of weaving for the betterment of the collective grows from well-tilled soil. In *The Craft of Zeus*, John Scheid and Jesper Svenbro consider the practical importance and symbolic meaning of political weaving in ancient Greece:

> Among the representations the Greeks made of society, of the bonds between men and the cohesion of human groups, or even of the city, there is one that seems to *fabricate* society more than any other: weaving. Domestic or political, profoundly ritualized, weaving brings into play an ensemble of notions capable of being inscribed in the collective memory, gestures that allow one to grasp, to touch, social organization. (1994/1996: 9)

"Weaving," these scholars added, "demonstrates for both the hand and the eye a possible, or desirable, way to conceive of life in society … [W]eaving unites what must be united. To weave is to unite, to interlace, to bind" (10).

With the social aspects of weaving in ancient Greece in mind, painting, for Varo, seems to have functioned as a weaving, an artistic practice undertaken to "give order to a great tangle of matters" in order to "put each matter in its proper place" (Scheid & Svenbro, 1994/1996: 12). Bogzaran added nuance to Varo's painted imaginal weavings, linking art and dreams with transformation and the presence of archetypal forces:

> Varo's paintings can be viewed as a process of transformation—a conscious narrative of an oneiric scene. The environments are dreamlike but the actions and interactions are lucid and deliberate. In each

painting she carries out a psychomagic act. Not only is the dreamer/ painter involved in the creation of the world: she is assisted by an invisible force. In her paintings, Remedios Varo clearly demonstrates that creation is a manner of working in concert with the magic of nature and the forces of the unknown. (2008: 181)

References

Akron, & Banzhaf, H. (1995). *The Crowley tarot: The handbook to the cards by Aleister Crowley and Lady Frieda Harris* (C. Grimm, Trans.). Stamford, CT: U. S. Games Systems.

Arcq, T. (2008). In search of the miraculous. In M. Orellano (Ed.), *Five keys to the secret world of Remedios Varo* (19–90). Mexico City, Mexico: Artes de Mexico.

Bogzaran, F. (2008). Dreams of alchemy. In M. Orellano (Ed.), *Five keys to the secret world of Remedios Varo* (159–86). Mexico City, Mexico: Artes de Mexico.

Colvile, M. (1988). *Beyond and beneath the mantle: On Thomas Pynchon's The crying of lot 49.* Amsterdam, Netherlands: Editions Rodopi.

Engel, P. (1986). *Remedios Varo: Science into art.* New York, NY: New York Academy of Science.

Fishbane, M. D. (1998). I, thou, and we: A dialogical approach to couples therapy. *Journal of Marital and Family Therapy*, 24(1), 41–58.

Guralnik, O., & Simeon, D. (2010). Depersonalization: Standing in the spaces between recognition and interpellation. *Psychoanalytic Dialogues*, 20(4), 400–16.

Hamilton, N. (1985). The alchemical process of transformation. Retrieved from www.sufismus.ch/assets/files/omega_dream/alchemy_e.pdf

Hanisch, C. (1969). The personal is political. Retrieved from www.carolhanisch.org/ CHwritings/PIP.html

Hillman, J. (2010). *Alchemical psychology.* Putman, CT: Spring Publications.

Hubert, R. R. (1994). *Magnifying mirrors: Women, surrealism, & partnership.* Lincoln, NE: University of Nebraska Press.

Jung, C. G. (1937/1968). Religious ideas in alchemy (R. F. C. Hull, Trans.). In H. Read et al. (Eds.), *The collected works of C. G. Jung* (Vol. 12, 2nd ed., 225–483). Princeton, NJ: Princeton University Press.

Jung, C. G. (1951/1968). The self (R. F. C. Hull, Trans.). In (H. Read et al., Eds.). *The collected works of C. G. Jung* (Vol. 9ii, 2nd ed., 23–35). Princeton, NJ: Princeton University Press.

Jung, C. G. (1954/1968). Psychological aspects of the mother archetype (R. F. C. Hull, Trans.). In H. Read et al. (Eds.), *The collected works of C. G. Jung* (Vol. 9i, 2nd ed., 73–110). Princeton, NJ: Princeton University Press.

Jung, C. G. (1948/1969). A review of the complex theory (R. F. C. Hull, Trans.). In H. Read et al. (Eds.), *The collected works of C. G. Jung* (Vol. 8, 2nd ed., 92–104). Princeton, NJ: Princeton University Press.

Jung, C. G. (1954/1969). Transformation symbolism in the Mass (R. F. C. Hull, Trans.). In H. Read et al. (Eds.), *The collected works of C. G. Jung* (Vol. 11, 2nd ed., 201–96). Princeton, NJ: Princeton University Press.

Jung, C. G. (1955–56/1970). *Mysterium coniunctionis* (R. F. C. Hull, Trans.) (H. Read et al., Eds.), *The collected works of C. G. Jung* (Vol. 14, 2nd ed.). Princeton, NJ: Princeton University Press.

Jung, C. G. (1921/1971). Definitions (R. F. C. Hull, Trans.). In H. Read et al. (Eds.), *The collected works of C. G. Jung* (Vol. 6, 408–86). Princeton, NJ: Princeton University Press.

Kalsched, D. (1996). *The inner world of trauma: Archetypal defenses of the personal spirit.* New York, NY: Routledge.

Kaplan, J. (1988). *Unexpected journeys: The art and life of Remedios Varo.* New York, NY: Abbeville Press.

Kaplan, J. (1998). Subversive strategies: The work of Remedios Varo. In M. Agosin (Ed.), *A woman's gaze: Latin American women artists* (110–28). Fredonia, NY: White Pine Press.

Luton, F. (2011). *Bees, honey and the hive: Circumambulating the centre.* Toronto, Canada: Inner City Books.

Marcus, J. (1987). *Virginia Woolf and the languages of patriarchy.* Bloomington, IN: Indiana University Press.

Miller, J. B. (1986). *Toward a new psychology of women.* Boston, MA: Beacon.

Navolio, L. M. (2004). *The process of individuation as embodied in symbols, images, and alchemical motifs: A psychological study based on 12 paintings by Remedios Varo* (UMI Number: 3618579) [Doctoral dissertation, Pacifica Graduate Institute]. ProQuest Dissertations.

Praglin, L. (2006, Fall). The nature of the "In-Between" in D.W. Winnicott's concept of transitional space and in Martin Buber's das Zwischenmenschliche. *Universitas, 1*(1), 1–9. Retrieved from universitas.uni.edu/archive/fall06/pdf/art_praglin.pdf

Pynchon, T. (1966). *The crying of lot 49.* New York, NY: Harper & Row.

Ramsay, J. (1997). *Alchemy: The art of transformation.* London, UK: HarperCollins.

Scheid, J., & Svenbro, J. (1994/1996). *The craft of Zeus: Myths of weaving and fabric* (C. Volk, Trans.). Cambridge, MA: Harvard University Press.

Singer, T. (2004). The cultural complex and archetypal defenses of the group spirit: Baby Zeus, Elian Gonzales, Constantine's Sword, and other holy wars (with special attention to "the axis of evil"). In T. Singer & S. Kimbles (Eds.), *The cultural complex: Contemporary Jungian perspectives on psyche and society.* New York, NY: Routledge.

Stewart, S. (1984). *On longing: Narratives of the miniature, the gigantic, the souvenir, the collection.* Baltimore, MD: John Hopkins University Press.

Thomson, S. A. (2003). *Pictures from the heart: A tarot dictionary.* New York, NY: St. Martin's Griffin.

Ulanov, A. (2005). *Spirit in Jung.* Einsiedlen, Switzerland: Daimon Verlag.

Varo, R. (1997/2018). *Letters, dreams & other writings* (M. Carson, Trans.). Cambridge, MA: Wakefield Press.

Von Franz, M.-L. (1980). *Alchemy: An introduction to the symbolism and the psychology.* Toronto, Canada: Inner City Books.

Warner, M. (2002). *Fantastic metamorphoses, other worlds.* New York, NY: Oxford University Press.

White, Y. (2014). The surrealist woman: The art of Remedios Varo. *Syracuse University Honors Program Capstone Projects.* 744. Retrieved from surface.syr.edu/honors_capstone/744

Whitmont, E. (1991). *The symbolic quest: Basic concepts of analytical psychology.* Princeton, NJ: Princeton University Press.

Woodman, M., & Sieff, D. (2015). Spiralling through the apocalypse: Facing the Death Mother to claim our lives. In D. Sieff (Ed.), *Understanding and healing emotional trauma: Conversations with pioneering clinicians and researchers* (64–88). New York, NY: Routledge.

Chapter 6

Voyage to the center of the inner world

The Feminine quest, the labyrinth, and the dangerous secret

Varo's experiences with death, both real and imagined, made a distinctive mark on her personal process of growth, the dangerous secret she harbored in the dream of the executioner and the egg, and the creative production of paintings that support social change. To ground our investigation into the crucial role the executioner plays in the alchemical process of transformation at work in Varo's dream of death, we follow Jung, who began researching alchemy in 1928.

That year, Jung received a package in the mail from a friend, Richard Wilhelm, who was writing to ask him to draft a commentary to his translation of *The Secret of the Golden Flower*, an eighth-century Chinese alchemical treatise of Taoist origin. Jung devoured the manuscript, surprised and satisfied to discover a striking similarity between individuation and the production of what the Chinese alchemists called the "diamond body" (Jung, 1929/1967: para. 29). Jung, according to Aniela Jaffé, recognized that the Chinese alchemists were working to achieve, through meditation and the creation of the diamond body, the same psychological transformation he had recognized and experienced as the goal of individuation: the shifting of the psychic center of the personality from the ego to the divine authority he called the Self (1968/1971: 51).

Jung was 81 years old when he finished writing *Mysterium Coniunctionis: An Inquiry into the Separation and Synthesis of Psychic Opposites in Alchemy*. For Jung, the book marked his final published attempt to elaborate on the methods, symbolism, and psychological dynamics and values at work in the ancient alchemical art first practiced in Greco-Roman Egypt, and in later centuries throughout Europe, Africa, and Asia. In a passage on the transformation of water, Jung linked alchemical symbolism with the unconscious workings of the psyche:

> The bath, submersion, baptism, and drowning are synonymous, and all are alchemical symbols for the unconscious state of the self, its embodiments, as it were—or, more precisely, for the unconscious

process by which the self is "re-born" and enters into a state in which it can be experienced. This state is then described as the "filius regius." The "old dragon" who prepared the bath, a primeval creature dwelling in the caverns of the earth, is, psychologically, a personification of the instinctual psyche, generally symbolized by reptiles. It is as though the alchemists were trying to express the fact that the unconscious itself initiates the process of renewal. (1955–56/1970: para. 548)

Elsewhere in *Mysterium Coniunctionis*, Jung pinpointed the alchemical relationship between psychological death and transformation: "Dissolution is the prerequisite for redemption. The celebrant of the mysteries had to suffer a figurative death in order to attain transformation" (para. 381). Psychologically speaking, symbolic death leads, for our purposes, to one of the more well-known conclusions Jung reached near the end of *Mysterium Coniunctionis*: the idea that *"the experience of the self is always a defeat for the ego"* (para. 778, emphasis in original).

This talk of transformation through the experience of ego death draws us into the underworld, which Jung said "signifies hell and the grave. The worm or serpent is all-devouring death. The dragon-slayer is therefore always a conqueror of death" (1955–56/1970: para. 482). Varo does not slay a dragon in her dream of the executioner; instead, she makes a specifically, archetypally Feminine, request: She asks for time to weave an egg, a symbol "of the transit between the underworld and the upperworld, death and life, and of what comes back in a stronger form" (Arias-Henao, 2019: 160). Varo's response to her execution is revolutionary in its courage and vulnerability: It defies the will to conquer and control (and the shadow of fear) embodied in the executioner and accepts the transit of death—both literal and figurative—as essential to new life. Varo's move in the dream suggests symbolically that she has encountered shadow material to the point where self-transformation and a generative relationship with death is concomitant to her communication of dangerous alchemical practices through her paintings.

In Jungian psychology, of course, the shadow, as an unconscious and potentially dangerous aspect of the Self, plays a crucial role in the individuation process. "The shadow," Jung wrote,

is a moral problem that challenges the whole ego-personality, for no one can become conscious of the shadow without considerable moral effort. To become conscious of it involves recognizing the dark aspects of the personality as present and real. This act is the essential condition for any kind of self-knowledge. (1951/1968: para. 14)

In *Mysterium Coniunctionis*, Jung meshed his psychology of the unconscious with the alchemical notion of the shadow:

Alchemy announced a source of knowledge, parallel if not equivalent to revelation, which yields a "bitter" water by no means acceptable to our human judgment... It is bitter indeed to discover behind one's lofty ideals narrow, fanatical convictions ... and behind one's heroic pretensions nothing but crude egotism, infantile greed, and complacency. This painful corrective is an unavoidable stage in every psychotherapeutic process. (1955–56/1970: para. 346)

Juxtaposing Jung's insight about "heroic pretensions" and his image of the archetypal "dragon-slayer" as the conqueror of death and thus the champion of the ego's rebirth reveals a deeply unconscious, compulsively heroic approach to individuation. We see this again where Jung linked alchemical symbolism with analytical psychology's notion of the shadow:

In myths the hero is the one who conquers the dragon, not the one who is devoured by it. And yet both have to deal with the same dragon. Also, he is no hero who never met the dragon, or who, if he once saw it, declared afterwards that he saw nothing. Equally, only one who has risked the fight with the dragon and is not overcome by it wins the hoard, the "treasure hard to attain." He alone has a genuine claim to self-confidence, for he has faced the dark ground of his self and thereby has gained himself. This experience gives him faith and trust, the *pistis* in the ability of the self to sustain him, for everything that menaced him from inside he has made his own. (1955–56/1970: para. 756)

Jung's ideas about the psychological integration of the shadow through conquest strike a chord of heroic invulnerability and dominance, concealing rather than integrating a deeper shadow of fear. The hero's winning of the hoard is turned on its head in Varo's dream of the executioner, in which Varo surrenders into her vulnerability to death and—rather than defeating death and claiming the treasure of life—enters into a partnership with death to create life.

This brings us to a pivotal moment in the dream: when the executioner questions Varo about her fear. Bogzaran pinpointed the psychological significance of what happens next:

Up until that point, she is caught in the narrative of the dream. She is seemingly at the mercy of her destiny until she is questioned about her fear. Anyone could experience such an archetypal dream and face the existential anxiety that leads us to question whether we have accomplished all we wanted to before our rendezvous with death. (2008: 177)

In the dream of the executioner, Varo meets her fear of death by parsing the difference between acceptance of death and her fear that she will leave her work incomplete.

Her psychomagic act begins when she sees an opportunity to transform herself and create a new self through her creative skills. Her desire to weave her lover's destiny into her own for eternity could be seen as the alchemical integration of the two powerful archetypes. (177)

As an image, the weaving of the egg speaks to a powerful alchemy at work in Varo's psyche. For in the making of the egg, Varo, as the dream ego, responds to the immanent death of the life she has known by the redemptive weaving together of the archetypal Masculine and Feminine into a synthesis contained in the vessel of the egg. In keeping with the ability of the symbol to release and transform energy, the question then becomes: what possibility can be born now that the opposites have been brought together in a new and more conscious way?

Quest of the Feminine: Art, psyche, and female initiation

To make a transit into and through Varo's symbolic world, it is necessary to realize that the transformative weavings of image and imagination are at work on multiple levels. On one level, images stitched together form a dream of an executioner, an egg, and a man that leads to the dreamer's awareness that she possesses a secret that could change the world. On another level, from within the symbolic spaces of the soul, images come alive on painted canvas as expressions of inner processes of transformation. Psychologically, what personal and transpersonal purposes are these images pointing to? Kaplan, Varo's biographer, examined several of the artist's paintings with initiation and transformation in mind. "Varo," Kaplan wrote,

> visualized the moment of spiritual breakthrough in a variety of ways. In *Emerging Light*, a woman steps from behind a wall, from darkness into light. Ripping layers of wallpaper like labial folds, she is born as a seeker of truth, carrying a flaming lamp. (1988: 165–6)

Kaplan looked, also, at *To Be Reborn*, a 1960 Varo oil on masonite. In this painting, the setting is a sacred room deep within a forest where

> a woman again bursts through a wall, coming to her revelation in naked innocence, as if newly born. Looking into a chalice filled with liquid, she sees reflected not her face but a crescent moon. She is ecstatic, her eyes wide with wonder, for she has been allowed a secret wisdom—a glimpse of the Holy Grail allowed only to the initiated. It is as though the fertile vegetation of the room, the magic of the chalice, and the magnetic power of the moon have pulled her forth, releasing her from confinement. (166)

By associating the woman's moment of spiritual breakthrough with the crescent moon, and by exposing her character's breasts, Kaplan believed Varo has painted an image of the experience of transformation "as essentially a female quest" (166). This is seen also, as described above, in *The Escape*, in which it is the female whose hand is on the tiller of the seed pod in which Varo and her lover travel toward their freedom. This sense of a female vision pervades Varo's mature work, Kaplan wrote, informing

> her choice of symbols (the crescent moon reflected in the chalice, figures emerging out of vaginal slits surrounded by labial folds) and her depiction of the figures who experience psychic awakening as specifically female. Women are central to these compositions, and Varo makes their experience paramount, reflecting the personal quest for spiritual awareness that she herself had undertaken. (166–7)

Varo worked again with initiatory imagery in *The Call*, a 1961 oil on masonite. In this painting, a flame-haired woman swathed in a bright orange dress and cloak walks down a narrow street under a dark and clouded sky showing the diffuse hint of three planets or stars. The woman's red hair rises from her head, appearing to coil around a celestial body—the sun?—in the sky above the town. "The Varo character in *The Call*," Kaplan wrote, "is literally enlightened: light from the star to which she is attached suffuses her body with an otherworldly glow" (167). Around her neck the woman wears a mortar, which is the vessel in which substances are ground or crushed with a pestle in alchemy. The flowing mane of red hair, almond shape of the face, and large dark eyes clearly mark this image as a projected vision Varo is having of herself. According to Kaplan, Varo is capturing a crucial moment in what Joseph Campbell called the mythological journey of the Hero. By answering the mythological call to adventure, Varo's character, as a representation of the artist herself, is responding to a summons, a destiny that asks the quester to transfer his or her "spiritual center of gravity from within the pale of his society to a zone unknown" (Campbell, 2008: 48). Varo's heroine, Kaplan wrote, "is similarly propelled forward, her illumination and movement in stark contrast to the gray, deadened figures asleep within the walls that surround her" (1988: 168).

Two other works by Varo evoke the female experience of spiritual and psychological transformation. "The intrepid traveler in *Exploration of the Sources of the Orinoco River*," Kaplan wrote,

> is a most determined woman who bears particular resemblance to Varo herself. A courageous heroine, she has set out on a solitary journey to find "the source." Although she is dressed in a marvelously adapted English trench coat and bowler hat, carrying wings overhead that seem to have been borrowed from a theatrical production, the seriousness

of her purpose is not compromised. The playfulness of her vehicle—a waistcoat transformed into a fragile little ship with notes in the side pocket and a compass instead of a watch fob—does not negate the intensity of her expression nor the somber watchfulness of the dark birds that attend her from the hollows of nearby trees. What she confronts is a simple wineglass, set on a modest table in a hollowed-out tree. A magical liquid flows out of the goblet, becoming the source of the river on which she travels. (168–9)

For Kaplan, Varo's use of the river as a metaphor for the spiritual quest of self-discovery exemplifies a contradiction "inherent in much of" the artist's work:

No matter how intrepid, her travelers are rarely if ever free. Here the traveling outfit, while a wonderfully inventive means of transport, acts also as a form of restraint, binding the woman into her boat with an elaborate network of interlaced cords. (169)

With these thoughts and with Varo's dream of the executioner in mind, the possibility arises that Varo was working in her paintings with the tension between containment and freedom, a psychological dynamic evoked in a seventeenth-century alchemical emblem in which a toad is chained to an eagle.[1] Alchemically, the images suggest that transformation requires the ability to transcend the duality of opposites and live instead in ambivalence—in Varo's case, simultaneous freedom and containment. The challenge psychologically is to develop the ability to consciously hold as creative partners the restraining concerns of material life and the longings of spirit as partners rather than seeing them as mutually exclusive opposites caught in ambivalent or even adversarial tension in the linear world of logic.

In the dream of the executioner, Varo weaves a containing egg, a vessel that hosts an imaginal process in which she frees herself from fear and accepts the death of her human experience to make way, perhaps, for the eternal soul, which, being a forever condition, is beyond containment. Von Franz noted that the egg is a containing symbol for the "psychic wholeness conceived as the thing which came before the rise of ego consciousness, or any kind of dividing consciousness" (1995: 229). Varo weaves around herself "a sort of cage in the shape of an enormous egg" made of "his substance and my own" (Varo, 1997/2018: 95–6). In doing so, she reverses the flow to complete the creative cycle from a divided consciousness to a conscious wholeness—a shift gestated in the egg that births a transpersonal awareness of self.

Spiral Transit: Spiritual gold and the journey of the soul

Varo depicted a different aspect of her experience of inner exploration in *Spiral Transit*, a 1962 oil on masonite. In this image, travelers navigate a spiraling course through the waterways of a walled medieval city "that rises like an island in the midst of a roiling sea" (Engel, 2008: 94). Kaplan, in the context of Varo's symbolic use of the journey as a metaphor, noticed a similarity between *Exploration of the Sources of the Orinoco River* and *Spiral Transit.* "As with the river explorer, theirs is a spiritual voyage, tracing the spiral of unfolding consciousness in egg-shaped boats that resemble the vessels in which the alchemical transformation takes place" (1988: 169). "This entire composition," Kaplan added, is

> remarkably similar to a Renaissance alchemical drawing of the Lapis Sanctuary, in which the tower at the center of the maze hides the Philosopher's Stone (a key element in alchemical transformation). Although it is possible that Varo might have come across a reproduction of this seventeenth-century Dutch rendering in her alchemical reading, it is more likely that such congruence of imagery ... reflects intuitive understanding or (in terms closer to Varo's way of thinking) her magic envisioning of a phenomenon never seen. (169)

Jung reproduced an image of the Lapis Sanctuary in *Psychology and Alchemy.* He described the seventeenth-century alchemical emblem as "a labyrinth, surrounded by planetary orbits" (1936/1968: 109, Fig. 51). In linking the labyrinth and the symbol of the mandala with the orbit of planets, Jung approached the inexpressible essence of the archetypal Self as a cosmos, a world within. In *Spiral Transit,* Varo seems to have imagined precisely this kind of alchemical journey: seekers travel in egg-shaped boats on the waters of the unconscious toward their own mysterious center. From a Jungian perspective, in *Spiral Transit,* Varo used the labyrinth as a symbol of the journey inward toward the deep Self. Psychologically speaking, the painting is Varo's attempt to express that which is inexpressible: the journey to the center of the labyrinth, the numinous place where "we touch the gold of our being" (Senensky, 2003: 40).

With the symbolism of the painting in mind, we can consider Varo's imagery from a more mystical perspective. In *The Mystic Spiral: Journey of the Soul,* Jill Purce explored the symbol of the spiral as a representation for the unfolding of the soul. As a symbol, the spiral is both "inherently asymmetrical" and entropic, that is, it depicts "unwinding movement from order to chaos, or, according to C. G. Jung, away from the conscious and towards the unconscious" (1980: 9).

Writing from a mystical perspective, Purce's words complement Varo's imagery in *Spiral Transit*—both seek to evoke the spiral nature of an individual's search for the divine:

> Each winding marks a containment and a completed cycle in the development of the whole; but, as each is a part of the whole, the completion

is also a beginning, so that the spiral shows the enclosure and "rounded" quality we experience, and the equivalent points reached at every new beginning. The recurrent moments of crisis and indecision, when understood, are growth junctures, points of initiation which mark a release or death from one state of being and a growth or birth into the next. "How many times," said Yeats, "man lives and dies between his two eternities." (15)

With the use of the spiral as a symbol, Varo trekked into a place of paradox. Purce pinpointed the dilemma:

Is the Absolute separated from us, the material world, by countless intervening spheres and planes, and perceptible to us only through emanations or manifested attributes? Or is this same Reality something implicit in the universe, in each one of us, in the Self at the heart of our being? (18)

Is the Divine immanent or transcendent? Purce considered the tension of opposites:

Does ... our two-dimensional spiral begin in the centre and travel out stretching ever further towards God Transcendent, or is the direction of the journey inwards through the unfolding levels of awareness, until, as St. Catherine of Genoa said, "My me is God, nor do I know my Selfhood save in Him"? (18)

Purce concluded that the spiral is a numinous symbol that draws the soul away from "the world of illusion" (19). Edith Schnapper, who wrote *The Inward Odyssey*, believed that the soul moves inward, away from the material world, drawn toward "the divine essence dwelling at the apex of man's spirit" (as cited in Purce, 1980: 19).

In *Spiral Transit*, Varo imagined both aspects of this theme. From the material world of the ego, seekers of soul travel in egg-shaped boats to the center of the city, toward the "God within," their movement an "inward process of regeneration and integration" (Purce, 1980: 19). From a depth psychological perspective, the image also depicts the outward pilgrimage of the soul—a journey originating at the center of the walled city, each seeker representing an aspect of the archetypal forces who seek to become birthed into, and embodied in, the experience of human beings in the material world (19).

According to Kaplan, Varo made the spiritual metaphor of a spiraling journey particularly overt in *Ascension to Mount Analogue*. In this 1960 oil painting, a cloaked traveler stands upon a small piece of wood and "rides the current of a river toward a spiraling mountain. The water miraculously flows up, and the figure navigates without a boat, powered by the wind that transforms his saffron-colored robes into billowing sails" (1988: 169). Varo wrote that the figure evoked "the effort of those who try to climb to another spiritual level" (as cited in Kaplan, 1988: 169).

The spiritual elements in Varo's paintings draw upon the artist's lifelong fascination with the occult. "As a schoolgirl," Kaplan wrote,

> Varo had been fascinated by the occult, had written to a Hindu yogi, had collected magic plants. As an adult, still psychically restless, she turned that energy toward other spiritual pursuits. As she studied mystic disciplines and read metaphysical texts, the quest for meaning and control through the development of her spiritual self became an obsession that dominated her work. Drawing on a wide range of mythic and hermetic traditions, Western and non-Western alike, Varo turned with equal interest to the ideas of Jung, G. I. Gurdjieff, P. D. Ouspensky, Helena Blavatsky, Meister Eckhart, the Sufis, legends of the Holy Grail, sacred geometry, alchemy, and the *I Ching*—seeing each as an avenue to self-knowledge and the transformation of consciousness. (1988: 163–4)

Varo presented the ultimate potential of such learning in *Hermit*, a 1956 painting in which

> a magical figure stands alone in the woods, its body in the form of a vaporous six-pointed star, the joining of upright and inverted triangles that symbolizes equilibrium and the conjunction of consciousness with the unconscious. Nestled in the deep cavity of its open chest sits the circle of yin-yang, the Chinese symbol that similarly represents the balance of opposites. The perfectly symmetrical figure is calm, its face serene, a corporeal emblem for the possibilities of inner harmony and balance that are the goals of the spiritual journey.
>
> (Kaplan, 1988: 165)

Varo moved simultaneously inward and outward in the labyrinthine spiral connecting psyche, world, and cosmos—movements held in her paintings. In her final painting, *Still Life Reviving,* and in her psychospiritual journey, Varo seems to have arrived at the still point that contains, and is contained, within all movement, and in this union of harmony, balance, the cyclical, and the eternal, she found St. Catherine of Genoa's revelation of a transcendent wholeness.

Dead Leaves: The labyrinth, Ariadne's thread, and rewinding the myth of the male hero

As Varo moved toward the culmination of her work in *Still Life Reviving,* she continued to experiment with a variation of the spiral, in the form of a labyrinth. With the symbol of the labyrinth in mind, Varo took her artistic practice of spiritual alchemy to new levels in *Dead Leaves*, a composition the artist completed in 1956, seven years before she died.

In *Dead Leaves*, Varo seated a woman on a bench on a carpet of grass in a room in which leaves blow in through an open window. The woman wears a flowing green gown that gracefully covers her shoulders but is scooped low at the neckline. Red hair cascades down her back. With her right hand, the woman gathers to herself a ball of blue yarn, thread that emerges from within a faceless black figure nearby whose torso is a series of vaulted stone passageways that recede and get increasingly smaller the further one travels into the figure's interior spaces. Two birds, one red, one white, fly toward the woman from within the labyrinth, leading into the body cavity of the faceless black figure.

Dead Leaves, like all of Varo's paintings, tells a story. In this painting, Varo's symbolic narrative invites us to imagine the journey women make into the sacred spaces of the archetypal Feminine. "The labyrinth," wrote Senensky, is a story "that takes us back tens of thousands of years to a time when the Great Goddess reigned, when the Feminine was revered and honored, and the mysteries of birth, death, and rebirth were ritualized and regarded with awe" (2003: 1). As a symbol for "the womb of the Great Mother," the labyrinth "offers us a contained space to re-experience the movement and struggle that growth, birth, and rebirth entail" (39).

In *Healing and Empowering the Feminine: A Labyrinth Journey*, Senensky highlighted the alchemical way in which a journey into the labyrinth blends opposing elements to create transformation: "Spirit underlies all things, and is always present. It is the matrix of compassion out of which we are born and in which we are held" (2003: 28). In contrast to the spirit, the soul

> is about the juiciness of life. It searches for ways to feel alive. It lives with the passions: despair, love, hate, rage, and jealousy. Soul, the lover of beauty, good music, chocolate truffles, and walks in the rain, is held in by the bosom of Spirit where it can sing its song, and push the boundaries of the known. (28)

According to Senensky, the labyrinth, as spirit, contains the movements of the soul as we walk the paths of our lives, "pushing ... boundaries to learn more about ourselves and growing into who we really are" (29).

With the symbolic labyrinths Varo painted in *Spiral Transit* and *Dead Leaves* in mind, what, precisely, do we mean when we refer to the divine, or archetypal, Feminine? "The Feminine is about process and relationship. It is about playing, experimenting, doing several things at once. It is not goal-oriented, although there may be a goal toward which we are heading" (Senensky, 2003: 16). "The Feminine," Senensky added, can appear illogical when we look at it from the perspective of the Masculine, but it has an inner logic that is its alone. The twists and turns, the forward and backward movement of the labyrinth, the dancing between quadrants, the act of allowing the unexpected to affect your journey, the still point at the center—that is static and containing while honoring the rhythms and movement of life and death—all form an exquisite portrayal of how Feminine energy manifests itself. (16)

For Senensky, the labyrinth acts alchemically as a *temenos*, that is, a sacred space "separated … from the profane world around it" (37). Blending alchemical psychology and mysticism, Senensky linked the labyrinth to the alchemical vessel:

> Within the contained space of the labyrinth, all the elements of who we are on a physical, psychological, mythic, and spiritual level have a chance to interact. Because the labyrinth is a container wherein movement can occur, it provides us with a boundary we can bump up against. This boundary creates a certain amount of tension, which produces the heat that stimulates transformation, just as fire catalyzes the alchemical transformation of base products into gold. (37)

In her painting *Personage*, Varo depicted the labyrinth as an inner alchemical container: The exposed midsection of an androgynous figure is shaped like an alchemical vessel. Inside the vessel, legs and feet can be seen descending stairs. Emerging from the imagination of an artist steeped in self-discovery, the image speaks symbolically of the journey inward, toward one's deep Self. "The labyrinth," wrote Helmut Jaskolski, "is a symbol of the path we have to travel" (1994/1997: 12). As a mandala image of antiquity, "the labyrinth remains today a meaningful symbol of birth, not of the physical process but of psychic birth, the spiritual entry into the world, a symbol of emancipation and self-realization" (46).

In *Dead Leaves*, Varo worked archetypally with imagery that is by nature both alchemical and mythological. In painting a woman, a ball of yarn, and a labyrinth, Varo evoked one of the earliest myths in Greek culture, the Minoan story of the Minotaur, the thing so monstrous and shameful it "had to be withdrawn forever from human sight" (Jakolski, 1994/1997: 16). Mythologically, here, too, is the thread of Ariadne, who gave to the hero, Theseus, a sword to kill the monster and a ball of yarn with which to find his way out of the labyrinth of the unconscious when the deed was done. With her imagery, we find Varo pulling on a thread of the patriarchy, for the Minotaur, hidden within the mythical labyrinth, has the body of a man but the head and tail of a bull. "If someone is bull-headed," wondered Senensky, "is he not stubborn? Wouldn't stubbornness describe an aspect of a patriarchal culture that wants to cling to its old powers and not change?" (2003: 132).

Born when Queen Pasiphae of Crete is tricked into copulating with a prize white bull given to her husband, King Minos, by Poseidon, the god of the sea, the Minotaur, the monstrous half-man, half-bull, symbolizes

> the union of unmitigated passion with power. How often has patri-archal culture led with brute physical strength and thrusting sexuality ... This bull-headed man destroys human beings. His unconscious, repressed, and locked-away terror has been devouring human potential and creativity for centuries.
>
> (Senensky, 2003: 132)

For Senensky, the depth psychological meaning of the myth of the Minotaur can be found on at least two levels. From a patriarchal perspective, the myth tells the tale of the triumph of the male hero, Theseus, the future King of Athens. Caught in a "heroic, mind-over-matter approach" to the initi-atory descent into the womb of the Great Mother, Theseus accomplishes his task (127). But in so doing, he betrays Ariadne, who provided the thread of imagination and feeling the hero needed to incorporate the aspect of shadow liberated by the symbolic death of the Minotaur.

From a patriarchal point of view, Senensky concluded, the myth of the Minotaur "seems to have to do with power over, rather than power from within" (133). From a Jungian perspective, the

> Minotaur is a great power contained within, and can be likened to a powerful unconscious complex that devours the life force of a person because it had been caged in the unconscious and not allowed the light of day. The Minotaur did not need to be killed, but befriended and integrated. (133)

According to Senensky, a fundamental message communicated through the myth of the Minotaur is one of pain and death at a missed opportunity. Theseus, she said, had everything going for him—the help of a woman whose feeling nature watched over his quest from the threshold of the laby-rinth, a guiding thread connecting the hero to the power of the earth and the Goddess, and a sword with which to cut, or discriminate, his way to transformation made possible through the encounter with an aspect of the shadow made monstrous by its repression.

What Theseus did *not* have "is the right attitude... He knows there is a force that devours and his only solution is to kill it" (Senensky, 2003: 133). In the heroic patriarchal version of the myth of the Minotaur, "Theseus is unable to relate to the world with his feminine nature healed and his shadow incorporated. There is death but no rebirth" (134). In Varo's painting, *Minotaur*, the monstrous creature has a feminine nature. The transform-ation of the gender suggests that Theseus was not only dissociated from his feminine nature but defended against it in a patriarchal world that saw the feminine as a threat to its survival (an idea we revisit in Chapter Eleven).

As suggested by the symbol of the labyrinth as a vessel that hosts transformation, Theseus was engaged in a process of personal growth that, although it perhaps inaugurated him into a new status of patriarchal manhood, failed as a ritual intended to incorporate wisdom and wholeness into his character. "Initiation," Senensky wrote,

> is the archetypal pattern by which the psyche, whether in individuals or in groups of people, is enabled to make a transition from one stage of development to another and, therefore, brings the theme of death and rebirth into focus. (2003: 38)

Did Varo understand the need to create a new initiatory pattern—one that was not a linear progression, but a movement into a new and more fluidly feminine paradigm? We might imagine the woman in *Dead Leaves* as Ariadne retrieving her thread, rewinding the patriarchal myth and with it raveling the knowledge that, from a matriarchal point of view, the death of the monster at the hand of the hero degrades into neglect, abandonment, and abuse—symbolized by a room filled with decay and dead leaves. In this room, the only vibrancy is in Ariadne, who was left behind, and the two birds flying toward her from the opening of the labyrinth.

In *Dead Leaves*, Varo chose not to depict the *minotauromachy*—the battle between Theseus and the Minotaur—a conflict that protects against the vulnerability that is part of one's relational and feeling nature by defeating that which dwells in the dark labyrinth of the unconscious. In her image of Ariadne withdrawing the yarn the princess of Crete gave to Theseus, we might wonder if Varo has given us an image of a woman withdrawing a projection, reclaiming her power from the patriarchal myth of the male hero who kills the monster but fails to cultivate the feeling nature that would free him from the fear of the feminine in women and in himself. Senensky pinpointed the heroic Masculine's fear of the primordial energy of the Feminine as a primary problem of patriarchy. The primordial Feminine

> is a force concerned with the continuation of life including giving birth, ripening, decay and death. The Feminine is nature without human intervention as it grows wild by following its own rhythm. It is like a rampaging forest fire whose heat releases new growth. When women give birth they are in the throes of Her energy. In sexual passion we know this energy. When we dance ecstatically we can be filled with it. Because of its uncontrollable nature and lack of consciousness, it has been feared by both men and women. Most of us are terrified of losing control. The terror of this unknown force is at the base of the

strictures of patriarchy. Some boundaries are necessary, but patriarchy is an example of the masculine gone overboard in its attempts to subdue that which it cannot command. (2003: 87)

In *Dead Leaves*, Varo fingered the thread connecting her to the female fullness of life, symbolized by the woman's red hair, partially exposed breasts, and by the carpet she sits on, which the artist has painted in the form of grass that thrives around the edges and in a circle at the center. From a Jungian perspective, the circle of grass growing at the center of the carpet carries potent psychological symbolism. A form of mandala, the circle of grass suggests the life-sustaining, growth-producing cosmic nature of the divine Self, which Jung described as "Formation, Transformation, Eternal Mind's eternal recreation" (1961/1963: 196).

Working with patients who brought their dreams into the consulting room, Jung discovered that the circle and square related to the mandala as symbols of totality that appear in the psyche's attempt to invite the ego to engage with the numinous archetypal forces that have as their goal the enlargement and revitalization of the personality (1950/1968: para. 634). For the ego, wrote Sharp, "experiences of the self possess a numinosity characteristic of religious revelations" (1991: 120). Jung, Sharp added, made no distinction between "the self as an experiential, psychological reality and the traditional concept of a supreme deity" (120). Jung himself emphasized that the existence of the Self "is a mere postulate and nothing whatever can be predicated as to its possible contents" (1936/1968, para. 247). He added, "Intellectually, the self is no more than a psychological concept, a construct that serves to express an unknowable essence which we cannot grasp as such, since by definition it transcends our powers of comprehension" (1928/ 1966, para. 399). In keeping with his belief in the religious function of the psyche, Jung concluded that the deep Self "might equally well be called the 'God within us'" (para. 399). In *Dead Leaves*, Varo revivifies the divine presence of the lost Feminine—an aspect of the transpersonal Self discarded as worthless by the patriarchal hero. Varo symbolizes this alchemical reclamation with the re-winding of the connecting blue thread that vitalizes the woman whose journey into the labyrinth has brought her back home to herself.

Jung, according to Sharp, believed that quaternary images, including the mandala, a word that comes from the Sanskrit, meaning *sacred circle*, appear in dreams, fantasies, and intentional interaction with unconscious forces through practices like active imagination—and in Varo's case, painting—when a person's ego is ready "to assimilate unconscious material" (1991: 111).

We will see shortly, however, that Varo's use of the mandala-like spiral and labyrinth may have different implications than posited by Jung and found in alchemy in the heroic attempt to square the circle.

Distinguishing between the circle and the square as quaternary images, in his researches Jung found that "the circle is a symbol of the psyche (even Plato described the psyche as a sphere). The square (and often the rectangle) is a symbol of earthbound matter, of the body and reality" (Jaffé, 1964: 249). The alchemical attempt, called *squaring the circle*, to unite these opposites produced the *lapis*, an arcane substance that symbolized a higher form of matter. Jung linked this process with the psychology surrounding the archetype of the Self. Direct experience of the Self, Jung wrote, "is exemplified in mandala symbolism, which portrays the self as a concentric structure, often in the form of a squaring of the circle" (1955–56/1970: para. 776). As a symbol, Jung added, the squared circle is numinous, the emotions constellated by the image represent an inexpressible transpersonal force ranging from relief at having distress or chaos contained "to an extremely intense experience of illumination. These aspects all appear in alchemy, the only difference being that there they are projected into matter, whereas here they are understood as symbols" (para. 776). Through the practice of working to unite opposites, the alchemical lapis "has therefore changed into a psychic event without having lost any of its original numinosity" (para. 776).

For the alchemists, squaring the circle was almost always a supremely challenging effort. Some practitioners, in fact, worked their entire life hoping to experience the numinous conjunction of human and divine. For those who use Jungian concepts and methods to follow the footsteps of the deep Self, pursuing personal growth through the practice of alchemical psychology can feel like trying to find one's way in the dark with only a small lantern and faith that one *might* find what one is looking for.[2] Of this pathless path, the late June Singer wrote:

> I would not want to suggest that any practical purpose is served directly, nor is that the intention behind active imagination, dream analysis or any other analytic procedure we may decide to use. Through the process, if seriously undertaken, transformations of the personality do occur. Narrow attitudes become broadened, one-sidedness gives way to the capacity to view a situation from several positions, aggression is replaced by productive activity, and passivity becomes receptivity. The changes are often subtle, but they go deep, and people who experience them know that they are living in a different way than they did before. (1994: 301)

In *Dead Leaves*, the rug with the grass circle at its center has enough straight edges and 90-degree angles to suggest a rectangle, but also has amorphous or amoebic edges, suggesting that its physicalness is not quite controlled or controllable, and has a "mind of its own." In other words, physical matter is inspirited, alive with intelligence that challenges the desire, enthroned in the patriarchal paradigm, for control and a rationally understood order. It suggests that the struggle to square the circle is grounded in the perceptual division of mind and matter that creates the illusion that one might control nature and unify that which cannot be divided. In *Dead Leaves*, Varo works from the ego to engage with and host the divine forces inherent in nature on their own terms. She does so for the purpose of personal growth and transformation, but also to enable archetypal patterns to become embodied in *their* experience of her human life, leading perhaps to a reality that, as she withdraws Ariadne's yarn from the myth of Theseus and the Minotaur, forms differently than that shaped by the assumptions of the patriarchal psyche.

In her use of the ancient motif of the labyrinth, Varo evoked the spiral path, marking "the symbolic passageway from the visible realm of the human into the invisible dimension of the divine" ("Labyrinth," 2010: 714).

In Mercurial fashion, the movement through the labyrinth veers back and forth, round and round, creating a dance whose steps eventually weave a vessel strong enough to hold what was at first intolerable experience. A transcendent pattern eventually emerges, which lifts one to a new vantage point. (714)

We have looked at Varo's use of the labyrinth as a symbol in a host of ways, including the artist's blend of art, alchemy, and Jungian depth psychology. Varo painted in a language of visual metaphor. She saw the connection between the human world and the divine world. To make the point even finer: It seems clear that Varo understood an old idea—that what is sick or injured in this world gets healed in the realm of the ancestors, and, conversely, what is injured or sick in the other world (the realm of myth or archetype) gets the medicine needed for healing from the actions and the lives of human beings.

The idea that a human life can be medicine is interesting, especially with *Spiral Transit*, *Dead Leaves*, and Varo's other paintings that focus on the motif of the labyrinth in mind. We do not know if Varo ever walked a labyrinth. If not, maybe it was because she did not need to. Maybe she was already following, in her personal search for self-discovery and through the practice of painting, the spirals of her life to the center of things. What did Varo see at the center? Do images of fruits as planets and explorers seeking new vistas suggest that the artist had found a sense of meaning in the sometimes-unbearable experiences of her life? All we know is how we feel in the presence of her images. In her paintings, Varo showed her sadness and fear, but also her longing for the harmony, wonder, and love she knew dwelled in the heart of the world.

As we complete this section of our look at Varo's use of alchemical psychology in her art and life, we can say that we know only what the artist showed us. But through imagination, there may be tasks that are now left up to us to figure out. For each of us must walk the spiral path of our own life. As Edinger once said, in the context of a discussion on the archetype of the Christ and consciously realizing "one's own particular pattern of wholeness," each of us must learn to bear our own cross (1972: 135). We know, from lingering with Varo and the figures who come alive in her painted worlds, that this was a person who followed the path of her life to the best of her ability. Maybe Varo died of a heart attack because she no longer needed to live a human life—she had accomplished what she came here to do. Maybe that something was to walk the labyrinth of life—her life, painful at times, playful, pouncing, and catlike at others.

With Varo's symbolic expressions of the labyrinth and the people who travel them in mind, Jaskolski offered these thoughts on the psychological and spiritual aspects of the experience of following the spiral path of the soul:

> He who ventures courageously into a labyrinth seeking to find the truth of his life is forced by its circuitous pathways to circumambulate the center of himself, to learn to relate with it and to perceive it from all sides. He can only reach it by passing through the entire interior space of the labyrinth beforehand, by relating to all of its dimensions, and integrating them all into the wholeness of his personality. (1994/1997: 77)

"The labyrinth," Jaskolski concluded, "is thus a representation of, and guide to, a complex movement from the outside inward and from the inside back out" (76).

Notes

1 The reference is to an alchemical emblem included in the *Viridarium Chymicum*, by Daniel Stolcius (Prague, 1624). From a Jungian perspective, the image of the eagle, a symbol of the spirit that longs to fly free, chained to a lowly land animal, a toad, speaks to the psychological challenge of holding the tension between opposites. To see the image, visit www.jcf.org/mythblast-sustaining-the-celebration/.

2 The metaphor of finding one's way in the dark with only a lantern comes from an alchemical emblem in *Atalanta Fugiens: Ein Alchemistisches Emblemwerk* by Michael Maier (1568–1622), published in 1617. The emblem can be seen in many places online including Wikimedia Commons.

References

Arias-Henao, D. (2019). *Walking on the moon: A depth psychology of Luna imagery* (UMI Number: TK) [Doctoral dissertation, Pacifica Graduate Institute]. ProQuest Dissertations.

Bogzaran, F. (2008). Dreams of alchemy. In M. Orellano (Ed.), *Five keys to the secret world of Remedios Varo* (159–86). Mexico City, Mexico: Artes de Mexico.

Campbell, J. (2008). *The hero with a thousand faces*. Novato, CA: New World Library.

Edinger, E. (1972). *Ego and archetype*. Boston, MA: Shambhala.

Engel, P. (2008). Places of the unconscious. In M. Orellano (Ed.), *Five keys to the secret world of Remedios Varo* (91–109). Mexico City, Mexico: Artes de Mexico.

Jaffé, A. (1964). Symbolism in the visual arts. In C. G. Jung, M.-L. von Franz, J. Henderson, J. Jacobi & A. Jaffé (Eds.), *Man and his symbols* (230–71). Garden City, NY: Doubleday.

Jaffé, A. (1968/1971). *From the life and work of C. G. Jung* (R. F. C. Hull, Trans.). London, UK: Harper Colophon Books.

Jaskolski, H. (1994/1997). *The labyrinth: Symbol of fear, rebirth, and liberation* (M. Kohn, Trans.). Boston, MA: Shambhala.

Jung, C. G. (1961/1963). *Memories, dreams, reflections* (A. Jaffé, Ed.; R. Winston & C. Winston, Trans.) New York, NY: Random House.

Jung, C. G. (1928/1966). The relations between the ego and the unconscious (R. F. C. Hull, Trans.). In H. Read et al. (Eds.), *The collected works of C. G. Jung* (Vol. 7, 2nd ed., 121–241). Princeton, NJ: Princeton University Press.

Jung, C. G. (1929/1967). Commentary on "The secret of the golden flower" (R. F. C. Hull, Trans.). In H. Read et al. (Eds.), *The collected works of C. G. Jung* (Vol. 13, 1–56). Princeton, NJ: Princeton University Press.

Jung, C. G. (1936/1968). Individual dream symbolism in relation to alchemy (R. F. C. Hull, Trans.). In H. Read et al. (Eds.), *The collected works of C. G. Jung* (Vol. 12, 2nd ed., 39–224). Princeton, NJ: Princeton University Press.

Jung, C. G. (1950/1968). Concerning mandala symbolism (R. F. C. Hull, Trans.). In H. Read et al. (Eds.), *The collected works of C. G. Jung* (Vol. 9i, 2nd ed., 355–84). Princeton, NJ: Princeton University Press.

Jung, C. G. (1951/1968). The shadow (R. F. C. Hull, Trans.). In (H. Read et al., Eds.). *The collected works of C. G. Jung* (Vol. 9ii, 2nd ed., 8–10). Princeton, NJ: Princeton University Press.

Jung, C. G. (1955–56/1970). *Mysterium coniunctionis* (R. F. C. Hull, Trans.) (H. Read et al., Eds.), *The collected works of C. G. Jung* (Vol. 14, 2nd ed.). Princeton, NJ: Princeton University Press.

Kaplan, J. (1988). *Unexpected journeys: The art and life of Remedios Varo*. New York, NY: Abbeville Press.

Labyrinth. (2010). In A. Ronnberg & K. Martin (Eds.), *The book of symbols: Reflections on archetypal images* (714–5). Cologne, Germany: Taschen.

Purce, J. (1980). *The mystic spiral: Journey of the soul*. London, UK: Thames & Hudson.

Senensky, S. S. (2003). *Healing and empowering the feminine: A labyrinth journey*. Wilmette, IL: Chiron.

Sharp, D. (1991). *C. G. Jung lexicon: A primer of terms & concepts*. Toronto, Canada: Inner City Books.

Singer, J. (1994). *Boundaries of the soul: The practice of Jung's psychology*. New York, NY: Anchor Books.

Varo, R. (1997/2018). *Letters, dreams & other writings* (M. Carson, Trans.). Cambridge, MA: Wakefield Press.

Von Franz, M.-L. (1995). *Creation myths* (Rev. ed.). Boston, MA: Shambhala.

Chapter 7

Cauldrons of color

Dead Leaves and the alchemical movement between death, life, and rebirth

Writing about alchemy and the lifelong unfolding of the personality he called individuation, Jung linked the "free-ranging psyche of the adept [who] used chemical substances" with the creative way "a painter uses colours to shape out the images of his fancy" (1955–56/1970, para. 687). With Varo's artistic practice of alchemical psychology and the layered symbolism in her images in mind, we wonder, as Jung did: "What is the psychological meaning of the procedure" Varo chose to evoke in making *Dead Leaves*? (para. 693).

The blackening: The human soul and its need for death to come alive

In *Dead Leaves*, Varo used color to create a composition that depicts her experience of the alchemical movement between life, death, and rebirth. Black, associated with the destruction of the original form, the first matter, sets the scene. Dead leaves, draping the walls and hanging from the ceiling, mark the move from summer and the fullness of life into the entropy of fall and the death-like dormancy of winter. Varo also chose black for the color of the faceless figure whose body is the origin of the thread being wound by the woman who has made the journey into herself and has now found her way back into life again. Alchemically, Varo told us, with the imagery, that the move inward, toward knowledge and experience of one's deep Self, begins with blackening, with the death of what has been.

The thread being wound by the woman on the bench connects the woman not only to the fire and fullness of life but also to decay and death—to the entropy waiting at the other end of life's string. In this sense, *Dead Leaves* depicts the initiation into the labyrinth of one's own being—the journey into, and through, the process of transformation in which complexed emotional patterns are gradually depotentiated, the personality re-animated into increasingly conscious, fulfilling, and meaningful experience. And in this case, given the partially exposed voluptuousness of the woman, unusual for Varo's painted figures, and her association with Ariadne, the Princess of Crete, the artist is clearly evoking a woman's revivifying and redeeming experience of the transpersonal Feminine

The blue thread: Imagination and initiation into the labyrinth of one's own being

Varo chose blue as the color of the thread being wound by the woman sitting on the bench in the circle of grass in the room with dead leaves. In alchemical psychology, as we mentioned earlier, blue heralds the appearance of the imagination (Hillman, 2010: 110–1). In *Dead Leaves*, through the use of the color blue, Varo revealed her allegiance to, and her faith in, the imagination. She was showing her devotion to the image, to the symbol, and to the artistic and transformative practices of painting and alchemical psychology. According to Tom Cheetham, the chief interpreter of the work of Henry Corbin, Jung's "rediscovery of alchemy as the language of the psyche is central to [the] practice of coming to terms with the unconscious" (2012: 209).

In *Dead Leaves*, the artist captured a moment in the collaboration between the surrendered ego (the woman winding the thread) and an autonomous figure of the objective psyche (the black figure with the labyrinth in the center of his or her body). Through the woman in her painting, Varo engaged with the black figure, from whom she draws the blue thread of what Cheetham called "a new kind of imaginative reality" (2012: 207). In this union of human and divine, both the woman and the faceless figure are drawn into an ongoing embodiment with the archetypal forces of life, death, and rebirth.

Weaving this thread with another we have been following, we see the embodiment of the theme of life, death, and rebirth in Varo's dream of the executioner. Perhaps Cheetham's allusion to a new *kind* of imaginative reality—one of a profoundly different nature—gives language to why the artist in the dream must be killed. Varo wrote that the central mystery in her dream is that she has knowledge, a piece of "absolute truth," that will destroy the world if everyone knows about it (1997/2018: 94). With Jung's belief that image is psyche in mind, we wonder: Why has the dream-maker used these particular images? Perhaps the answer has to do with the way Varo, as the dream ego, responds to her own execution: She surrenders, but with an asterisk. She asks Death for time to weave an egg—symbol of birth, death, and rebirth—into which she weaves her destiny with the man to whom she wished to be connected for eternity.

Varo painted, grew as a person, and placed high value upon the imagination as her way of living a conscious and meaningful life that supports all beings, including the earth we live on and the expansive cosmos that surrounds us. What if the imagery in the dream of the executioner is meant in part to model for us how Western patriarchy kills imagination (beheads it) and thus the wholeness and possibility of change that challenges the known order? What if Varo, not as a projected image of the artist as the dream ego, but as an expression of the soul itself, exemplifies the imaginal presence needed to respond to patriarchy's annihilating fear of vulnerability? What if the dangerous knowledge Varo possesses in the dream has something to do with cultivating soul, in ourselves and in the world, through attending to images and working to transform what is base in our nature into recast and increasingly conscious forms?

Guided by unconscious forces, Varo, in *Dead Leaves* and other works, may have left painted clues for us to follow as we travel further into the artist's imaginal realm. Varo's paintings, engaged with from a symbolic sensibility, become more than pretty pictures—they transform into alchemical recipes, symbolic instructions for cooking the armored oppressions of patriarchy into food that is nourishing to everyone, not just those with privilege and power. From a Jungian perspective that sees symptoms as seeds of healing, Varo's images become imaginal couriers whose intent is to communicate meta-phoric messages sent from the archetypal realm to expose the problems of patriarchy. Perhaps this is an aspect of the secret Varo knew. Perhaps this is a piece of the absolute truth that Varo had discovered (or had revealed to her) in the dream of the executioner, a secret so dangerous that the patriarchy, in the form of the executioner, could not afford to let her bring it into the world.

There are, as Cheetham acknowledged, risks and pitfalls to traveling in imaginal terrain. To safely explore "the suprapersonal world of the arche-typal realm," a person must "cultivate a truly visionary Imagination, freed from the limitations of the ego" (2012: 208). "This realm," Cheetham added,

> truly transcends the world of the ego—entry into these spaces is a "living birth," in Jung's own words, and here we are kept off-balance continually. Here dynamic equilibrium, and even disequilibrium, are the norms. Here we find life on the edge of chaos, or at least on the edge of our ability to *know*, to predict, and to understand. [The *mundus imaginalis*] is creative, powerful, and deeply unsettling. (208–9, emphasis in original)

In *Dead Leaves*, by fingering the blue thread, Varo has followed the path into the unknown of herself. Through the character in her painting, the artist has traveled into, and become an active partner with, the *mundus imaginalis*, the term Corbin gave to "the place of visions and the visionary imagination" (Cheetham, 2012: 208).

With the imagery in *Dead Leaves*, Varo hinted further at the dangerous truth she dreamed about. Imaged as a woman winding a blue ball of string, the artist draws back the thread of the imagination from Theseus, who lacked the imaginative capacity to see anything other than a monster and do anything other than kill the beast. Alchemically and artistically, Varo evoked the collaboration between the human being and the archetypal forces that people the imaginal realm. Her painting suggests a dangerous truth—a secret so subversive it could cut open the fabric of the material world and rip apart an inflexible patriarchal mind that must see things in a literal and concrete way. Symbolically, Varo's character has found the opening in her psyche and is re-winding the thread of life, her life, back into herself. One alchemical way of speaking this truth: The reddening of life is inseminated by the blackness of death. Hillman spoke to the fear one can feel in the presence of the "cosmic forces that shape the soul apart from human beings. What civilized society fears is black magic: the magical pull of black attraction, the soul's desire to descend into darkness, like Persephone into Hades" (2010: 91).

Why does the human soul need death to come alive? Hillman believed a crucial ingredient is imagination:

> Alchemy advises "beware of the physical in the material." It is not the "material" of suffering that poisons the work with despair, but the "physical," that is, the substantive naturalistic mind that prevents an imaginative appreciation of the material. (92)

It is threatening for a mind caught in delusional literalism to fathom, but from Varo's painting, the truth is there for the imaginal eye to see: The thread connecting life and death comes from the darkness, from within the labyrinthine passageways of the psyche that lead into personal and cultural complexes, as well as archetypal forces that transcend the human. The journey to enlightenment is often difficult, but usually worth it. The traveler, in this case Varo, follows the thread of the soul into the unknown; with each step, each experience, she gathers into herself both the finality of material death and the eternal life of a soul powered, like one of the artist's magical conveyances, by imagination. From a Jungian perspective, psychological life is created in the vessel of the unconscious. For here is a protected space, a womb, in which the essence of who we are can be conceived, inseminated, cooked, and ultimately birthed into embodied knowing: This is who I am.

In *Dead Leaves*, a composition painted on cardboard in 1956, seven years before her death, Varo symbolized a process of transformation that is working on unseen levels to prepare her to live her truth. Living one's truth is not always easy, in fact, it is often painful, and for Varo, even traumatizing. From a Jungian perspective, living into the individuation demands of the deep Self involves surrender: The ego must give up its need for control and predictability, and agree to support and host the archetypal forces at work in one's life. As illuminated in the above discussion of *Dead Leaves*, the work of individuation becomes an alchemical reunion between ego and Self, human and divine, feminine and masculine, life and death. The result of the pairing of one thing with another is a new form, a more conscious life, in which a person, now more aware of debilitating complexes and destructive aspects of shadow, can consciously co-create animating and unexpected possibilities instead of breeding conflict, injury, and harm.

Blending the metaphor of the labyrinth and the experience of the life-enhancing transit toward one's authentic self with the image of dead leaves, Varo symbolized her experience of the archetypal forces of Death and Life. With the painting, Varo depicted a powerful conjunction: the interplay between the instinct for life and the entropy and inevitable death of all living things. She evoked the impersonal quality one can experience when an ego surrenders into service to the archetypal Self. The woman in the painting, a projected image of an aspect of Varo, looks away from the scene and sees without seeing; her hands, winding the blue thread, seem to know what to do automatically, without instruction or attention. The ego of the human being who surrenders to such forces is relativized, then reanimated by the archetypal forces waiting within suffering and complexes for release into embodied experience.

The two whitenings: The furnace of distress and the death of innocence

In the mirror of Varo's painting, we see an even more subtle alchemical process at work: the whitening of the artist's soul under the silver light of the moon. In *Dead Leaves*, Varo located the woman winding the blue thread in a room where the walls, ceiling, portions of the floor, even a chair, stone fireplace, and the drape billowing into the space from a breeze blowing in through an open window are tinted in silver, the color that appears at the point in the process of alchemical transformation when the substance has been whitened, is now ready to be assimilated, and needs reducing.

For Hillman, following Jung and the alchemists, the process of alchemical transformation aims ultimately at a reddening, or vivifying, of the first matter. The original state of one's personality needs to be blackened as a first step toward re-solidifying things as the psyche prepares a person to host the archetypal forces that are trying to birth themselves into material life. For this transformation to take place, the original pattern of the personality, the first matter, which has been destroyed, must then be whitened. "In alchemical color symbolism," Hillman wrote, "white is the principal stage between black and red, a transition of soul between despair and passion, between emptiness and fullness" (2010: 154). Borrowing from Jung, Hillman added, "the phase called whitening in alchemy refers to the emergence of psychological consciousness, the ability to hear psychologically, and to perceive fantasy creating reality" (158).

Hillman related the whitening, the alchemical *albedo*, with the *anima*, in Jungian psychology a Latin term for soul that refers to the feminine aspect of a person's personality.

Anima consciousness, or the *albedo* in alchemy, offers a different mode of perception. Seeing, listening, attending all shift from the gross attachments of the *nigredo* to a new transparency and resonance. Things shine and speak. They are images, bodies of subtlety. They address the soul by showing forth their souls. (158)

In the practice of alchemical psychology, Hillman wrote, "all whites are not the same white" (129). In fact, in the alchemical process of transformation, whitening happens two times. Hillman called the first whitening *primary*. "Primary white is immaculate (without stain or blemish), innocent (without hurt, harmless), ignorant (without knowing, disregarding), unsullied and unsoiled" (155). This first whitening is characterized by "childlike naivety, unawareness, immaturity and a lack of experience" ("White," 2010: 660). As a part of the *albedo*, the alchemical cooling of the unconscious matter, the second whitening indicates that the substance has undergone a fiery purification that first blackened it and then burned away what was inessential (Marlan, 2005: 97).

Unexpected Journeys, Kaplan's biography of Varo, includes several photographs that allow us to track the artist's evolution from the primary whitening, the "unworked innocence" of childhood, a time "of marshmallow dreamings, sweet, shy virginity," into the alchemical "*albedo*, a cooling that results from violent tortures, long-suffering patience, and intense heat" (Hillman, 2010: 129). A family photograph shows Varo around the age of four. The future artist poses with her father, Rodrigo, and older brother, also named Rodrigo. "They are a pensive, handsome group," Kaplan wrote, "very Spanish, with sharp features, dark skin, and dark eyes strikingly set against strong aquiline noses" (1988: 11). In the formal portrait, Varo wears a white dress with a ruffled neckline. An intricate pattern of lace has been sewn into the garment. Lace appears in another family photograph, taken, Kaplan estimates, when Varo was seven years old. In this grouping, Varo poses with her grandmother, older brother Rodrigo, and her mother, who holds the future artist's younger brother, Luis, born since the first family portrait was taken. In this black-and-white photograph, Varo wears a dark dress that features a large white lace collar. A delicate white piece of jewelry hangs from her neck, framed within the plunging lines of the intricate lace collar, and set off by the dark fabric of the dress. Varo's lively expression continues in adolescence. In one photograph she poses at the beach with her younger brother Luis and four female cousins. In another image, Varo, now a young woman, poses with her parents and extended family. The look on her face, like that of the adolescent girl next to her, blooms with a grin that is both shy and exuberant. She is filled with spirit, animated in the way the archetypal maiden Persephone might have been before the team of horses broke through the ground and Hades came to abduct and rape her in the underworld.

Like Persephone, for Varo the innocence of childhood and adolescence gave way to suffering that left indelible marks upon her personality. There were good times, to be sure. In 1930, Varo, 22 years old, earned a diploma as a drawing teacher and married fellow artist Gerardo Lizarraga. "Fascinated by the Surrealist ideas that had been filtering into Spain," Varo and her young husband lived for a year in Paris "to find the avant-garde at its source" (Kaplan, 1988: 35). In Paris, Varo signed up for a series of no-cost art courses—and promptly dropped out. Kaplan, referring to the stifling experience Varo had in a Roman Catholic convent school as a girl, explained the young artist's reasoning:

> She soon realized that she did not want to place herself, once again, within the confines of the classroom. Young and eager, she was just beginning to feel the growth of her own wings and she wanted no institution to limit their span. (35)

Varo and Lizarraga lived in Paris for a year. The couple returned to Spain in 1932. "Still savoring their taste of Parisian life," Varo and Lizarraga settled in Barcelona, home to an avant-garde atmosphere that "was liberal, optimistic, and very anticlerical in outlook and had become, by the early 1930s, much more of an intellectual and artistic center than Madrid" (Kaplan, 1988: 35). Barcelona offered Varo "distance, both geographical and psychological, from the watchful eyes of her family and a chance to experiment with her life as well as her art" (35–6).

In Barcelona, Varo made a bold break from "the strict moral code under which she had been raised" (Kaplan, 1988: 36). Married to and living with Lizarraga, she took a lover, Esteban Francés, also an artist "interested in the experimental and the surreal" (36). According to Kaplan, Varo's decision to share her bed and a studio with Francés "established a pattern she was to maintain for the rest of her life: multiple relationships, all open, nothing hidden, which developed into friendships that lasted long after any romantic connection had ended" (36).

Like her first husband, Esteban Francés "was part of Varo's life in Spain, France, and Mexico" (Kaplan, 1988: 36).

> Although open sexuality and the flouting of conventional morals were a virtual credo in the bohemian set, Varo was rare in her ability to conduct affairs that matured into friendships with little jealousy and few recriminations ... [and that] endured across great spans of distance and time, remaining intact despite the wrenching upheavals of this chaotic period of history. (36)

Sharing a studio "in an area of Barcelona frequented by young artists," Kaplan wrote, "Varo and Francés thrived in the highly charged atmosphere—buoyed by the early Republic's extraordinary effusion of hope" (37). The artist-lovers "set to work producing paintings, drawings, and collages that expressed a commitment to Surrealist ideas" (37). A photograph taken in Barcelona at the time shows Varo arm in arm with Francés at her left and another young male artist at her right.

> Smilingly broadly, she looks bright and happy, and her companions seem suave and debonair. All smartly dressed in sophisticated clothing, they project an air of being young people on the move. Francés, small and dark, with boyish good looks and sultry eyes, has a cigarette tucked in his fingers and a coat draped over his arm. He has turned slightly toward Varo, protectively clutching her hand in his own, as if to make clear for the camera which two of the three are the couple. (37)

By 1936, however, Varo had been abducted into a blackening of unconscious cultural and personal complexes brought forth in the traumas of war and exile. The exuberant girl and young artist flying high on the current of Surrealism were gone, replaced by a frightened woman with nervous eyes and a cigarette in her hand. Varo's smile and spirit would never leave her. But in photographs taken of her after World War II, the smile often fades. In one image she looks away from the camera, staring soft focus to her left, dark eyes searching, perhaps, for the unblemished whiteness of the girl and young woman she once was (Kaplan, 1988: 50). No longer a maiden, this Varo still sports a crisp white blouse trimmed in delicate lace. But now the incandescent light in her eyes is darkened by the menacing densities of murder, by the shrieks and screams of people strafed by German planes, by the visceral fear of death and the memories of her capture and confinement in a French prison camp in the winter of 1940.

Like Persephone, Varo emerged from darkness, the inessential burned away in a second whitening. Starting in the early 1950s, the artist began to find herself. In the compositions Varo painted over the last decade or so of her life, the traumatized maiden emerges from the underworld a woman who belongs not to a man or her family's patriarchal God, but to herself. Persephone's story, linked to the second whitening, signifies that an aspect of this phase of alchemy is that the virgin (as distinct from the maiden) is also Queen of the underworld and a bringer of spring. Eating a seed of the pomegranate, a symbol of fertility offered to her by Hades, invests Persephone (as maiden become Virgin and Queen) with the obligation to return annually to that which lurks below human life in its foundations, in the unconscious, to bring new life back into the day-world.

In her 1957 self-portrait, *Witch Going to the Sabbath,* Varo revealed herself as the witch, or Virgin Queen, who, having called upon numinous forces in the continual cycle of the rebirthing of the world, now attends the symbolic day of rest—the fallow period between movement into and out of life as we have created it. In Varo's painting, the witch is cloaked in the vibrant cascading red of her own hair, the color of blood, symbolic of that which flows from the heart and the womb. She holds on one upturned palm an imaginal bird bearing her same face with brightly colored feathers that look like those of a peacock. In the painting, the tail feathers of the peacock touch the dark cavern of the witch's heart—the mysterious liberating power of love.

Mythologically, the sign of the peacock, "considered sacred to Juno, the Roman goddess of lunar light and protector of childbirth," connects the witch to the Persephone principle of rebirth that emerges from the imprisoning darkness of the underworld (Hauck, 1999: 230). As an alchemical emblem, the peacock refers to "the indwelling 'spirit'" (230) or "the inner experience of the astral world" (McLean, 1979: 3). Alchemically, the appearance of the peacock signifies awareness of etheric forces and of the astral body connecting the human self to the transpersonal cosmos. The appearance of colors in the alchemical flask confer upon the alchemical adept an experience "equivalent to seeing through the eyes of the gods or to having visions and making the connection to the divine mind through the imagination" (Hauck, 1999: 230).

In Varo's painting, the witch's face is blue, a subtle symbolic indication of the *imaginatio,* in which the artist now sees through the literal into that which is possible, real, and divine. The stage represented by the peacock arrives as a result of the alchemist having made herself open to initiatory spiritual experiences by entering the blackening or *nigredo,* a forceful putrefaction that involves "the absolute suppression of the ego" (Hauck, 1999: 114). "Putrefaction," Hauck wrote, "is often perceived as a dark depression in which the ruling principle of the personality must die to make room for a higher identity" (114).

Silvered imagining: The hammered soul and the symbol as a living presence

Seeing alchemically, we now find Varo, devoted to searching for her true nature, sitting at her easel and opening her mind and heart to unseen worlds that appear under the silver light of the moon, wishing to conjure themselves on her canvas. She begins a painting with a sketch, maybe several sketches, drawings done in pencil, images forming and reforming, ideas and feelings cooking slowly in the cauldron of her imagination.

A hallmark of Varo's work is her use of color. According to Hillman, color is crucial to the psychological use and experience of imagination. "Colors," he wrote, "are a primary presentation of archetypal differentiation, each color a celebration of the sensuality of the cosmos, each shade and hue tincturing the psyche with a set of moods and attaching it to the world with particular affinities" (2010: 116).

In *Dead Leaves*, Varo colored her canvas carefully. The black of death and the bleakness of decay ground the scene. There is the blue thread that we have associated with imagination and the ability to engage with the animating presence of the divine through metaphoric means. The red hair of the woman winding the blue thread is also an important aspect of the symbolism of the painting. "Hair is incredibly potent," wrote one essayist; "its root follicles, fed by tiny blood vessels, lie invisibly under the skin, associating hair with interior, involuntary fantasies, thoughts and longings" ("Hair," 2010: 346). The fullness and redness of the hair flowing down her back in *Dead Leaves* may have been Varo's expression of the erotic longing she felt for and vitality she received from the beings who supported the creative unfolding of her life and art from their origins in the imaginal realm.

With these alchemical operations taking place, it might be possible to miss the most important color Varo used in *Dead Leaves*. By tinting the floor, ceiling, walls, and furniture in layers of silver, silver-white, silver-gray, and charcoal flecked with white and silver, the essence, or soul, of the painting shines brightly for us to see. In *Dead Leaves*, Varo stilled the movement of the alchemical opus. The moment caught on canvas is the altering of the white room (the room a symbol for the artist's psyche) with the tarnish of silver—the light of the moon illuminating mysteries held in the darkness of the labyrinth. With the formative experiences of Varo's personal life in mind, in *Dead Leaves* the artist rendered visible[1] the alchemical shift from innocence destroyed and then whitened by imagination to a hard-won capacity for what Hillman called "silvered imagining," a fermentation process that adds "weight to light" and rubs "the silver to more clarified reflections" (2010: 186–7).

From a Jungian perspective, we can say that with a silvered imagination, Varo surrendered to the inherent worth and dignity of images, and to symbols as living presences with their own desires to become embodied and cared for in and through the work we do in our human lives. As a person and an artist, Varo consciously chose to live from the imagination.

In her dream of the executioner, Varo appears as a woman of surrendered intent, a person whose faith in the imagination, in the image, and in the numinous workings of unseen realms, is put to the ultimate test. In the dream, Varo, who is not limited to a literal interpretation of things, is willing and able to engage with opposites (her wish for more life, and acceptance of her own death) in a way that allows a new possibility (weaving her destiny with the man) to emerge. Varo wrote that in her dream, when told she is to be executed, she asks and receives permission "to do something of the greatest importance before dying" (1997/2018: 95). In an imaginal act she weaves an egg around herself and the man with whom she wishes to be connected for eternity. It is psychologically important to note that the egg—an ancient symbol of wholeness and new life—is woven from both their substances, an imaginal and alchemical conjunction of feminine and masculine.

From a Jungian perspective, personal transformation is only a beginning, for transformation is required to prepare a person to bring what they are supposed to bring into the world. The qualities at the foundation of Varo's imaginal act in her dream are ones that she discovered through her personal work of transformation and that she offered the world through her painting: unwavering curiosity, belief in the numinous workings of the psyche and the transformative nature of imagination and image, and a profound valuing of the connective quality and cyclical nature of the feminine. With change at the level of community and culture in mind, Varo's dream of the executioner suggests a possibility that may be threatening to those who defend against ambivalence and multiplicity by encasing themselves in a mindset Hillman called *delusional literalism*—the belief that what one sees, as well as how one sees one's self and world, comprises reality (2010: 192).

In the dream, the projected version of Varo shows a range of imaginal sensibilities, including the willingness to engage with images not from a place of objective understanding but according to their subjective meaning and possibilities. This way of living may be why the executioner is ordered to kill Varo. For what would happen if people choose to live from a place that recognizes and values the relationship one has with one's images and inner life—that which is other than and appears and sees differently than the familiar, known, or assumed? This might lead to the threat of being connected not only to one's self but to others.

The imagery in Varo's dream of the executioner offers imaginal evidence of what we see being enacted in cultures around the world: Patriarchal forces want to kill ambivalence and multiplicity. Clinging to what is literal, the executioner, who fears the overwhelming vulnerability of relationship, with others and with himself, decapitates the head of the woman who commits a menacing act: She surrenders her art and life to feeling, to connection, to the symbolic vitality of the image, and to the liberating presence and power of imagination.

But the imagery of decapitation proves that the practice of alchemical psychology is not all one thing or another. For Varo, the imagery might also be commenting on the soul's attempt to free itself from an identification with the dense literalisms of the blackening. "Alchemical psychology," Hillman wrote,

> teaches us to read as accomplishments the fruitlessly bitter and dry periods, the melancholies that seem never to end, the wounds that do not heal, the grinding sadistic mortifications of shame and the putrefactions of love and friendships. These are beginnings because they are endings, dissolutions, deconstructions. (2010: 89–90)

In a chapter titled "The Seduction of Black," Hillman wrote: "Of all alchemical colors, black is the most densely inflexible and, therefore, the most oppressive and dangerously literal state of soul" (2010: 91). Hillman noticed how painters engage with the "many saturations of black. Part of the painter's opus is the differentiation of blacks: blacks that recede and absorb, those that dampen and soften, those that etch and sharpen, and others that shine almost with effulgence—a *sol niger*" (91), or black sun, an alchemical term Jung said "coincides with the *nigredo* and *putrefactio*, the state of death" (1955–56/1970: para. 113). For Hillman, the *sol niger* is one way to speak about the personal experience of what he calls a black that is blacker than black—a black so dense it carries "the archetypal essence of darkness itself" (2010: 92). In the context of soul-making and the transformation of the human personality, Hillman wondered: "What can release the soul from its somber identification" (92) with the dense and delusional literalisms of the blackening? "The alchemist answer: decapitation. According to Jung, the black spirit is to be beheaded, an act that separates understanding from its identification with suffering" (92).

Alchemically, Hillman wrote, decapitation "emancipates" the mind from its identification with the body (2010: 92). "Blackness remains," he added, "but the distinction between head and body creates a two, while suffering imprisons in singleness. The mind may begin to recognize what the body only senses. Decapitation allows the mind to be freer from the body's identity" (92). In the context of the theory and practice of alchemical psychology, Hillman concluded that decapitation, as both a symbol and as an imaginal operation at work in the psyche of the individual,

> is therefore a *separatio*—to use an alchemical term for the basic therapeutic move of making distinctions, or analyzing. Despite the fixity of *nigredo* moods and their repetitive thoughts, analysis separates the material—dreams, moods, projections, symptoms—from the mind's literal identification with this material. The dense and oppressive material becomes images that can be entertained by the mind. Mental images emancipate us from the slavery to the *nigredo*; though the material remains dark, decapitation allows the mind to cogitate the darkness. (92)

The imagery in the dream of the executioner, therefore, might be looked at as a sign of Varo's final freedom from the confining perspective of delusional literalism, which devalues anything that cannot be quantified or controlled.

However, as an agent of the reigning order that Varo's knowledge threatens, another meaning of her dreamtime beheading arises. Philosopher Rene Descartes's declaration in 1637, "I think therefore I am," is emblematic of the patriarchal association of the mind with the archetypal Masculine and a sense of the self that bypasses and is valued above the body, embodied experience, and soul. Hillman argued that "the place of soul" is "a world of imagination, passion, fantasy, reflection, that is neither physical and material on the one hand, nor spiritual and abstract on the other, yet bound to them both" (1975: 68). The soul's movement is that of descent into embodied experience. Soul is patient, it is "vulnerable and suffers; it is passive and remembers. It is water to the spirit's fire, like a mermaid who beckons the heroic spirit into the depths of passions"—and into the *nigredo*—"to extinguish its certainty" (69). As such, the body, as the vessel of soul—and in particular a woman's embodied experience of her Self and oppression—are dangerous to the patriarchal mind and must be severed from it.

Paradoxically, we also might see the act of beheading as the separation that is needed to relieve the person of the mind's rejection and subjugation of the soul, the relational aspect of the Self that is connected to Eros, claiming a new reality where everything has its rightful place (Hillman, 1975: 69). This is the trick that Varo plays on the executioner as henchman of the State. She turns her beheading into what is needed for the imagination to work soulfully and generatively in the space created by the distance between the conscious attitude and unconscious complex, the patriarchal fantasy and her embodied experience.

These psychological moves require a silvering imagination to lighten the fixity of the blackening—to see, welcome, and be changed by its form rather than dismiss it with a too-quick assumption of its meaning by the intellect. As the soul is silvered, the gold of revelation is mined. For Hillman, the amalgamation of the two elements requires a hammer:

> The test of the amalgamation of silver with gold is not witness of itself in the day world, imagination witnessed in literality, fantasies "coming true." The test is rather standing to the blows of the hammer as silver: that mental and imaginational realities are ungraspable elusives, quick and silver, and yet remain self-same, as they are ... They can take every sort of pounding (query, analysis, concentration, reproduction, emotional challenge) without coming apart into two interpretive halves, a physical side and a psychic side, a good side and a bad, a female side and a male—or the image and its meaning. (2010: 196)

In Varo's case, suffering and trauma hammered her personality into new outlines, the contours of her inner and outer lives re-shaped by her steadfast silvering imagination and, as seen in *Dead Leaves*, infused with the healing and insight brought forth by unseen archetypal presences. In Varo's dream egg, we find her alchemical amalgamation woven with ribbons of an imaginal substance that blends masculine and feminine in a conjunctive emblem of that which is sacred, transcendent, and immortal.

As important as silver is to the seasoning of the soul, there is more yet to come as a person works to re-invent outworn attitudes of thought and feeling. "Silver," Hillman wrote, "is hard and it likes heat and truth; its eventual telos is yellow and red: vivification" (2010: 188).

Three ravens: Black, white, and the red that brings all things to an end

In *Dead Leaves,* movement out of the labyrinth is symbolized in the flight of birds. Varo included a winged aspect of the whitening in the form of two birds that emerge from the stone passageway in the torso of the faceless black figure. Although the first whitening in alchemy refers to "unworked innocence," and thus the patriarchal definition of virginity, the second whitening is suggested in the form of a bird, "a white and gleaming condition of the soul" (Hillman, 2010: 129, 128). In Varo's painting, the flight from the labyrinth of the white bird hints at the presence of a woman who is "one-in-herself," which Esther Harding describes as the older meaning of *virgin* (1971: 105).

Varo also hinted at the crystallization of the alchemical process, the *rubedo*, or reddening, in *Dead Leaves* by painting a red bird emerging from the labyrinth. In the alchemical reddening, the passionate activity of the soul, the feminine Eros, is resurrected "and revivifies matter, crowning it in beauty and pleasure" (Marlan, 2005: 190). This " 'final stage' of the alchemical transformation," wrote Jungian analyst Stanton Marlan, brings about "the final dissolution of sunlit consciousness" (191), for the reddening—and the goal of alchemy—has at its core a relationship to darkness that holds the mysterious forces of the transcendent Self and the unknowable essence of the unconscious. That the white and red birds fly out together points to the relationship between the alchemical opus and the second whitening, brought forth through the distillation and assimilation of complexes, the differentiation of the numinous Self, and a relationship with its transcendent forces such that one belongs to, and is one in, one's Self. Alchemically speaking, the reddening, or revivification and birth of new forms, requires the white virgin, the archetypal state in which soulful creativity is perpetually inseminated from the spirit within (which is why women do not need muses).

In revisiting Varo's painting *Sympathy*, we find the artist linking revivification and vibrancy with her relationship with the objective unconscious. In this painting, the cat, the table and cloth, and the woman and the chair the woman sits on, are all colored richly in red. Because of their ability to hunt at night, cats are associated with the ability to see in the dark, and thus with the moon and the underworld. Alchemically, the cat in *Sympathy* brings in the reddening, the reconstituted and revivified personality now animated with cosmic energy, symbolized by gold sparks of revelation shooting into the room. A gold liquid spills from the table onto the floor, soaking the foundation of the room in knowledge and insight.

In her painting *The Weaver of Verona,* Varo provides a different glimpse into the process of reddening: The personality, solidified by storm and stress, is woven from an inner figure (Edinger, 1985: 85). In this image, a dark-haired woman with bluish-grey skin sits in the back of a room, in a black chair. With knitting needles, the woman weaves a surprising garment—a giantess, a woman with red hair made from golden threads that loop and swirl into the air on an invisible loom. In Varo's painting, the red woman being woven from the golden threads appears as if she is ready to fly from a room high in a tower out into a city filled with other towers.

In a similar painting, *The Red Weaver*, an image Varo painted in 1956, the same year she created *The Weaver of Verona*, the skin and clothing of the woman weaving the red giantess is colored a blue so deep as to almost appear black. The woman weaves the red giantess from blue thread that spools into the room through a window, a blue mist of clouds hinting at the source of the thread being used to give life to the red giantess who is readying herself to take flight through an opening in the tower wall.

In the foreground of the painting, a black cat paws a black-and-blue colored ball of yarn. The yarn is both a toy and the material from which the cat comes into being. Play, Varo seems to suggest, is for the kitten a self-generating, life-giving process. "Black cats," wrote Sandra Thomson, "are often considered symbols of death and darkness and, therefore, associated with the moon and all that is 'dark' (shadow) about the feminine, including feminine calculation, mystery, and hidden wisdom" (2003: 91). In *The Red Weaver*, the animating presence of the black kitten seems to place an emphasis on the looming birth of the woven red giantess. With the imagery, Varo seems to suggest that the alchemical reddening, the consolidation and revivification of the personality, is made possible through a playful engagement with shadow and imagination, symbolized as a conjunction of color (the kitten whose fur is both black and blue).

One of the more obvious places Varo used the color red, as a possible hint at the reddening and the coagulation of new elements coming together within her psyche, is in the flowing manes of hair of the women in her many painted self-portraits. For a woman artist such as Varo, hair carries symbolic power. "The vitality of hair is stunning," writes an essayist in *The Book of Symbols* ("Hair," 2010: 346). In all three paintings in her triptych—*Toward the Tower*, *Embroidering the Earth's Mantle*, and *The Escape*—the hair of the maidens is *light* red, suggesting a latent *rubedo* and innate vitality. In the third panel, *The Escape*, the maiden's hair is longer, a clue that the woman has escaped the conformity enforced in her early training in the convent and that her connection to the man with whom she escaped is maturing beyond the naiveté of an innocent girl. A striking difference is found when we compare the red hair in each of the paintings in the triptych with that of the woman in *Dead Leaves*, whose richly-dark reddish-orange hair flows down below her waist, suggesting her potency in relationship to the *rubedo* as she winds into herself the ball of yarn that had been knitted into the unseen passageways of the labyrinthine unconscious.

Note

1 The words "rendered visible" are from the artist Paul Klee. They signify his thought that "art does not reproduce the visible; rather it makes visible" the invisible. See: Klee, P. (1961). *Notebooks, Volume 1: The Thinking Eye* (J. Spiller, Ed.) (p. 76). London, UK: Lund Humphries.

References

Cheetham, T. (2012). *All the world an icon: Henry Corbin and the angelic function of beings*. Berkeley, CA: North Atlantic Books.

Edinger, E. (1985). *Anatomy of the psyche: Alchemical symbolism in psychotherapy*. La Salle, IL: Open Court.

Hair. (2010). In A. Ronnberg & K. Martin (Eds.), *The book of symbols: Reflections on archetypal images* (346–9). Cologne, Germany: Taschen.

Harding, E. (1971). *Women's mysteries*. Boston, MA: Shambhala.

Hauck, D. W. (1999). *The emerald tablet: Alchemy for personal transformation*. New York, NY: Penguin Press.

Hillman, J. (1975). *Re-visioning psychology*. New York, NY: HarperCollins.

Hillman, J. (2010). *Alchemical psychology*. Putman, CT: Spring Publications.

Jung, C. G. (1955–56/1970). *Mysterium coniunctionis* (R. F. C. Hull, Trans.) (H. Read et al., Eds.), *The collected works of C. G. Jung* (Vol. 14, 2nd ed.). Princeton, NJ: Princeton University Press.

Kaplan, J. (1988). *Unexpected journeys: The art and life of Remedios Varo*. New York, NY: Abbeville Press.

Marlan, S. (2005). *The black sun: The alchemy and art of darkness*. College Station, TX: Texas A&M University Press.

McLean, A. (1979). The birds in alchemy. *Hermetic Journal, 5*. Retrieved from www.levity.com/alchemy/alcbirds.html

Thomson, S. A. (2003). *Pictures from the heart: A tarot dictionary*. New York, NY: St. Martin's Griffin.

Varo, R. (1997/2018). *Letters, dreams & other writings* (M. Carson, Trans.). Cambridge, MA: Wakefield Press.

White. (2010). In A. Ronnberg & K. Martin (Eds.), *The book of symbols: Reflections on archetypal images* (660–1). Cologne, Germany: Taschen.

Chapter 8

Birds and eggs

Symbol of the liberated soul and image of immortality

On the patio of her home in Mexico City, Varo kept "numerous birds in cages" and birds appear often in the artist's paintings (Kaplan, 1988: 90). In a passage exploring the symbolic meaning of doves, Hillman suggested that these birds "are the *emotions of images*, the animal in the air, in the mind, the mind as winged animal; and they are the excitation and tenderness released by imagining" (2010: 183, emphasis in original). Hillman linked "these doves of alchemical fantasy" to "the mediating power of fantasy itself" (183). Doves "express, as they do in the traditional symbolism of the Third or Holy Ghost, Jung's transcendent function of active imagination" (183).[1] Alchemically, doves, a smaller species of bird in the pigeon family, suggest "an experience of emotional relief, a lightening after blackness and leaden despair, as if something else is there besides; within the misery, the tremor of a bird" (166).

In this passage, Hillman linked with Jung, who suggested that a "tender pair of doves," as a theriomorphic symbol representing animal instinctuality, "would be capable of 'an interpretation from above downwards'" (1955–56/1970: para. 205). "Interpretation from above downward," Hillman explained,

> follows [a bird's] descending motion that announces a new vision of things. This is the moment, in Corbin's language, of *ta'wil*, that shift in mind enabling us to experience the sensate world of perception by means of the imaginal world. And it is this move that tames the lion [a symbol for literalism], depriving him of his usual power as king of the physical world. (2010: 185–6)

Many of Varo's painted works are themed around creation, the alchemical process of making something new from the raw matter of what has been destroyed. Birds, with Varo's life and imagery in mind, evoke the metaphor of the new insights that are possible after one has survived the emotional and psychological difficulties of the blackening. In *The History of Magic and the Occult*, artist Kurt Seligmann reproduced a series of alchemical illustrations that show birds taking flight as symbols of a soul in the process of making its way into conscious partnership with the divine. In Varo's painging *Dead Leaves*, a white bird flies out of the labyrinth of the unconscious. Edinger said that the whitened soul (that is, a more conscious soul) "is often represented by a white bird being released from the material being heated. One picture shows a man being cooked in the water bath with a white bird emerging from his head" (1985: 120–1). Commenting on the released bird as the white soul, Edinger noted, quoting an alchemical text: "At the end of the sublimation there germinates through the mediation of the spirit, a shining white soul which flies to heaven with the spirit" (120).[2] Henderson and Sherwood, in their study of the symbolism in the *Splendor Solis*, a sixteenth-century German alchemical treatise, found many parallels to the image of a man being cooked in a bath with a white bird emerging from his head. These images

> show spirit arising from the chaotic material of the unconscious. They refer to an *increatum*, something that was not created by God but created by the human being from the depth of suffering, the white soul brought forth to enrich higher consciousness and the whole of his [or her] life.
>
> (Henderson & Sherwood, 2003: 101)

With such symbolism in mind, Arcq examined Varo's 1957 painting, *Creation of the Birds*, along with *The Guardian of the Egg*, a tempera on wood panel by Varo's close friend, Leonora Carrington. In these pieces, Arcq wrote, "the women portrayed have undergone a metamorphosis: one has been transformed into a giantess, the other into a woman-owl hybrid, and both have acquired the power of 'creating' birds" (2010: 106). As metaphors of metamorphosis, birds, as painted by Varo and Carrington,

> represent the moment when the alchemist finally manages to separate the soul and the spirit from the body and thus liberate them. From this perspective, these two paintings grant women exceptional powers that allow them to transform not simply matter, but the very essence of human beings. (106)

Varo's meticulous and elegant paintings move something in us. We are moved, in a simple way, because she was moved. This artist's life and art convey, symbolize, and embody vital truths about the alchemical process of transforming suffering into seasoned awareness. But can Varo's paintings help shift the harmful impacts of patriarchy? From a Jungian perspective, the process of exploring possible answers must start with, and stick to, the image. On his Alchemy website, Adam McLean presents a host of alchemical engravings culled from medieval manuscripts. In one engraving, a woman stands in a fountain, bathed by golden light filtering down from the heavens.[3] Another image shows a woman and child glowing in the golden light of a sunbeam.[4] For Jung, such images carried the beauty and terror of numinous forces. One alchemical text, Jung wrote,

> says that in order to acquire the "golden understanding" (*aurea apprehensio*) one must keep the eyes of the mind and soul well open, observing and contemplating by means of that inner light which God has lit in nature and in our hearts from the beginning. (1937/ 1968: para. 381)

In *Solar Music*, a 1956 painting that features a woman who plays a stringed sunbeam, Varo evoked what Jung called "the longing of the darkness for light" (1955–56/1970: para. 345). Music from the woman's bow breathes life into birds that nest in nearby trees. Light from the sun colors the forest floor, bringing life to vegetation and turning green the shawl the woman wears. Estella Lauter, who studied Varo's image in the context of the relationship between art and nature, wrote,

> The creator in *Solar Music* has the power to [affect] her environment not by accident or by fate but because she is *attuned* to the sunlight. She must see the sun's rays as strings in order to play them, and she must play them well in order to [affect] the life of the birds so profoundly. (1984: 83)

In the forest, a symbol for the unconscious, the woman in *Solar Music*

> dares to play the sun. The sun responds by making the forest green. The music that she makes awakens and releases the birds who fly away. The woman knows what she is doing, enjoys it, feels no surprise at her results, and experiences no need to be observed or appreciated ... Her achievement is their flight. (84)

Lauter saw *Creation of the Birds* as a more mature vision of the alchemical transformation that is possible when a human being collaborates with the divine. In the painting, the woman with the bow from *Solar Music* has now assumed the form of an owl. Seated at a table, the creature brings birds to life with a brush powered by paint mixed in an alchemical vessel in which the substance from the stars and the moon is stored. This image of creativity, Lauter believed,

> is both more radical and more conscious than the one presented in *Solar Music*. The woman/owl gives wing to *her visions* of the birds. By careful arrangement of the violin, the alembic, and the [magnifying] glass, she

enables the music of her own life, the substance of the stars, and the light of the moon to "feed" her paintings and confer life on them. The image differs strikingly from the related stories of Pygmalion and Pinocchio. Their creators brought them to life out of a desire to be loved. They did not make use of cosmic forces, nor did they undergo transformation themselves. In [*Creation of the Birds*], the self-transformation appears to be crucial. The act is a collaborative one. Her creation is the product of her love rather than of her desire to be loved. The effect of the painting is to stress the power of empathy with non-human forms of life. (84–5)

For Lauter,

Varo's paintings offer all of us powerful images for aspects of the visionary processes of creation which have been difficult to articulate in "scientific" terms. In *Solar Music* we find an image for the sense of being in tune with powerful non-human forces; of being fully conscious, yet detached from the concerns of the ego; of acting spontaneously on behalf of others without self-consciousness. In *Creation of the Birds*, Varo shows us the degree of self-transformation and collaboration with forces beyond ourselves required if we aspire to bring something new into the world. (97)

By highlighting female empowerment, Varo's work subtly challenges a solely masculine way of engaging with the world and the nonrelational patriarchal will to power. In her depiction of a creative process that is transformative, Varo hints at the need to add a feminine perspective to the cooler, more distant light of ego consciousness. As Barbara Stevens Sullivan observed, if masculine consciousness exists in the bright light of day, "feminine consciousness develops in the soft light of the moon, or even in the dark" (1989: 22). Masculine logos separates components and exerts judgment in a "directed, disciplined, logical way" (22). In contrast, "Feminine knowing," as illustrated in Varo's composite figure of an owl/human with a violin heart, "orients toward a state of wholeness that includes imperfection and that blurs edges and differentiations" (22). Devoted to the embodiment of the Feminine principle, Varo evokes female experience not only as a way to express the experience of self and Other holistically and metaphorically, but also because its orientation toward relatedness and wholeness is inclusive and transformative.

Art and the alchemical symbolism of the egg

Travel further into the imaginal underworld of Varo's dream of the executioner and we come to the weaving of "a sort of cage in the shape of an enormous egg" (Varo, 1997/2018: 95). Featured often in creation myths, the egg is a symbol of "regeneration and rebirth" ("Egg," 2010: 14). Symbolically, "the egg means a new germ, a new life possibility" (von Franz, 1995: 265). Von Franz, who helped Jung with alchemical research and wrote several books on the topic, added:

> If you think of the many cosmogonic myths where the egg is the beginning of the world, it acquires the dignity of a cosmic principle. It is the very beginning, something out of which the whole universe can be born. (265)

Von Franz believed the egg plays a decisive role in the practice of alchemical psychology: "Giving birth out of itself without addition, [the egg] symbolizes the innermost nucleus of the individual, the Self, to which we cannot add or take away" (265). Fariba Bogzaran added nuance to the egg as a mythological motif:

> The notion of the Cosmic Egg is found in many traditions, particularly in Hindu mythology. According to one Indian myth, the world was created out of non-being and was formed into an egg. The hatching of the cosmic egg produces various forms and they eventually dissolve back into nothingness to start all over again. (2008: 178)

Laurinda Dixon, a professor emerita at Syracuse University, studied the egg as an alchemical symbol in *The Garden of Earthly Delights*, a triptych by Hieronymus Bosch, a fifteenth-century painter whose work is often considered a forerunner to Surrealism. As an art student in Madrid in the 1920s, Varo studied the bizarre and often macabre imagery Bosch created to explore human desire and fear, most often in paintings with overt religious themes. Exploring the symbolic importance of the egg in alchemy, Dixon wrote:

> Continuity between the organic and inorganic worlds was a basic alchemical concept, and changes in substances were likened to changes in a growing embryo or seed. In the symbolic language of alchemy, the vessel in which the transmutation took place was termed the "egg," so named because of its ovoid shape. Real eggs as well as the retort of the same name were considered a microcosm of the world containing all the qualities of life—the four elements perfectly conjoined. (1981: 23–4)

Alchemical psychology connects the egg to the hermetic vessel—the temenos or container in which the transformation of the first matter takes place. "For the alchemists," Jung wrote, "the vessel is something truly marvelous: *a vas mirabile...* It is a kind of matrix or uterus from which the *filius philosophorum*, the miraculous stone, is to be born" (1937/ 1968: para. 338).

Equated with the round alchemical vessel, "the egg stands for the chaos apprehended by the artifex, the *prima materia* containing the captive world soul" (para. 306). Alchemical theory, applied to the symbol of the egg in Varo's dream, leads us to a new possibility: the egg as both cage and womb, a "luminous incubator" ("Egg," 2010: 14) from which "the liberated soul" is born from its gestation in the unconscious (1937/1968: para. 306).

Contained in the vessel of painting, Varo warmed images inside the egg of her creations. Varo, however, was hardly the only surrealist painter who worked with the egg as a symbol of creative power. Kay Sage, a painter and poet, used the egg to explore architectural themes. One of Varo's lovers, Esteban Francés, combined the ovoid form of the egg with the swirling inward and outward movement of the spiral. Gordon Onslow one of the last surviving members of the surrealist artists close to André Breton, experimented with circles, spores, and egg-like spirals. Bright and sometimes chaotic, Ford's images evoke a feeling of life teeming with energy and exuberance—sometimes to the point of overwhelm.

Salvador Dalí, a classmate of Varo's at the San Fernando Royal Academy of Fine Arts in Madrid in the 1920s, played with the image of birth from within the philosopher's egg in several paintings. As one example, in his work *Geopoliticus Child Watching the Birth of the New Man*, exhibited in 1943, Dalí painted a man emerging from a terrestrial egg that has broken open and is leaking placental blood. For Dalí, the image of the man being born from the egg represented new values emerging from the destruction of violence and war.

The egg in the alchemical paintings of Leonora Carrington

In Part II, we look at the creative synergy between Remedios Varo and Leonora Carrington. Here, let us look from a Jungian perspective at Carrington's use of the egg as a symbol of fertility and the raw matter from which the cosmos is conceived. One of Carrington's more well-known works, a tempera she painted on wood panel, is called *The Giantess*, the alternative title of which is *Guardian of the Egg*. The painting, which sold at auction to a private collector for $1.5 million in 2009,

> shows a cloaked female figure, her tiny face surrounded by a wheat-field halo, towering over an earth featuring farmers, animals, trees, boats and fishes. Amidst swooping birds and against a thunderous sky, the outsize female is holding something very precious and very small: an egg, which seems to represent the future.
>
> (Moorhead, 2017: 226–7)

Carrington, who was born and lived as a girl in the north of England, evoked the hermetic aspects of the egg motif in at least two other works that grew from the mythological ground of her British background. Carrington titled a 1955 transcendent occult work, *The Chair, Daghda Tuatha dé Danaan*. According to Susan Aberth, the Daghda is the High King of the Tuatha dé Danaan, a fairy people from Irish legend (2010: 82). "The glowing red room," Aberth wrote, "refers to his epitaph as 'The Red One of Perfect Knowledge' and the chair, with his name carefully inscribed in the lower left of the back, is his throne" (82). "The central protagonist in this occult transubstantiation," Aberth wrote,

> is the large egg—this is the cosmic egg of creation, which is also some-times likened to the alchemical vessel, known as an alembic, in which the alchemist performs the distillation process... The white alchemical rose represents the feminine principle necessary to commence trans-formation. The white rose is also the moon and is usually coupled with the red rose, signifying the masculine principle and the sun. Moisture drips from the ceiling (heavens) on to the rose, instigating a process of percolation, which causes water to run off the table and float through the air on to the seat of the chair. What ... we are witnessing ... is a marriage, between the Daghda and the Great Goddess, between the white rose and the red (symbolized by the red room), between opposites (black and white)—an alchemical conjoining. (82)

Carrington worked again with alchemical imagery in *Ab Eo Quod*, a 1956 painting that recreates the Eucharist, the Christian ceremony com-memorating the Last Supper. The image features a large egg upended in the middle of a cloth-covered altar-table in a room with red walls. Next to the egg is a wine beaker, two glasses filled with wine, a stem of grapes, a husk of grain, and a pomegranate, a fruit that Aberth associated with Persephone, the maiden who was abducted, raped, and held by Hades in the underworld, emerging through her ordeal as a Queen or Goddess.

In the alchemical scene Carrington painted in *Ab Eo Quad*, the eye moves from the egg upward: liquid drips from a white rose dangling, Aberth wrote, like a chandelier from the ceiling. When water drips onto the egg, steam rises, imagery representing the heat generated by the warming of the base matter being refined in the alchemical furnace. Carrington symbolized the transformation of the first matter with white moths (or are they butterflies?) that hatch from cocoons and flutter about the room, allusions, Aberth believed, "to processes of transformation and metamor-phosis" (2010: 93). Art historian M. E. Warlick added: "Moths, butterflies and other insects, which have traditionally represented the transform-ation of the human soul, here underscore the desire for a metamorphosis to release the hidden powers of the unconscious mind" from the egg (2017: para. 18).

The egg, the liberated soul, and the dream of the executioner

In her dream of the executioner, as alchemist and dream ego, Varo weaves the egg around herself in an eternal union of the feminine and masculine principles. Although she is now enclosed in the egg, the feeling is one of liberation and contentment. Jung, as we have said, wrote about the liberated soul being born from within the temenos of the philosophical egg (1937/ 1968: paras. 305–6, figure 98). Jung's context is both the outcome of the alchemical opus and the practice of alchemical psychology. However, he might as well be evoking the experience of Varo as artistic and alchemical practitioner. Varo's movement through the various operations in the alchemical opus can be traced through her art. Indeed, according to Bogzaran, Varo's painting, *The Gypsy and the Harlequin*, an oil on canvas produced in 1947, contains some of the elements of the egg she later weaves with ribbons in her dream of the executioner:

> Although the painting was completed many years prior, it could be seen as a precognition of this dream. It depicts an emotionally cold atmosphere with a walled alley littered with hatched eggs and broken pots. Alien faces without mouths hide behind walls. A woman is shown holding a giant bubble or egg. A white thread winds around her body and neck, with a stone tied to one end and hanging down her back, strangling her. She is accompanied by a male or androgynous figure wrapped in ribbons and without proper feet to hold him up. (2008: 180)

A decade later, in *Dead Leaves*, Varo painted a silvering room in which a white and a red bird fly out of the labyrinth toward a redheaded woman, prefiguring the relationship between the white Feminine (or archetypal Virgin), the silvering of moonlight, the Masculine principle (or inseminating spirit) and the red revivification in an alchemical union.

Consider a final image related to the egg as symbolic container for psychological and spiritual transformation—and to the practice of art as a mode of deep inquiry. The image is that of art as gestation or brooding, new life being heated in the oven of the womb (the painting). Just as life gestates in and then hatches from the egg,

> in ancient healing rituals would initiates withdraw into a dark cave or hole to "incubate" until a healing dream released them reborn into the

upper world, in the same way the chick crawls out of the egg. Similarly, in deeply introverted, self-reflective states [such as painting], brooder and brooded become one in egglike, nuclear processes of crystallization. Here, too, the egg evokes the beginning, the simple, the source. The egg is the mysterious "center" around which unconscious energies move in spiral-like evolutions, gradually bringing the vital substance to light. ("Egg," 2010: 14)

"Alchemy," an essayist in *The Book of Symbols* wrote, quoting John Dee, an advisor to Queen Elizabeth who practiced alchemy, divination, and Hermetic philosophy,

depicted the germ of the egg contained in the yolk as the "sun-point," the infinitesimally small, invisible "dot" from which all being has its origin. It is also the creative "fire-point" within ourselves, "the soul in the midpoint of the heart," the quintessence or golden germ "that is set in motion by the hen's warmth" of our devoted attention. ("Egg," 2010: 14)[5]

And so, in Varo's dream of the executioner, we might see her having woven into her death a beginning: an egg with the union of masculine and feminine at its golden center that sets in motion the eternal spirals of life, warmed by the imagination.

Notes

1   Hillman cites Jung's essay, "The Transcendent Function" in *The Collected Works of C. G. Jung* (Vol. 8, 67–91). See also Jeffrey Miller's book, *The Transcendent Function: Jung's Model of Psychological Growth through Dialogue with the Unconscious* and *Jung on Active Imagination*, edited by Joan Chodorow. One of the best explications of active imagination is by June Singer in *Boundaries of the Soul: The Practice of Jung's Psychology* (272–315).
2   The alchemical text Edinger referred to is identified by Jung as *Pretiosa margarita novella*, written by Petrus Bonus of Ferrara, an Italian physician, between 1330 and 1339. "This text," Jung wrote, "shows beyond all doubt that the connection between the mystery of Christ and the mystery of the lapis was even then so obvious that the philosophical opus seemed like a parallel and imitation— perhaps even a continuation—of the divine work of redemption" (*Psychology and Alchemy* [1937/1968], paras. 462–3).
3   From the frontispiece to "Brunnen der Weissheit" (1757). See image A023 of Alchemical and Hermetic Emblems on Alchemywebsite.com (www.alchemywebsite.com/amclglr1.html).
4   An engraving by Karl von Eckhartshausen (1794). See image A169 of Alchemical and Hermetic Emblems on Alchemywebsite.com (www.alchemywebsite.com/amclglr1.html).

5 For more on Dee and the "sun-point" in the egg, as "the point originated by God," see a passage by Jung in *Mysterium Coniunctionis* (1955–56/1970, para. 41).

References

Aberth, S. (2010). *Leonora Carrington: Surrealism, alchemy and art.* Burlington, VT: Lund Humphries.

Arcq, T. (2010). Mirrors of the marvellous: Leonora Carrington and Remedios Varo (M. Suderman, Trans.). In S. Begley (Ed.), *Surreal Friends* (98–115). Burlington, VT: Humphries.

Bogzaran, F. (2008). Dreams of alchemy. In M. Orellano (Ed.), *Five keys to the secret world of Remedios Varo* (159–86). Mexico City, Mexico: Artes de Mexico.

Dixon, L. (1981). *Alchemical imagery in Bosch's Garden of delights.* Ann Arbor, MI: UMI Research papers.

Edinger, E. (1985). *Anatomy of the psyche: Alchemical symbolism in psychotherapy.* La Salle, IL: Open Court.

Egg. (2010). In A. Ronnberg & K. Martin (Eds.), *The book of symbols: Reflections on archetypal images* (14–5). Cologne, Germany: Taschen.

Henderson, J., & Sherwood, D. (2003). *Transformation of the psyche: The symbolic alchemy of the splendor solis.* New York, NY: Brunner Routledge.

Hillman, J. (2010). *Alchemical psychology.* Putman, CT: Spring Publications.

Jung, C. G. (1937/1968). Religious ideas in alchemy (R. F. C. Hull, Trans.). In H. Read et al. (Eds.), *The collected works of C. G. Jung* (Vol. 12, 2nd ed., 225–483). Princeton, NJ: Princeton University Press.

Jung, C. G. (1955–56/1970). *Mysterium coniunctionis* (R. F. C. Hull, Trans.) (H. Read et al., Eds.), *The collected works of C. G. Jung* (Vol. 14, 2nd ed.). Princeton, NJ: Princeton University Press.

Kaplan, J. (1988). *Unexpected journeys: The art and life of Remedios Varo.* New York, NY: Abbeville Press.

Lauter, E. (1984). *Women as mythmakers: Poetry and visual art by twentieth-century women.* Bloomington: Indiana University Press.

Moorhead, J. (2017). *The surreal life of Leonora Carrington.* London, UK: Virago.

Sullivan, B. S. (1989). *Psychotherapy grounded in the feminine principle.* Asheville, NC: Chiron.

Varo, R. (1997/2018). *Letters, dreams & other writings* (M. Carson, Trans.). Cambridge, MA: Wakefield Press.

Von Franz, M.-L. (1995). *Shadow and evil in fairy tales* (Rev. ed.). Boston, MA: Shambhala.

Warlick, M. E. (2017). Leonora Carrington's esoteric symbols and their sources. *Studia Hermetica Journal, VII*(5). Retrieved from portfolio.du.edu/mwarlick/page/65131a

Chapter 9

The dream of the executioner
A paradigm shift

Linking in with the dream of the executioner, and with the alchemical practice of breaking down a substance—in Varo's case, the distressing ingredients of psychological trauma—in order to reconstitute it in a new form, the imagery of the egg in the artist's dream about death suggests that, from the perspective of the soul, a new way of being is animating in the unconscious. The significance of this way of being is conveyed in the synchronicity of this dream of death being the tenth, and last, in a sequence the artist recorded in her diary.

Jung defined synchronicity as occurring when two things arise simultaneously and have an acausal but meaningful connection. Varo, as we have mentioned, recorded ten dreams in her diary, the dream of the executioner being the final dream in the series. Jung could have been addressing the link between Varo's dream series that culminated in the dream of the executioner in his comments on the total number of illustrations—ten—in the *Rosarium philosophorum*, a sixteenth-century alchemical treatise. Jung followed the alchemists in calling the number ten the *denarius*, "which stands for unity on a higher level" (1946/1966: para. 525). For the alchemists, Jung added, "the denarius forms the *totius operis summa*, the culminating point of the work beyond which it is impossible to go" (para. 526). As an alchemical symbol for the "result of the completed work," that is, for the alchemical project in its entirety, Jung concluded that "the real meaning of the denarius is [as] the Son of God" (para. 525).

Writing about her dream of the executioner in the tenth and final entry in her diary, Varo may have been unconsciously expressing in alchemical terms the birth into a new state that her death would bring: "When I finished weaving that egg-like object, I felt at peace" (1997/2018: 96). As the symbolic image of the culmination of her artistic and alchemical work, weaving a giant egg out of ribbons has profound meaning. "In most cultures the egg is viewed as a symbol of immortality," and "ribbons have been associated with immortality and absolute realization" (Bogzaran, 2008: 178). Varo's dream-hands not only weave the egg, they are the source of the *prima materia*, including the masculine substance, out of which the ribbons emerge. From the unified substance of masculine and feminine, Varo weaves an egg to contain a woman (herself) and a man. In so doing, she dissolves the mythic clash between these opposing forces in her absolute realization of them as intertwined principles. In keeping with the power of the symbol to constellate and release energy from the unconscious, the *coniunctio*, or union of opposites, within each partner begets their union in the egg, yielding "a living birth that leads to a new level of being, a new situation" (Jung, 1958/1969: para. 189).

The archetypal Masculine and the man in the egg

Psychologically, it is natural to wonder about the man woven into the dream egg. Is he an image representing Walter Gruen, Varo's husband of her later years? Is it a symbol for Benjamin Péret, her second husband, the surrealist poet Varo married in France? Perhaps the man in the dream is an imaginal reflection of Gerardo Lizarraga, the prize-winning fellow artist Varo married in 1930. There are still other possibilities. The image of the man in the egg might be that of her father, Don Rodrigo, whose shrunken head, Varo wrote, was the one she dropped into the well in her 1960 oil on canvas, *Woman Leaving the Psychoanalyst* (Varo, 1997/2018: 108). The man with whom she needed to weave her destiny might also be an image of what Jung called the *animus*—the unconscious aspect of a woman's psyche (1939/1968: paras. 511–2), understood by post-Jungians to inhabit the inner lives of both men and women as the archetypal Masculine.

Varo may have painted an image of her inner masculine in *The Escape*, the third painting in the triptych that included *Toward the Tower* and *Embroidering the Earth's Mantle*. In this work, the young woman from the other two paintings (with Varo's red hair and facial features, clearly intended to be a projected version of herself) flees with a man. The couple travels toward a mountain in what Varo has playfully painted, and Kaplan just as playfully described, as "a magical vehicle that looks like a furry inverted umbrella floating on a foggy mist. Their capes billow out behind them, catching the wind and acting as sails" (1988: 23). Is the man in the orange cape an image of Varo's inner masculine? Does the union of this male figure with the girl who has escaped the stifling convention of working to perpetuate the way things have been signify a symbolic inner marriage—the alchemical *coniunctio* that completes the work of the opus?

Writing in the context of psychotherapy informed by the feminine principle, Barbara Stevens Sullivan may as well have had Remedios Varo in mind when describing the balance between feminine and masculine: "Reason," as one aspect of the Masculine principle, "offers a soothing hold for the patient's inner chaos, but each element of that inner chaos must be directly felt before it can be contained" (1989: 132). The act of feeling requires the relational, inclusive Eros of the Feminine. In *The Escape*, in close embrace with a man, Varo steers her boat through turbulent waters toward an opening into the solidity of a mountain. With Sullivan's thoughts and this image in mind, we might consider *The Escape* as Varo's symbolic attempt to contain emotions related to traumas in her life and to the storm and stress of inner change that solidifies the personality (Edinger, 1985: 85).

The Juggler: The alchemical androgyne and the union of opposites in the world

Such speculations are stimulating as we return to stick with the image in Varo's dream of the executioner a little longer. Brooding over an imaginal hatchling warming in the egg of Varo's imagery, we are reminded that it is the weaving of the two destinies, not necessarily the identity of the man, that was so important to Varo. What if we "stay with the dream-soul and look at things its way" (Hillman, 1979: 106)? From this perspective, it is possible that the meaning of the image of the man in Varo's dream with whom she wishes to weave her destiny has nothing to do with an actual man. Luis-Martín Lozano reminded us that

> dreams themselves, transferred to paintings, were not what Varo found interesting about surrealism. What fascinated her was the symbolic metaphor that artistic imagery was capable of translating from the inner world—even the subconscious—to the outer, through a conscious creative process like painting. (2000: 27)

Beyond our amplification of her images through the nonliteral lens of depth psychology, we know a few things about Varo, from visual clues left in the artist's painted images, from published letters, diary entries, notes on paintings, and from the events of her life. Instead of asking who the man is, we might consider what happened in the dream. The dream begins with Varo's execution for possessing knowledge that is a threat to the established social order, so we might suspect that the rest of the dream involves this secret. But what is the secret and how does it relate to the imaginal act of weaving an egg? The artist left clues for us to follow: her paintings. Symbolically speaking, Varo's images are alchemical treasure maps. Like working with dreams, decoding the mysterious messages is the challenge.

We know from Jung's researches into alchemy that the imagery of medieval alchemical emblems was often bizarre, the descriptions by the alchemists of the process of transforming base substances into refined properties even more so. We also know that Varo, as Engel wrote, read widely:

> Tenth-century German mysticism, Gregorian chants, medieval alchemy, the novels of Herman Hesse, the reincarnation theories of G. I.

Gurdjieff, the painting[s] of Hieronymus Bosch and Pieter Breughel, were her sources; but also astronomy, physics, mathematics, engineering, biology, and psychoanalysis. (1986: 1)

Lozano linked Varo's interest in alchemical psychology and hermeticism to *The Juggler*, the artist's 1956 oil and inlaid mother-of-pearl on masonite:

Underlying apparently lyrical or even fantastic themes, Varo conceived intricate discourses that are hard to interpret, influenced by Western as well as Eastern thought. One of the sources Varo seems to have used [as inspiration for the imagery in her paintings in general and for *The Juggler* in particular] was the manifesto of the invisible Rosicrucian brotherhood, founded by Christian Rosencrantz in the seventeenth century. This order of initiates in the study of alchemy tried to revive an erudite tradition inherited from antiquity ... through the ... theories [of] Paracelsus. (2000: 49)

Varo invoked Paracelsus, a Renaissance healer, in her image of *The Juggler*, an androgyne jester working astral magic before a "group of gloomy people who all look alike" (Lozano, 2000: 49), with a vessel at his feet surrounded by a quaternity of substances, representing perhaps the world of the *prima materia*. The juggler's hat is blue, the alchemical color of *imaginatio*, as is the dress of the woman in the cart who, with eyes closed in a serene posture, seems to be focusing inward, perhaps dreaming. In the cart with the woman in blue, in the green Gothic tower on wheels next to the juggler's stage, are emblems of fundamental polarities: the lion of literalism; the owl of insight and wisdom; small birds flying free, dove-like creatures whose ascent seems heavenly; and the horned goat whose ascent among the mountains is earthbound.

Charging her images with potent occult symbolism, in *The Juggler* Varo seems to suggest that the Feminine principle is the motor that powers alchemy, for here, with the image of a woman dreaming, her eyes closed, her hands clasped and resting over her womb, the artist evokes the archetypal presence of the lunar psyche as the inner secret of the alchemical work of transformation. With the imagery in *The Juggler*, Varo sends a symbolic message: The imaginal power of the Feminine is the generative heart that beats at the center of the work. But not forgotten in the painting is the androgyne juggler—the archetypal wizard or magician, whose beard might instead be a collar and whose cloak symbolizes the red of revivification— a resplendent display and magical enactment of the alchemical union of opposites in the world. With the image of an androgyne-as-alchemist in mind, Lozano added, "Varo seems to be referencing" the alchemical beliefs of the Rosicrucians, who believed in the next coming of the Holy Spirit, harbinger of a period of joy and freedom for the human race. The jester, then, is not so much a juggler as he is a prophet of the times to come, which could change the gray and uniform existence of his audience. (2000: 49)

Still Life Reviving: Image as soul food

The androgyne appears time and again in Varo's imaginal world. Psychologically, these images suggest that the artist is working to combine aspects of her own personality, aspects that appear in projected form as characters in her paintings. In this light, Varo's dream in which she is to be beheaded evokes an initiatory separation—an enforced movement, or transition, from one place (an ego rooted in material life and in the fear of death) to another (the underworld, where images of death depict the movement of the psyche as it travels along the arc of life, death, and rebirth). To accomplish this inner movement, Hillman explained,

> the psyche needs to be fed... The alchemists had an operation called *cibation* ("feeding") and one called *imbibition* ("soaking" or "steeping"), in which the psychic stuff that one was working on required the right food and drink at a certain moment during the opus of soul-making. (1979: 172–3)

In Varo's artistic process of individuation, we clearly see, as Hillman observed, that

> what we eat in dreams is not food but images... In our dreams, eating is a moment of transubstantiation, where what is only natural becomes also metaphorical. It is a primordial ritual for keeping the Gods alive, keeping in communion with presences beyond our selves. (174)

Considering Varo's last painting, *Still Life Reviving*, Hillman's thoughts bring her images to mind in a new way. The image of fruit dying and regenerating depicts death in service to life, transforming "eating into a ritual for the psyche" (172). "Images," Hillman added,

> are the soul's best food. May this mean as well that foods are the soul's best images? With this I am suggesting that eating in dreams nourishes the mouths of our ghosts, giving back to the other souls and our own dream-soul some part of what grows in our psyche... Eating in dreams would therefore have little to do with a hunger instinct and much to do with a psychic need for nourishing images. (174)

Considered her final self-portrait, in *Still Life Reviving* Varo is present in the scene without appearing in it. The painting is a mirror in which Varo reflects her movement through the cosmos of herself. The artist no longer needs to see herself as a human being. She has *become* the image. She feeds the cosmos with herself and, in the absence of a human self-image, moves beyond even the androgyne to a sublime oneness in which what is differentiated is the light at the center of the cosmic spiral or mandala, the fruit of the soul, and the uniform empty plates.

Facing death without fear: Dream 9 and the menace within

Given the dissolution of Varo's sense of self into the spiraling perpetuity of life reviving in this last painting, we can ponder with heightened awareness Walter Gruen's question about the meaning of the painting in connection with Varo's death by heart attack: Had Varo cultivated the courage and wisdom "necessary to face death without fear?" (Bogzaran, 2008: 181). Varo's last dream, Bogzaran wrote, answered Gruen's question. Carrying a message from the depths of her psyche, Varo's dream of the executioner suggests that the artist *did* face her fear of death in realizing the alchemical power and wisdom of love to transform opposing forces into an ultimate creative act—living, dreaming, painting, all in service to the rebirth that comes about through the death of what has been (181). As the dream ego, Varo responded to her imminent execution with an imaginal act—born from her process of individuation reflected in her paintings—that placed her of her own accord back into the egg of creation. From this, we might surmise that, in addition to facing death without fear, Varo discovered that in life, the ultimate creative act is a conscious death.

Symptoms of the artist's trauma—"anguish, worry, upset and fear"—and the densely alienating *nigredo* it left her in—permeate Varo's sequence of dreams that lead up to the artist's encounter with the executioner (Bogzaran, 2008. Importantly, Varo's confrontation with an inner figure that would prevent her from awakening to the archetypal gold within complexes formed by trauma and misogyny is depicted in Dream 9. In her notes on this dream, Varo wrote, "I sensed with frightful horror something behind me that instead *was coming out of myself* ... This 'thing' behind me filled me with enormous terror and with a sensation of heavy, tormented sleep" (1997/2018: 93–4, emphasis in original). Varo struggled in her dream to awaken,

> but the mysterious creature grabbed me tightly by the back of my neck ... and with his other hand he squeezed the bridge of my nose. All the while, he was saying: "This is so you don't wake up, I don't want you to wake up. I need you to sleep soundly so that I can do what I have to do." (94)

Varo woke from the dream "in great torment and drenched in sweat" (94).

Who is the malevolent male creature that menaces Varo in the dream? From Kalsched's psychoanalytical perspective, the figure could mark the appearance in Varo's psyche of the Protector/Persecutor. The male creature in Varo's dream, in other words, could be an inner figure, or subpersonality, whose job is to protect Varo from future trauma by persecuting her in the present. In Kalsched's theory of the self-care system at work in the human psyche, the archetypal presence of the Protector/Persecutor often defends against trauma with withering criticism aimed at discouraging vulnerability. Over time, this protective strategy becomes persecutory as it further degrades (and retraumatizes) an already weakened and vulnerable sense of self. What once served to keep aspects of the self in hiding, protected from injurious circumstances and people, now traps "an anxiety-ridden child-ego" in toxicity and tyranny imposed on him or her from within the psyche (Kalsched, 1996: 41). Add a feminist viewpoint to the threatening figure in Varo's dream who does not want her to awaken, and the Protector/Persecutor can be seen as working to protect the individual and cultural psyche.

Psychologically, the role of the Protector/Persecutor fits perfectly with the paradigm of the patriarch as the defender of established order of male domination in the world, and as a figure introjected from exposure to that world defending the individual psyche against disruption to its cultural conditioning. As such, the Protector/Persecutor is a force that works within the individual to sustain the hypnotic trance of the familiar order as the only order by redacting imaginal access to alternatives. Given these dynamics, it seems crucial that, although the series of dreams Varo recorded in her diary are undated, Dream 9 apparently occurred before Dream 10. To face the executioner and her fear with courage, Varo would have needed to overcome the presence of internalized oppression, symbolized in Dream 9 by the malevolent male creature who menaces her.

In 1948, Varo seems already to be working on the meaning of, and her relationship with, death. *The Pollution of the Water*, painted that year, features, like her dream, the figure of an executioner. In the painting, Varo's reaper appears in the form of a skeletal man with a scythe. Looking at the painting, we wonder what, exactly, has been polluted, and how? The backdrop of the painting suggests the vast blue of the sea, symbolic perhaps of the unconscious and more specifically of the archetypal Feminine, "our mother of mothers, the Great Round within whose fluid containment life began and from whose fertile precincts" it continues to evolve ("Ocean," 2010: 36). The skeletal figure is associated archetypally with mortality, and with the Grim Reaper as the bringer of Death. Symbolically, given the title of the painting, we might reflect on the possible meaning of the image: In the pollution of the water, has the Grim Reaper killed the Great Round, poisoning the waters of the unconscious with fear such that we avoid digesting the truth held there, leaving us severed from our roots in the soil of the feminine and the cyclical nature of life? Have we become, like the marketplace the skeletal executioner has walked through in Varo's painting, devoid of life, with all that remains two tables holding vegetables that seem a bit limp, disconnected from the source of life and a third table, surprisingly, holding bolts of fabric that seem more alive than the vegetables? With this image of fabric—symbols for Varo of the creative potential held in the domain of the divine Feminine—has the artist painted hope and a clue to what can transform the deadening influence of patriarchy?

Two Varo paintings, *Star Catcher* from 1956 and *Celestial Pablum* from 1958, offer clues to the process through which Varo may have ameliorated the internalized patriarchal black-out of potentially transformative elements in her psyche. In *Star Catcher*, the painted figure has caught the moon—a symbol for that which provides the silvering illumination of what is covered in blackness, what psyche and culture have redacted—and placed it in a cage. Interestingly, in the dream of the executioner the artist describes the egg she weaves as *cage-like*, suggesting the notion that a cage can function in a process of personal growth both as an enlivening womb as well as a deadening prison—a tomb. In defiance of the Protector/Persecutor that appeared in Dream 9, Varo needs to find the moon in the night of her own soul's journey, capture it, and in *Celestial Pablum*, nourish it with the gentle glow of the stars to strengthen its light and her relationship with it. Keeping in mind Jung's observation that the unconscious treats the ego as the ego treats it, we can see in this act of feeding the moon a conscious, life-giving relationship between Varo and the darkness that has its own light—one that transforms fear of the unknown into the experience of generativity.

Arguably, the fear of death is a central motivating factor in human life and stands behind the fear of the unknown and change. As such, it is arguably at the core of the will to power that seeks control over the future and the mythic lineage of the search for eternal life. In her image of the egg—a symbol of the "repeating of the archetypal birth of the cosmos" (Eliade, 1958/1996: 414)—Varo suggests that eternal life does not flow from a linear temporal line, nor does it function within the paradigm that prioritizes the individual. Rather, it follows the spiraling, cyclical feminine in which the individual is a small portion held within the whole, and death, including one's own, is recognized as necessary "for the continuance of life" (Sullivan, 1989: 26). Recalling Varo's affinity for cats, in the artist's dreamtime engagement with her death we can see her cat-like nature as she captures her prey—feeding on and digesting death—by "perfectly attuning her own being to the life currents [and needs] of the larger world" (25).

The Encounter: The egg, an owl, and an image of the dangerous secret

From a Jungian perspective, the symbolism of the egg carries within it the dangerous secret that would free us from fear and the grip of the patriarchy, for the egg emerges from the womb of the Feminine. In one of Varo's last works, *The Encounter*, a vinyl painted on bristol board in 1962, the artist

Figure 9.1 The Encounter, Remedios Varo, vinyl on bristol board, 1962. © Artists Rights
Society (ARS), New York. Photo credit: Private Collection, Christie's Images/
Bridgeman Images.

reveals a dual realization: She paints herself as a tall figure cloaked com-
pletely in silver and blue with her hand over the mouth of a face (her face)
that peers out from her womb.

She has come from the dark wood of the unconscious in the background
of the painting with the knowledge that there is a secret held in her womb—
a secret that has been silenced. The imagery is uncomfortably ambivalent: Because the secret is dangerous, it must be kept silent to be protected.
In the painting, the woman opens a door. Inside a dark room on the other
side of the door is an owl with human hands and legs who peers out at her.
The owl, in connection to the egg, the womb, and the silencing of the secret,
brings us to the story of the goddess Athena as a mythological narrative
unfolding in Varo's art and life.

In older, goddess-worshipping cultures, the owl's powers of death were understood as transformative, part of "the perpetual functioning of the cycle of life, death, and regeneration embodied by a central feminine force—the Goddess" (Gimbutas, 1997: 351). In today's cultural context, however, the owl's "stunning power of death" is subsumed by the interests of the patriarchy's will to power (254). Thus, the owl's spiritual and magical associations with the archetypal Feminine, with night, and with the lunar psyche, have given way to narrow typecasting in which the owl is most often linked as a symbol "of acute … awareness" with Athena, the Greek goddess of wisdom and war ("Owl," 2010: 254).

Psychologically and culturally, Athena is a representation of a daughter of the patriarchy. This unofficial status is confirmed in Athena's unusual birth—from the head of her father, Zeus, who, fearing that a son would overthrow him, swallowed Metis, his pregnant consort. In an act of domination and dismissal of the feminine by Zeus, Athena, as unborn daughter, was gestated and born from the god's forehead, her connection to the mother, the feminine, the womb—and thus the pre-patriarchal province of the owl—severed. Like Athena, Varo was a father's daughter: Her paintings feature the meticulous and intricate brush strokes she honed as a girl while executing mechanical drawings for her father, a hydraulic engineer.

In the play *Hamlet*, as daughter, sister, and potential wife, the character Ophelia captured what the psychological dynamics of patriarchy are like for girls with owlish inner natures: "They say the owl was a baker's daughter. Lord, we know what we are, but know not what we may be" (Shakespeare, as cited in Woodman, 1980: 8). Woodman said of Ophelia that she "is a little walking owl, bewitched by her unconscious feminine, her father," and, we might add, the patriarchy (9). "She never finds her own voice. She never finds her own body or her own feelings and therefore misses life and love in the here and now" (9).

In *The Encounter* we meet Varo, a daughter of the patriarchy with subordination to the authority of the father as her first matter. It is 1959. Varo has four years left to live. In this painting, Varo makes one of her stronger and more overt symbolic statements about what it is like to be a woman in a patriarchy. The story in the painting unfolds like this: A woman has walked out of the dark woods of the unconscious to stand before a door. She stands cloaked in a delicate silver and blue flowing robe, with a face peering out from her womb. With her left hand, the woman cradles the face—her own face—her fingers cupped tightly over the mouth. With her right hand she opens the door. Standing on the other side of the door, inside a dark room or closet, is a creature with human legs but the upper body and face of an owl. What message is Varo sending about patriarchy through her image?

Here, we pause to consider two crucial details: the transformative power of the metaphor and the alchemical importance of color. First let us look briefly at the ability of the metaphor to combine "what is already known in a new way to produce a new thing not yet fully understood" (Siegelman,

1990: ix). In his essay, "On the Relation of Analytical Psychology to Poetry," Jung called symbols, as the larger class to which metaphors belong, "bridges thrust out towards an unseen shore" (as cited in Siegelman, 1990: x). For Jung, wrote Ellen Siegelman, "the unseen shore can be thought of as the unconscious as well as the unseen" (x).

> Metaphors offer a passageway to the unconscious, not perhaps the royal road of dreams, but an important thoroughfare, nevertheless. They also serve as bridges between affect and insight, since the hallmark of a living metaphor is the intense feeling that surrounds it. Metaphor is a way to mobilize and release affect. (x-xi)

In *The Encounter,* the colors (silver and blue) Varo chose for the garment worn by the woman facing the owl figure at the door are crucial to decoding the metaphoric message the artist is sending with the imagery. "Color," Philip Ball wrote, "underpins the alchemical belief in transmutation. A substance's color was deemed an outward manifestation of its inner properties" (2001: 76). What do the colors of the cloak of the woman emerging from the forest reveal about the processes of transformation at work in Varo's life? From a Jungian perspective, we see from the silver and blue of her garment that the soul of the woman is bluing, having entered the realm of imagination, and at the same time it is also silvering. Alchemically speaking, the imagination of the whitened soul has been enriched by the tarnish of time and experience, seasoned by suffering. Now, having found the silver light of her lunar nature, the woman knows the secret held in her womb—the female truth about patriarchy—that she has had to silence, her hand over the mouth of the self she carries within her. Having come from the dark woods of the unconscious, depicted in the background of the painting, the woman holds her truth within her and can travel beyond the parameters of patriarchal oppression to reclaim her voice. As Woodman, who did pioneering work to revalue the feminine from a Jungian perspective, believed, "only by discovering and loving the goddess lost within her own rejected body can a woman hear her own authentic voice" (1980: 10). And, we might add, in so doing redeem the owl in its wisdom and relationship with death from being subsumed by the patriarchy and by the war-like violence inflicted upon women by misogyny and hierarchies that demand the inferiority of females and the feminine.

In *The Encounter*, the owl at the door of Varo's consciousness is no longer little, but stands tall on long human legs, asking to be let out of the room that limits her movement into life. Remembering that the psychological purpose of a metaphor is to constellate emotion that has remained unconscious, what do we feel in the presence of the woman and the owl? The feeling of the image is ambivalent. There is the sweetness of a reunion and the hope of redemption. But the meeting also brings sadness in the reminder of a shameful psychological crime: a woman's voice, the song of her soul, silenced by patriarchy.

For Varo, *The Encounter* marks the artist's transit into "what Winnicott ... designated as the transitional space, which is midway between fantasy and reality and is the domain from which art and culture spring" (Siegelman, 1990: xi). Here, in symbolic space, Varo, as an ego surrendered into service to the designs of the emerging Self, is free to build a bridge between a woman's confinement in patriarchal conformity and her release into a place of freedom where she can once again hear, and act upon, the sound of her own voice. From a Jungian perspective, the painting comes alive as a living metaphor that carries the pain of the patriarchal past but also the symbolic seed of future change.

It seems, from our look at the dream of the executioner and at the imagery in *The Encounter*, that Varo did what Woodman believed a woman must do: let the Goddess in, succeeding, in the process, at reclaiming Her emissary, the owl, from the suffocating grip of the patriarchy. In doing so, Varo liberated herself from the fear of death and the silencing of feminine wisdom. In the dream of the executioner, Varo gives voice to what has been hidden in her womb's relationship with the cycles of death and birth, weaving around her the egg and giving herself to the regenerative nature of death, life, and love. As we have also seen, in her last painting, *Still Life Reviving*, Varo gave form to the archetypal, or cosmic, nature of her insight.

The artistic diary: Toward the culmination of the work, the *coniunctio*

Why did Varo die from a heart attack soon after she rendered visible her alchemical work in *Still Life Reviving*? Is there any way to really know? As a final entry in an artistic diary of sorts, Varo's last completed painting, seen in the light of our amplifications, suggests that the alchemical opus of her life had, in fact, come to a place of completion.

As mentioned earlier, Varo did not date the dreams she recorded in her diary. But we do not really need to know when the executioner came to kill her in the last recorded dream. Through her paintings and dreams, Varo told us what was important: She had completed her work. Having done what she came to do—having been put, as the prophet Isaiah said, in the fire like silver and "tested in ... the furnace of distress"—it was time to go to the next place (as cited in Edinger, 1985: 31). It was time for her to leave life because she no longer needed to keep searching for herself. Alchemically speaking, Varo had found within herself the *archeus*, or inner alchemist, that Paracelsus claimed is in each of us. Philip Ball elaborated:

For Paracelsus, purification by separation was the essence of alchemy. Alchemy, he says, "is nothing but the art which makes the impure into the pure through fire ... it can separate the useful from the useless, and transmute it into its final substance and its ultimate essence." And just as the alchemical adept labors to do these things in his workshop and thereby create gold or medicines, so there is an alchemist inside man himself, whose job it is to separate those elements in food that nourish from those that poison. Paracelsus called this inner alchemist the archeus. (2006: 239)

Jung had a similar idea. Instead of *archeus*, Jung referred to the inner alchemist as *Mercurius*. "In a psychological sense," Jung wrote, "Mercurius represents the unconscious" (1955–56/1970: para. 700). More particularly, in "The Spirit Mercurius," an essay he wrote in 1942, Jung referred to Mercurius as "the process by which the lower and material is transformed into the higher and spiritual, and vice versa" (Jung 1948/1967: para. 284).

For the alchemists, Mercurius served as a multifaceted symbol used to represent various aspects of the process of transformation. Seen psychologically, Mercurius is an image used by the alchemists to represent "the agency of consciousness which, as it comes into being, increases our awareness of our own potentials for discriminating and evaluating" (Singer, 2000: 100). "Mercurius," June Singer added, "is frequently depicted as a hermaphrodite, an image designed to reflect the nature of Divinity, which is 'All in One'" (100). Jung commented on an alchemical emblem, the *Mutus Liber*, that depicts Mercurius as a child inside the philosopher's egg. An image of the conjunction of opposites, he "stands on the sun and moon, tokens of his dual nature" (1936/1968: 66, Fig. 22). The ability of Mercurius to bring opposites together into a new wholeness is an inner experience imaged in Varo's paintings and in alchemy as the androgyne and found in the egg she weaves in the dream of the executioner.

The androgyne and the alchemical union of opposites can also be linked with the young feminine held in the beehive house, girls who, in *Toward the Tower*, rode away from conformity in service to the surrounding culture. Frith Luton told of Apollo's gift to his newborn trickster brother, Hermes, of three bee maidens, who speak truth through insight attained by drinking mead and eating honey (2011: 73). This oracular capacity of the feminine calls to mind Hillman's notion of the soul's need for images and food as image—honey imbibed as a sweet intoxicant that frees the imagination and nourishes the fertility that sustains the collective. The bee maidens, Luton added,

represented something other than the oracle of Apollo the sun god. Apollo's kind of wisdom took the form of logos-based, solar, far-shooting insights (like his golden arrows) and knowledge, whereas the white-faced bee maidens divined in a less straightforward way. They were Mercurial, embodying knowledge of a more flowing nature than only solar insights. The knowledge or wisdom of the bee maidens came to consciousness through a process in which the solar and lunar have been combined. (73)

In this same vein, we can revisit the transformation of the girl who cycles away from the beehive house in Varo's 1961 painting, *Toward the Tower.* Having awakened from her bewitchment to conformity, the girl secretly weaves herself with her lover into a fold of the garment of a new world. From their hiding place in the fold of the garment, which spills from the tower in *Embroidering the Earth's Mantle*, Varo and her beloved elope, setting out, in the third painting in the triptych, *The Escape*, "in a special vehicle, across a desert, toward a grotto," a cave carved into the cleft of a mountain (Varo, 1997/2018: 109).

With the image of the mountain, Varo and her beloved traveled into numinous symbolic terrain. "The mountain," wrote an essayist in *The Book of Symbols*, "is one of our very oldest images of deity, distant sky gods of thunder and rain, gods of erupting intensity, divine metallurgists fanning the volcanic bellows of creativity" ("Mountain," 2010: 108). As a metaphor, the mountain evokes an even older presence:

the mother goddess of Asia Minor and India. The mountain is the throne from which she rules and protects, seated, immobile, eternal. Her snowmelt and rainfall stream down the mountainside fertilizing everything. Wild animals and raptors shelter in her slopes and clefts. Rock materializes her bulk and gravity, the greatness of her thighs and breasts, her towering, gigantic, generative strength. Gestating with the mountain's hollow, uterine interior are precious metals, an image alchemy adopted to describe the mysterious *prima materia*, the undifferentiated stuff we start with when we mine our depths, which gradually reveals its potential forms and values. (108)

Associated with "revelation and transition," mountains "suggest arduous, painstaking ascent and sublimation, the widened perspective," and "reflect the mythic goal of sacred quests and the pinnacle of self-knowledge" (108).

It is quite a distance between the mountain where Varo's triptych is destined to end and the girl who realizes in the first painting that she is trapped in deadening conformity as she rides her bicycle to her job. The growth of the girl over the course of the three paintings could not be more profound. Once hypnotized, the girl leaves the beehive house—only to be trapped in a tower, a symbol used to represent a woman's imprisonment in the phallic enclosure of patriarchy. Something important happens to the girl in the tower: she awakens to the presence of the deep Self, symbolized in the third painting by the image of the mountain. Animated from within by a conscious connection to archetypal forces, the girl feels the blunt impact of a boot on her neck: the world of men is a menacing place. Making matters worse, somewhere along the line, the girl realizes she has another problem: she has lost her voice. The girl, no doubt, feels anger, sadness, and confusion as she works to find her way back into a connection with the love and wonder that animate the world.

In the end, the girl, a projected image for Varo herself, makes it out of the tower. She suffers her suffering and grows beyond her suffering. This one girl, seen three times, grows before our eyes into a Bee Maiden, an oracle who speaks divine truth. And we might even venture to say that what makes the girl wise enough to convey messages from the divine or archetypal Feminine is her relationship, depicted in Varo's 1958 painting *Celestial Pablum*, with the silvering light of the moon that illuminates hidden Eros and creativity so that the imaginal and the physical can birth new images and meanings, alchemical amalgamations of silver and gold.

The bee maidens seem to hold within themselves the coming together of opposites expressed alchemically, not only in the figure of the androgyne, but also in the image of the marriage of the red king and white queen. Symbolically, this may have been Varo's way of hinting at the idea that her escape with her male lover from the tower in the second painting was both an inner and outer experience—an emergence from confinement into a newly made world that defies the divisive and hierarchical patriarchal value system that assigns superiority to men and the masculine and inferiority to women and the feminine. The same paradigm also applies to other aspects of Varo's attempt to be herself in a patriarchal world in which thinking and rationality are used to defend against the unbearable vulnerability of feeling, relationality, and the intimacy of human connections nourished by Eros.

According to Kaplan, "Varo believed in the potent interdependence of people as well as of objects" (1988: 181). In *Three Destinies*, an oil painting on masonite from 1962, Varo presents three robed monks. One figure is writing. The second paints. A third drinks. All three are shown alone in a tower but still connected, fates permanently interwoven by what Varo called

> a complicated machine from which come pulleys that wind around them and make them move (they think they move freely) ... [but] the destiny of these people ... unbeknownst to them, is intertwined and one day their lives will cross.
>
> (as cited in Kaplan: 181)

"Surveying the line between free will and determinism," Kaplan added, "Varo felt that all humanity was 'bound by a cosmic, mysterious destiny,' by an interconnectedness that she saw as the magic underlying existence. It was a magic she believed in as life's motive force" (181). *Three Destinies* also suggests the interdependence of the logos and linearity of language; the

Figure 9.2 Creation of the Birds, Remedios Varo, oil on masonite, 1958. © Artists Rights Society (ARS), NY. Photo Credit: DeA Picture Library/Art Resource, NY.

wholistic, imaginal world of form and color; and the realm of the body and the sweet sensual ecstasy of libation.

For Kaplan, Varo imaged the magic of interconnection in *Creation of the Birds*, an imagined scene, as we have said, in which a composite creature—part human, part owl, and part violin—sits at a desk drawing a bird.

Kaplan evoked the numinous nature of this androgynous alchemical figure:

> Using primary colors distilled from the atmosphere, she draws with a pen that is connected through a violin to her heart. Moonlight (the domain of both owl and woman), captured and magnified through a triangular lens, illuminates the drawing, stimulating the drawn birds to come to life and take flight out a window ... Here is the true interconnection of art, science, alchemy, and nature, each nurturing the other in a cycle symbolically represented by the two vases in the corner, which feed their golden contents back and forth to each other. (181)

In *Creation of the Birds*, Kaplan believed Varo chose specific symbols to depict the blending of disciplines, and to image the numinous experience of co-creating a human life animated through partnership with divine forces:

> She used an egg-shaped alchemical vessel, like the one in *Embroidering the Earth's Mantle*, as the receptacle of transformation, in which is created the palette of primaries, the trinity [red, yellow, blue] that is the foundation of all color in art. (181)

In *Creation of the Birds*, Varo, Kaplan wrote, "chose a triangular magnifier, like the triangular prism that Newton, the master scientist, had used to separate light into the colors of the spectrum" (181). Kaplan added,

> By creating birds that fly off the page, Varo placed herself within the tradition of mythological artists such as Pygmalion, whose creation was said to have come to life, and Daedalus, who sculpted wings that offered flight.
> In aligning herself with these traditions, Varo made a claim for the artist as one who goes beyond mere imitation of nature to actual creation itself. This painting of the owl-woman-artist-alchemist creating beauty and life through the conjunction of color, light, sound, science, art, and magic is the very image of creativity to which Varo aspired in her life. As creativity and harmony are at the center of this painting, so they were at the very core of Varo's being. Thus, *Creation of the Birds* can be seen as the paradigmatic image of the fulfillment of her quest. (181–2)

In artistic and symbolic ways, Varo's painting of an owl painting birds reflects a crucial aspect of the artist's experience with and understanding of the alchemical practice of uniting opposites through a "belief in the intrinsic numinosity and animation of matter itself: as sacred and living substance" (Mather, 2014: 103). In terms of combining and unifying opposites, Mathew Mather wrote that alchemical processes

> afford an image of the *coniunctio* as an above (spiritual) and a below (chthonic), as well as a left (queen) and a right (king). Effectively, an alchemical process in the *vas* finds ... a correlate in a supposedly profound ontological transformation of the alchemist ... This journey ... captures the essentials of the alchemical opus as a tortuous mystical rite which Jung likened to a mystery comparable, at least, to the passion of the Christ ... [an ordeal] which mirrors not only [the alchemist's] own psycho-spiritual transformation but also a mysterious transpersonal process. (103–4)

It is important to note that the *coniunctio*, or coming together, that coalesced for Varo is multifaceted rather than dualistic. In unifying the feminine and masculine as the opus of a female quest, multiple elements are brought into partnership, including those that are archetypal, cosmic, and other than human, both discovered and yet to be discovered.

We see this in Varo's painting, *Cosmic Energy*. The image, a gouache on cardboard that Varo painted in 1956, features two figures—one appearing female, the other male. Both are silvered, with gold tendrils of hair sprouting from their heads, suggesting their engagement with the alchemical amalgamation of silver and gold, insight and revelation. The bodies of the two figures are ghostlike, as if astral—a union of human form and the etheric Self with its cosmic nature. The figures are in a room, looking across at each other, seeming to be engaged together in a creative performance as golden grass begins to cover the room's foundation. The female figure pets a red cat, joining animal instinct, the cat's ability to see in the dark, its relationship with the moon, and its silver emanations with their performance. The male figure plays a red violin, enjoining the sacred in the terrain they are creating between them. These two openings—through the cat to the embodied unconscious, and through the music to sacred terrain—Varo has painted as two holes in the walls, one beside the female figure, the other beside the male. Light streams through each hole in the wall; each shaft illuminates a flower growing from the floor of the room. In the *coniunctio* depicted here, we see unified through the creative play between feminine and masculine the embodied unconscious, cosmic forces, and the flowering of the mantle of the world.

Manifesting the sacred

In *The Sacred and the Profane: The Nature of Religion*, Mircea Eliade proposed the term *hierophany* to designate the transpersonal and metaphysical "*act of manifestation* of the sacred" (1957/1987: 11, emphasis in original). A historian of religion, philosopher, and interpreter of religious experience, Eliade worked etymologically to represent that moment when "*something sacred shows itself to us*" (11, emphasis in original). "Man becomes aware of the sacred," Eliade said, "because it manifests itself, shows itself, as something wholly different from the profane" (11). In a passage on the difference between "space that is sacred … and all other space," Eliade wrote:

> When the sacred manifests itself in any hierophany, there is not only a break in the homogeneity of space; there is also revelation of an absolute reality, opposed to the nonreality of the vast surrounding expanse. The manifestation of the sacred ontologically founds the world. (20–1)

In a number of Varo's paintings, music seems to provide such a break in the homogeneity of life: the surprise that birds are created from a pen connected to the owl being's violin heart, the numinosity of the woman in the forest playing a sunbeam with a violin bow, and the woman playing a flute in the background as girls in a tower weave the garment of a new world. These painted musical interludes are perhaps for Varo moments when she is able to not only *detach* (to use a word Eliade might have chosen) from the pain of her personal traumas, but also touch and be transformed by the archetypal forces split off by and held within them. Through the images emerging onto her canvas, Varo midwifes the birth of the sacred.

"Revelation of a sacred space," Eliade wrote, "makes it possible to obtain a fixed point and hence to acquire orientation in the chaos of homogeneity, to 'found the world' and live in a real sense" (1957/1987: 23). "The sacred," Eliade added, "reveals absolute reality and at the same time makes orientation possible; hence it *founds the world* in the sense that it fixes the limits and establishes the order of the world" (30, emphasis in original). Painting, for Varo, functioned as a ritual act of reorienting her attention away from collective conformity and the psychological and physical violence in which the will to power is saturated toward offering an artistic and alchemical alternative born of love and imagination. Bringing images alive with paint and brush, the artist re-animated the raw matter of her suffering, in the process reweaving the thread connecting the human with the divine.

To use Eliade's language, Varo's paintings allowed her to break through the plane of profane existence into a religious universe in which the sacred manifested itself through the images that formed on her canvas. The images enabled Varo, from Eliade's point of view, to take "possession of a territory" (1957/1987: 30). The artist did not intend to colonize the space as her own, that is, she did not hope to possess or own the divine. Instead, the artist worked to consecrate the imaginal space she now inhabited through the sacred practice of painting—the equivalent, as Eliade would say, to making the territory "a cosmos, to *cosmicizing* it" (30, emphasis in original). By occupying sacred space in a conscious way, Varo used painting as a profound ritual act of creation. Engaged with the divine in this way, Varo followed Eliade, who believed that

> what is to become "our world," must first be "created," and every creation has a paradigmatic model—the creation of the universe by the gods. When the Scandinavian colonists took possession of Iceland ... they regarded the enterprise neither as an original undertaking nor as human and profane work. For them, their labor was only repetition of a primordial act, the transformation of chaos into cosmos by the divine act of creation. (31)

With these thoughts in mind, Varo's paintings become more than her attempt to heal from trauma, or even her soul's attempt to express through art the beauty and terror of a world founded and made sacred through devotion to the will of the gods. Varo's paintings, to use Eliade's words, become "*images of an opening*"—portals to spaces made sacred through sometimes excruciating experiences of setback and suffering (1957/1987: 26, emphasis in original). Psychologically, they become what Eliade called "paradoxical point[s] of passage from one mode of being to another"—experience of profane existence made sacred through the revelation provided by images of opening (26).

The dream of the executioner and the dangerous secret: A paradigm shift

With these reflections, the implications of Varo's dream of the executioner, the weaving of the egg, and the serious nature of the knowledge the artist said she possessed come into clearer focus. What if the dangerous knowledge Varo possessed was a style of seeing, a psychological and spiritual practice of acknowledging and working with images as openings into numinous or sacred experience? And more than this, what if the experience of the sacred requires openness to and integration of what is seen as Other, of what threatens one from the dark within oneself, of qualities of love and relationality that make one vulnerable, of the willingness to be changed? From a concrete and literal point of view, it is threatening for a person to engage with the psyche as a surrendered, collaborative partner for the purpose of growth and transformation not only at the level of the individual but at cultural levels as well. In this light, we can see more clearly the possibility that the executioner in Varo's dream represents an aspect of the cultural paradigm, or ruling principle, invested not in stretching beyond a comfort zone, but in using any means necessary to protect it.

With these psychological potentialities in mind, a particular problem emerges with how a patriarchy splits opposites and assigns them to fixed, mutually exclusive positions in a linguistic paradigm that does not know how to weave feminine and masculine together—a social structure that cannot *unknow* them as separate. By joining the feminine and masculine in an egg she weaves of their substances, Varo engages in a transformative and ouroboric act: in death, the product of life is consumed to produce the new egg. The implication of the imagery seems to be that the union of the opposites is not a single point or a linear trajectory of an individual life everlasting, but a spiraling, generative act—feminine and masculine, knowable and unknowable, human and divine, in a cyclical interdependency of life and death.

Weaving the personal together with the cultural, our reflections on Varo's imagery make clear how the artist sacralized the inclusive, imaginal, and will to love of the feminine by seeing through the fear, powerlessness, and agony that, in our collective trance, we project onto others by disenfranchising, oppressing, and terrorizing them. In opening human life into the terrain of the sacred spiral that transcends it, Varo made a final escape—freeing herself, and us if we follow her spiral transit, from the fear of death.

Western religious and political systems depend on fear to execute programs of domination and control. Our sense, after engaging with the numinous images in Varo's paintings and through engaging with the artist's experience of living as a woman in a patriarchal world, is that the religious and political power systems in the West are threatened by, and are therefore intolerant of, the openness to wonder and to the larger, unseen forces that Varo images in her art.

Patriarchal norms and the experience of war are at the heart of Varo's *prima materia* and thus beat at the heart of her transformations. Writing about war, Hillman contended: "The failure to understand may be because our imaginations are impaired and our modes of comprehension need a paradigm shift" (2004: 5). Likewise, the failure to conceive of and collectively practice an alternative to war and hierarchical systems is a consequence of the impairment of imagination by the predominance of fear produced by the hegemonic nature of the will to power. Varo's work provides us with a way into a feminine paradigm that would shift our relationship with both death and life—asking us to live and die with a more expanded consciousness, challenging androcentric and anthropomorphic, linear, literalizing, nonrelational and non-inclusive, hierarchical, and hyper-competitive perspectives.

Varo's secret, as dreamed through the images of the executioner and the weaving of the egg, encompasses a feminine approach to alchemy, Surrealism, and psychology as distinct from an approach that seeks to include and value female experience but remains founded in a patriarchal paradigm. Brought forth as an invitation from the unconscious, the secret asks that patriarchal men do the inner and outer work of opening into the relational, vulnerable terrain of the feminine within themselves, evolving in the process into conscious carriers of wholeness who are able and willing to embrace that which is perceived as other, sacrifice the will to power for love and understanding, and imagine both psychological and physical births and deaths as meaning-rich enactments of love and generativity.

Dreams of alchemy: Love, wonder, and the creative forces that animate the soul

Novelist John Fowles once said that questions are a form of life. Answers, he added, are a form of death (1977: 23). As this first part of our exploration of the symbolic world of Remedios Varo nears its end, a problem presents itself: How to end where we began—in death—without killing the images Varo painted to bring us alive? Maybe the only thing left to do is stick with the image. Maybe the conscious psychological move that is needed now is to cease all speculations and trust the vision of the dream.

Remedios Varo did. Hidden in this tormented and traumatized artist's treasure chest of images is a drawing of a sleeping figure. Varo called the piece *Dreams*. The figure in the drawing sleeps in what appears to be a cocoon—a chrysalis of a kind, gestating not a butterfly but dreams. The cocoon is suspended from an axle or drive shaft that extends from beyond the foot of the dreamer's bed to a wall just beyond her head. In the manner of a gramophone, the rod acts like a spindle, a turbine powered by a wheel affixed to the ceiling of the room above the bed. The wheel is connected by a pipe to unseen forces beyond the sleeping figure's bedroom and to a gear down below. Power for this apparatus of dreams is generated by a belt connecting the wheel and gear. Energy created by the movement of the parts travels along the drive shaft through the sleeper's space. Above and beyond the dreamer's head, the energy of imagination passes through a wall.

What happens on the other side of the wall is a possibility that could only have been dreamed up by someone who believed implicitly in the unseen powers that animate human experience, for through the flared horn of a gramophone, moving along the drive shaft, are ... people. In Varo's image, the apparatus of dreams produces not sound, but other selves. Depicted as stick figures, these imaginal beings move along a series of passageways that lead into and through a black-and-white realm of lines and cubes. The unfolding narrative here is of a sleeping person awakening, not in a physical sense, but in imaginal, psychological, or spiritual ways: a human dreamer coming alive through participation in the wonder of creation. Here, perhaps, in a simple pencil drawing, is another attempt by Varo to symbolize knowledge that is deadly to paradigms of living based on the concrete, the literal, fear of the unknown, and the need to objectify and dominate the unfamiliar. Here, perhaps, is a distilled essence, the curiosity of a woman's soul, an image rendering visible an unspeakable longing, the "urge to see the unseen" (Adams, 2014: 15) and the willingness to be changed by it.

Such is the symbolic power and mission of metaphor: to link what we know with what we do not—or cannot—know. Jung, as mentioned earlier, called symbols "bridges thrown out towards an unseen shore" (1922/1966, para. 116). In a depth psychological sense, the unseen shore can be thought of as the unconscious aspect of psyche and of life. From a Jungian perspective, a symbol points beyond itself as the best possible expression for something unknown. A metaphor is a type of symbol. A hallmark of what Jung called a *"living* symbol" is the intense feeling that surrounds it (1921/1971: para. 819, emphasis in original). Informed by a belief in the intelligence and love of the unconscious psyche, Varo painted and drew images that evoked what it felt like to live intimately with the creative forces that animate the soul. Feeling into these symbolic spaces, we touch into the wonder of forces we cannot know or understand.

Varo's message, culled from her paintings, from the experiences of her life, and from the imagery in her dream of the executioner and the egg, is this: If we can persevere through ambiguity and ambivalence, we come into a place of right relationship with ourselves, with others, and with the sometimes painful and almost always challenging experience of human life. Through imagining, painting, and living, Remedios Varo found this place. The intention underlying her alchemical practice of painting was to help others find it, too.

References

Adams, M. V. (2014). *For the love of the imagination: Interdisciplinary applications of Jungian psychoanalysis.* New York, NY: Routledge.

Ball, P. (2001). *Bright earth: Art and the invention of color.* New York, NY: Farrar, Straus and Giroux.

Ball, P. (2006). *The devil's doctor: Paracelsus and the world of Renaissance magic and science.* New York, NY: Farrar, Straus and Giroux.

Bogzaran, F. (2008). Dreams of alchemy. In M. Orellano (Ed.), *Five keys to the secret world of Remedios Varo* (159–86). Mexico City: Artes de Mexico.

Edinger, E. (1985). *Anatomy of the psyche: Alchemical symbolism in psychotherapy.* La Salle, IL: Open Court.

Eliade, M. (1957/1987). *The sacred and the profane* (W. Trask, Trans.). New York, NY: Houghton Mifflin.

Eliade, M. (1958/1996). *Patterns in comparative religion* (R. Sheed, Trans.). Lincoln: University of Nebraska Press.

Engel, P. (1986). *Remedios Varo: Science into art.* New York: New York Academy of Science.

Fowles, J. (1977). *The magus.* New York, NY: Little, Brown.

Gimbutas, M. (1997). *The Kurgan culture and the Indo-Europeanization of Europe: Selected articles from 1952 to 1993.* Washington, D.C.: Institute for the Study of Man.

Hillman, J. (1979). *The dream and the underworld.* New York, NY: Harper & Row.

Hillman, J. (2004). *A terrible love of war.* New York, NY: Penguin Press.

Jung, C. G. (1922/1966). On the relation of analytical psychology to poetry (R. F. C. Hull, Trans.). In H. Read et al. (Eds.), *The collected works of C. G. Jung* (Vol. 15, 65–83). Princeton, NJ: Princeton University Press.

Jung, C. G. (1946/1966). The psychology of the transference (R. F. C. Hull, Trans.). In H. Read et al. (Eds.), *The collected works of C. G. Jung* (Vol. 16, 2nd ed., 163–323). Princeton, NJ: Princeton University Press.

Jung, C. G. (1948/1967). The spirit Mercurius (R. F. C. Hull, Trans.). In H. Read et al. (Eds.), *The collected works of C. G. Jung* (Vol. 13, 191–250). Princeton, NJ: Princeton University Press.

Jung, C. G. (1936/1968). Individual dream symbolism in relation to alchemy (R. F. C. Hull, Trans.). In H. Read et al. (Eds.), *The collected works of C. G. Jung* (Vol. 12, 2nd ed., 39–224). Princeton, NJ: Princeton University Press.

Jung, C. G. (1939/1968). Conscious, unconscious, and individuation (R. F. C. Hull, Trans.). In H. Read et al. (Eds.), *The collected works of C. G. Jung* (Vol. 9i, 2nd ed., 275–89). Princeton, NJ: Princeton University Press.

Jung, C. G. (1958/1969). The transcendent function (R. F. C. Hull, Trans.). In H. Read et al. (Eds.), *The collected works of C. G. Jung* (Vol. 8, 2nd ed., 67–91). Princeton, NJ: Princeton University Press.

Jung, C. G. (1955–56/1970). *Mysterium coniunctionis* (R. F. C. Hull, Trans.) (H. Read et al., Eds.), *The collected works of C. G. Jung* (Vol. 14, 2nd ed.). Princeton, NJ: Princeton University Press.

Jung, C. G. (1921/1971). Definitions (R. F. C. Hull, Trans.). In H. Read et al. (Eds.), The collected works of C. G. Jung (Vol. 6, 408–86). Princeton, NJ: Princeton University Press.

Kalsched, D. (1996). *The inner world of trauma: Archetypal defenses of the personal spirit.* New York, NY: Routledge.

Kaplan, J. (1988). *Unexpected journeys: The art and life of Remedios Varo.* New York, NY: Abbeville Press.

Lozano, L-M. (2000). *The magic of Remedios Varo* (E. Goldson & L. Valenzuela, Trans.). Washington DC: National Museum of Women in the Arts.

Luton, F. (2011). *Bees, honey and the hive: Circumambulating the centre.* Toronto, Canada: Inner City Books.

Mather, M. (2014). *The alchemical Mercurius: Esoteric symbol of Jung's life and works.* New York, NY: Routledge.

Mountain. (2010). In A. Ronnberg & K. Martin (Eds.), *The book of symbols: Reflections on archetypal images* (108–9). Cologne, Germany: Taschen.

Ocean. (2010). In A. Ronnberg & K. Martin (Eds.), *The book of symbols: Reflections on archetypal images* (36–9). Cologne, Germany: Taschen.

Owl. (2010). In A. Ronnberg & K. Martin (Eds.), *The book of symbols: Reflections on archetypal images* (254–5). Cologne, Germany: Taschen.

Siegelman, E. (1990). *Metaphor & meaning in psychotherapy.* New York, NY: Guilford.

Singer, J. (2000). *Androgyny: The opposites within.* York Beach, ME: Nicolas-Hays.

Sullivan, B. S. (1989). *Psychotherapy grounded in the feminine principle.* Asheville, NC: Chiron.

Varo, R. (1997/2018). *Letters, dreams & other writings* (M. Carson, Trans.). Cambridge, MA: Wakefield Press.

Woodman, M. (1980). *The owl was a baker's daughter: Obesity, anorexia nervosa and the repressed feminine.* Toronto, Canada: Inner City Books.

Mystical sisters

Varo, Carrington, the eternal Feminine,
and the unmaking of patriarchy

Medical matters

Chapter 10

Kindred spirits

Varo, Carrington, and the possibilities of woman's creative power

While male surrealists were dismembering the female body in a bid to annihilate their own disavowed inner feminine, artists like Remedios Varo and Leonora Carrington painted to embody wholeness and a sense of the sacred in their lives. That Varo and Carrington are mentioned together is not only fitting but obligatory. The friendship between the two women was long and close (Berland, 2010: 33). In Parts II and III, we focus on the creative partnership between two artists brought together to contribute to a great work: "reintegration of female powers in a world brought to holocaust by the demands of the male ego" (Chadwick, 1991: 12).

The partnership between the two women was grounded in both life experiences and intellectual interests. Like Varo, Carrington was deeply interested in Jungian psychology and alchemy. Alchemy, in fact, became one of Carrington's abiding interests late in the 1930s when the young artist studied painting at the Ozenfant Academy of Fine Arts in London (Warlick, 2017: paras. 4, 6). M. E. Warlick, a retired art professor who studied the use of esoteric symbols in Carrington's paintings, wrote that Carrington's studies under Amédée Ozenfant, a French cubist writer and painter, included an "emphasis on the chemistry of art materials" (para. 6). Inspired, Carrington "began collecting books on alchemy in used bookstalls around London" (para. 6).

Jungian psychology was also a strong influence on Carrington, who read Jung's published researches into alchemical psychology when they were first published in the mid-1930s (Warlick, 2017: para. 12). Carrington's studies of Jung continued into the 1970s and 1980s. Living in New York and Chicago after leaving Mexico City in the wake of the government repression of student protests in 1968, Carrington frequented the Kristine Mann Library, founded by the Analytical Psychology Club of New York in the 1940s (para. 22). Jung's "emphasis on the alchemical feminine" resonated strongly with Carrington, who worked, and reworked, alchemical symbolism into a host of paintings (para. 13). These include *The Garden of Paracelsus*, in 1957; *The Chrysopoeia of Mary the Jewess*, in 1964; and *Cornelia and Cornelius*, a 1973 work in which the red king and white queen bathe together—a reference to the sixteenth-century series of images of the alchemical union of the *vir rubeus* and *muliere candida* in the *Rosarium philosophorum*. Carrington worked with similar alchemical imagery in *Sol Niger*, a 1975 painting in which black and gold partners nestle close to one another in a cocoon-like vessel. Intimate relations between opposites show up again in *The Lovers*, a 1987 painting where the alchemical king and queen are this time red and blue, surrounded on all sides of the bed by a group of robed and hooded figures dressed in black and white sacred garments.

For Varo and Carrington, friendship formed a crucible, the word used to describe a container in which different elements interact, leading to the creation of a new synthesis, but also a situation of severe trial. Traumatized by the violence of war and patriarchy, the artists used alchemical and artistic practices to animate new ways of being. For these surreal friends, painting was a way to express and transform suffering that animated contact with numinous forces. But there was more to their bond than the common ground of overwhelming upset related to war and exile. These women were brought together by circumstance and by archetypal forces underlying the operation of the material world to do something neither could attempt on their own. Their task: to help unmake the patriarchy and re-enchant a world that can now embrace the imaginative power of women.

In what follows, we look in some detail at the ways in which each woman engaged with the practice of spiritual alchemy. A point of emphasis is on how the relationship as an alchemical vessel helped each woman come home to herself in a way that nourished her inner well-being. In this context, we look at the life and art of Leonora Carrington, whose personal experiences of trauma and transformation mirror Varo's. Blending personal history with amplifications of symbols in each artist's creative work, we see expressed through life experience and images the raw components of affliction and torment recast into new symbolic forms. These forms, in their paintings and other creative works, highlight the presence and power of female insight, wonder, and love. New in what follows is a connection featured for the first time: the art of Varo and Carrington, produced in the crucible of friendship, not only for personal growth but as a way to address and resolve complexes at work at the group or cultural level.

"Cultural complexes," wrote Samuel Kimbles, "shape the individual's psyche through highly charged group memories of specific traumas and historical assumptions that operate within the individual's connection to present conditions" (2000: 166–7). When a cultural complex has been constellated, "people literally cannot see one another for who they really are" (167). Individuals caught in the grip of a cultural complex work to protect the underlying vulnerability of the group—that aspect of the shadow the group finds so unacceptable it must be denigrated, disavowed, gotten rid of, by projecting it out into the world.

As women, Remedios Varo and Leonora Carrington both got caught in the gears of patriarchal machinery—male-dominated and misogynistic power complexes at work at a cultural level that damaged their well-being. Art was a way these artists pushed back on the oppressions and suppressions of aristocracy, Catholicism, Surrealism, and violent patriarchal Fascism. We have looked at the ways in which painting helped Varo heal from trauma, discover a feminine lens and way of operating in the psyche and world, and symbolize her transformative experiences with the numinous presence of the divine. We will look shortly at the artistic and alchemical responses Carrington made to resist the patriarchal suppression of her female voice. Later in this chapter, we look again at Varo's dream of the executioner, and at several of the artist's paintings, attuning more finely to her images as revelatory of androcentric bias in psychology and as acts of defiance meant to protest the patriarchal debasement of women and the Feminine.

When Remedios Varo died of a heart attack in the fall of 1963, Leonora Carrington felt like she had lost a sister (Moorhead, 2017: 217). The two women had been inseparable for two decades, forming what Joanna Moorhead, one of Carrington's biographers, described as an "almost conspiratorial friendship" (177). For years, the women saw each other almost every day. The women "shared their dreams, their nightmares, their obsessions, and their deepest secrets" (Kaplan, 1988: 93). "Secrets," according to Walter Gruen, Varo's companion during her later years, "that Remedios would talk about with no one but Leonora" (as cited in Kaplan, 1988: 93). Janet Kaplan added:

> Building on the strange powers of inspiration that each felt so intensely, on a shared belief in the mystical and the powers of magic, the two women developed a deep rapport, finding themselves able to communicate in a way that fed their lives and their work. (93)

"Varo and Carrington," Kaplan wrote,

> shared the sense that they were both uniquely inspired by strange inner powers, that they had been chosen for a special psychic journey. Traveling together into what poet Adrienne Rich called "the cratered night of female memory," they undertook a shared process of self-discovery, working together to probe the possibilities of woman's creative power. (216–7)[1]

The foundation of the bond between Varo and Carrington was their deep trust of a like-minded creative person and a mutual understanding of "the pain and despair each had known" (Kaplan, 1988: 93). The implicit affinity each felt for the other seemed to set them apart as "confidante[s] in an otherwise hostile world" (93). Seeing herself as "an eccentric that others couldn't understand," Varo "looked to Carrington as a soul mate who would need no explanations, an ally who would not try to explain away her anxieties with facile logic or undermine her visions with common sense" (93). That Carrington felt similarly is

> a sentiment she expressed through one of the characters in her novel *The Hearing Trumpet*: "I often feel like Joan of Arc, so dreadfully misunderstood... I feel I am being burned at the stake just because I am different from everybody else because I have always refused to give up that wonderful strange power I have inside me and it becomes manifested when I am in harmonious communication with some other inspired being like myself." (93–4)

At a fundamental level, the sister-like attachment between Varo and Carrington was possible because they felt safe together. We have looked at the way in which traumatic suffering tormented Varo personally but also transformed her work as an artist. For her part, Carrington's early life mirrors Varo's troubling experiences with patriarchal family and cultural religious values in Spain.

Crookhey Hall: Carrington and the *prima materia* of childhood

Born in the spring of 1917, Carrington grew up in Clayton Green, in the north of England, near Chorley, South Lancashire, home for generations to families working in the textile mills. Late in life, Carrington remembered the place as the Black Country for the soot and pollution that came along with industrialization (Aberth, 2010: 11). The Carrington family wealth stemmed from her paternal grandfather, a mill hand who invented and patented a new loom attachment that "led to the development of Viyella, a popular blend of cotton and wool" (11).

If Varo felt stifled by her mother's adherence to Catholicism in Spain, Carrington felt similarly trapped by the suffocating demands and dictates of aristocracy. In 1947, Carrington evoked the pain she experienced as a prisoner of patriarchal aristocracy in her painting, *Crookhey Hall*, which she titled after the Edwardian manor she lived in with her family for a time as a young girl (Aberth, 2010: 11). In the painting, a young woman in a flowing white dress races along a path. From behind, a flying figure dressed in black reaches for her with outstretched arms. A likeness of Crookhey Hall broods in the background, its square stone entrance shaded black. Psychologically, Aberth wrote, Crookhey Hall symbolized for Carrington the "forbidding and restrictive prison that represented parental authority" (11).

Remembering Hillman's reference to the two whitenings, *Crookhey Hall* seems to hold both, as well as the transition between them. In Carrington's

Figure 10.1 Crookhey Hall, Leonora Carrington, color lithograph on woven paper. © Artists Rights Society (ARS), NY. Photo Credit: Princeton University Art Museum/Art Resource, NY.

painting, white clothed figures in the background play in a pool of water, naively unaware of any difficulty. Another figure in white is on the path leading from the Hall, her hand over her mouth, as if in shock, or perhaps to silence the scream of dawning awareness as she looks at the figure in the black of the *nigredo* nearby, further along on the path. A second woman in white, the one in the white dress, flees the dark Hall of her childhood, her hand raised before her in a fist of determination and defiance, signifying the second whitening of the *albedo*. From the perspective of alchemical psychology, Carrington painted the inner movement between the naiveté of the first whitening through the suffering of the *nigredo* into the *albedo* and "the emergence of psychological consciousness" (Hillman, 2010: 158).

Further applying a depth psychological perspective to the image Carrington painted, we turn to Jung, who wrote that the *nigredo* "was felt as 'melancholia' in alchemy and corresponds to the encounter with the shadow in psychology" (1943/1968: para. 41). In her painting, Carrington evoked the torment of imprisonment in the shadow, symbolized by the mansion, and by the black figure who may be trying to keep the young woman in the white dress from escaping. Carrington painted the moment in time when the young woman in white has nearly reached the end of the path leading away from the prison of parental authority. From the way the image is painted, it seems possible—if not likely—that the young woman *will* be able to break free from the pull of the psychological space that has imprisoned her.

But we note that the black figure who might impede her movement is flying *back* toward the manor. What does the presence of this figure suggest psychologically? As a symbolic aspect of Carrington's *prima materia*, the black figure and the threat this aspect of shadow represents to her psychological freedom lurks in the childhood housed in her unconscious. The image suggests that the element of destruction as the raw matter of lived experience persists, waiting to be reconstituted in a new form.

Jung saw the experience of alchemical work involved in the movement through the blackening, whitening, and reddening as a tortuous mystical rite in which "the substance suffers torments" (Mather, 2014: 104) in a bid to eventually bring forth the golden aspects of soul imprisoned in the embodied or somatic unconscious. According to Jung, the alchemist would experience this ordeal as mirroring not only his or her own psychospiritual transformation, but also a mysterious transpersonal process: In the ordeal of transformation, "it is not the adept who suffers, rather *it* suffers in him, *it* is tortured, *it* passes through death and rises again" (1955–56/1970, para. 492, emphasis in original). If Jung is right, the flying black figure in *Crookhey Hall* shapeshifts from a symbolic representation of a shadow problem into an image of an untransformed potential still waiting for deliverance through the ongoing process of engaging with dreams, emotions, and the conflicts of life. From Carrington's life history, it is possible to consider the flying black figure in *Crookhey Hall* as a multivalent symbol representing not only unconscious suffering associated with parental authority that the artist has become aware of, but also material still unseen and waiting for development.

Although it is safe to say that the family home in the painting represents Carrington's attempt to heal and transform her experience of feeling imprisoned by parental authority, we can peer into the psychological presence of the black figure even further. With the shapeshifting, or mercurial, nature of psychological complexes, in mind, the black figure flying back toward the prison of parental authority suggests a new psychological possibility. What if the figure flies back toward the prison of parental authority not to entrap the young woman running for freedom, but because he or she (the black figure) must return to the prison, the shadow, until Carrington's waking ego is able and willing to engage with unconscious contents that are not yet ready to be brought into awareness and that resonate through her later experience of sociocultural forces?

Down Below: The onset of war and the female body as alchemical vessel

We meet these forces, perhaps, in Carrington's painting, *Down Below*, which visually expresses aspects of the trauma the artist also chronicled in a prose memoir, also titled *Down Below*, first published in *VVV*, an American journal devoted to Surrealism, in 1944 (Suleiman, 1990: 171). In her memoir

Down Below, Carrington chronicled a bizarre and frightening imprison-ment: involuntary commitment in an asylum for the insane in Franco's Spain after fleeing across the border of Nazi-occupied France (1944/1988a).

Carrington was young at the time, just 23 years old and alone, "disowned by her family," and feeling "powerless against a terrifying and swiftly approaching war" (Aberth, 2010: 46). The memoir *Down Below* opens with Carrington in terror. It was the summer of 1940. The French police had captured and imprisoned her lover, surrealist artist Max Ernst (Carrington, 1944/1988b, 164). To the French, who were at war with Germany, Ernst was an "enemy alien" (Chadwick, 1991: 9). With Hitler's Third Reich on the move, Carrington made a gut-wrenching decision: with Ernst in a French prison, she sold the farmhouse the two artists had been living in near Avignon and fled for Spain (Moorhead, 2017: 110–1). What followed was a surrealist nightmare: Carrington and two friends set out by car from Andorra, a small independent principality tucked into the Pyrenees moun-tains between France and Spain. Driving all night for Spain, they got trapped at the border. Eventually, Carrington's father pulled strings that allowed the three refugees to enter a country ripped open by the violence and conflict of the Spanish Civil War. Nearly seven decades later, the artist could still call up the fear she felt as the three friends "drove all day, and then on through the night, passing trucks from which dangled arms and legs, and along roads lined with coffins. It all stank of death, Leonora remembered" (115).

At the time, Spain was in the process of recovering from the atrocities of the civil war fought between anarchists and Republicans loyal to the elected, left-leaning Second Spanish Republic and Nationalists aligned with monarchists, conservatives, and Catholics, factions defended by the army of General Francisco Franco. Having just abandoned her intense relationship with Ernst, and now caught in a cultural cauldron boiling over with violence, Carrington wrote that she found herself feeling terrified and overwhelmed. "I was choked by the dead, by their thick presence in that lacerated country-side" (1944/1988b: 170). By the time she and her friend, Catherine, reached Barcelona, Carrington found herself in "a great state of exaltation" (170).

Things were shifting quickly: impending world war, the end of her love affair with Max Ernst, the lethal political conflict swirling in Spain. With life in upheaval all around her, and before the destructive *nigredo* that led to her imprisonment in an asylum, Carrington responded by trying to gain some control in a situation in which she was powerless. She convinced Catherine to ditch their car and take the train to Madrid. Why Madrid? Carrington explained:

> I convinced myself that Madrid was the world's stomach and that I had been chosen for the task of restoring this digestive organ to health. I believed that all anguish had accumulated in me and would dissolve in the end, and this explained to me the force of my emotions. I believed

that I was capable of bearing this dreadful weight and of drawing from it a solution for the world. The dysentery I suffered from later was nothing but the *illness* of Madrid taking shape in my intestinal tract. (1944/1988b: 170–1, emphasis in original)

In this passage, Carrington describes her instinctive turn to alchemical practice. In a moment of terror, the young artist makes her own body into an alchemical vessel in a bid to digest the hatred, oppression, and violence occurring in the world. The aim of this mini opus: to embody and metabolize lethal aspects of war and violence, reconstituting these distressing experiences into safety, freedom, and love.

During this time of her life, between 1937 and 1941, Carrington wrote short stories replete with the motifs of food, appetite, and eating. In an essay, "Gardens of Delight, or What's Cookin'? Leonora Carrington in the Kitchen," Sonia Assa described Carrington's *Down Below* as an "exceptionally clear, tense and pitiless account of her experience" in Spain (1991: 223). "Carrington's characters," Assa wrote, "speak and cook too much, too fast, delight in hunting and tearing, but fill their mouths with words more often than with food, trying to cover up or quench a want through their dizzying skill" (215). Assa suggested that through the female characters in Carrington's short stories, a culinary alchemy was at work as the artist processed unresolved inner conflicts and identity issues arising from the stifling options offered within a patriarchal culture:

Her female characters are divided into the flesh-eaters, who eat ravenously, outrageously, and the cookies-and-greens eaters, the delicate eaters, who may offer food, may not eat at all, or may well *become* food. They play out, in food terms, as Carrington must have fantasized them, the two optional role-models presented to the young girl at the threshold of the adult world: on the one hand, the unladylike, powerful and lustful ogress, on the other, the subdued, observant, passive and hostile anorexic. (218)

In a short story in *The Seventh Horse and Other Tales*, Carrington imagined herself as Virginia Fur, a feral girl with "a mane of hair yards long and enormous hands with dirty nails" (1988: 3).

This was something to see: fifty black cats and as many yellow ones, and then her, and one couldn't really be altogether sure that she was a human being. Her smell alone threw doubt on it—a mixture of spices and game, the stables, fur and grasses. (3)

Of Carrington's short fiction, Assa wrote, "the delicate world of bourgeois home and garden is wrecked ... gardens are untidy and profuse, kitchens dirty and cluttered, ladies unlady-like beasts of prey, while men's virility is unambiguously in question" (1991: 220). Carrington described one of her male characters as wearing "an enormous gold wig with rose-coloured shadows, like a cascade of honey. A variety of flowers, growing here and there in his wig, moved in the wind" (as cited in Assa, 1991: 226, fn. 12). Carrington often portrayed men in her short stories as

> showy birds of paradise, clad in the bright attire of the males of the animal kingdom, but smelling feminine scents and with a weakness for "feminine" colors (pink, violet and purple: colours of the flesh, of the inside of the body). Delicate and androgynous, they give us the uneasy feeling that they could well end up in the stewpot, making a trifling "bouché" for their devouring females.
>
> (Assa, 1991: 220)

From a Jungian perspective, in these images we can see patriarchal males and females exhibiting in themselves the qualities they have projected onto one another. Exposed is men's fear of their feminine qualities, which if acknowledged would make them androgynous, but also, given a patriarchy that sees feminine qualities in a man as inferior and demasculinizing, vulnerable to being shamed and devoured.

Regarding Carrington's somatic attempt to metabolize what she saw and felt as the sickness of Spain, Assa noticed that the first symptom of the artist's "illness was an obsessive desire to control her appetite" (1991: 223). Feeling powerless, Carrington "indulged in voluntary vomitings and limited her diet, like so many of her 'passive' heroines, to salad and potatoes" (223). Carrington, in *Down Under*, said she wanted to get beyond the "brutal ineptitude" she saw around her in Spain as the violence of World War Two escalated (1944/1988b: 164). To do so, the artist responded with what Assa called "a self and body centered" process of purification (1991: 223). Carrington wept and repeatedly induced vomiting "by drinking orange blossom water" (1944/1988b: 164). "I had realized the injustice of society," the artist wrote, adding that by throwing up she was hoping to cleanse herself and the world around her made sick by the machinery of war and the terror of the will to power (164).

Carrington's experiences in Spain remind us of Varo's transformative move in the dream of the executioner: using her own substance to weave an egg that harbors the embryo of loving relatedness, qualities that threaten the underlying vulnerability of the male-dominated status quo. In the dream, Varo, as the dream ego, is willing to suffer death at the hands of the patriarchal executioner. But in surrendering to her own beheading she is at peace, her sense of fulfillment created through engagement with archetypal forces. Like Varo, Carrington responded alchemically to the demands of her moment in history. The artist intended to bear the dreadful weight of war and trauma at both individual and archetypal levels, metabolizing the suffering into something new: a solution for the world. In this way, Carrington became a physical vessel for the transformation that was needed. In this process, Assa wrote, "the woman's body is itself the cooking pot"—or in Varo's symbolism, the egg—"the place of transformation" (1991: 224).

Alchemically, Carrington and Varo worked to ingest and then metabolize the aspects of patriarchal life that are menacing, and even murderous, to both men and women. In a patriarchy, wrote Carol Gilligan and Naomi Snider, women are forced to "disavow or dissociate themselves from an honest voice—the voice that speaks from experience—thus disabling their ability to register and protest against experiences of violation or subordination" (2018: 90).

Men in patriarchy, Gilligan and Snider added, defend against vulnerability, and the loss of intimacy and love, by disconnecting "from their emotional radar, disabling their ability to empathize or care, and by doing so undermine their ability to register what is going on around them, or to repair the violations they suffer and inflict on others" (90). Patriarchy instills and enforces a "psychological pathology" in which "dysfunctional defenses against loss [of intimacy] not only stand in the way of love but undermine the ability to resist injustice" (90).

Later in her life, Carrington used writing and painting to infuse feminine values into what was cooking in the alchemical vessel of her life and in the world around her. In Spain, even amid the blunt impact of war and the disorientation of an impending mental breakdown, Carrington's experiences can be seen as following an alchemical process of transformation, progressively balancing love and subjugation in order to find a new synthesis that fosters feminine agency. As upsetting as it was for Carrington to abandon Max Ernst and to flee the terror of the German invasion of France, the young artist's ordeal was just beginning. For what happened to Carrington next in Spain clipped the last thread connecting her to the reality she thought she knew.

From mayhem to madness: Carrington in the asylum of the patriarchy

Carrington's somatic and imaginal attempt to purify herself (and others) of the annihilating presence of war and patriarchal Fascism brings to mind Jung's comments on the importance to the alchemical work of imagination. "Imagination," Jung wrote, quoting *Ruland's Lexicon*, "is the star in man, the celestial or supercelestial body" (1937/1968, para. 394). "This astounding definition," Jung explained, makes clear that "we have to conceive of these processes not as the immaterial phantoms we readily take fantasy-pictures to be, but as something corporeal, a 'subtle body,' semi-spiritual in nature" (para. 394). "The *imaginatio*, or the act of imagining," Jung continued, is a physical activity that could be fitted into the cycle of material changes, that brought these about and was brought about by them in turn. In this way the alchemist related himself not only to the unconscious but directly to the very substance which he hoped to transform through the power of imagination. (para. 394)

Jung concluded that imagination is a psychic and physical "concentrated extract of the life forces," which means that the alchemist, who "works with and through his own quintessence and is himself the indispensable condition of his own experiment," must "have a sound physical constitution" (para. 394). Hillman traveled in similar terrain in a passage on the union of opposites:

> Alchemical soul-making proposes that the final idea of sun conjuncted with moon means nothing less and no other than a condition of being in which solar brilliance and awakeness and moon-madness are marvelously conjoined. The *mysterium conjunctionis* is illumined lunacy... After all, is alchemy not a prolonged witness to mad men at work upon themselves? (2010: 125–6)

In Spain, sometime during the middle part of 1940, Carrington's experience moved from high upset to nervous breakdown. She was kidnapped by a Dutchman whose passport was "infested with Swastikas" (Moorhead, 2017: 119). Taken by car to a house where she was raped, the young woman was then dumped in a park in Madrid. She wandered around the park in torn clothes until a policeman took her back to her hotel. "I spent the rest of the night," Carrington wrote, "taking cold baths and putting on nightgowns" (as cited in Moorhead, 2017: 119–20). Shortly after, Carrington had another encounter with the Dutchman, a man she was convinced was "the evil master behind Spain's troubles" (120). The Dutchman thought Carrington had gone insane. Carrington's woman friend agreed. Carrington spent another night wandering in the street and taking cold baths. Soon, a doctor was called.

Here is where Carrington went from being the wild child expelled from every school in which her parents enrolled her to a danger to the family reputation and possibly to herself. "Presumably on the family's orders," Moorhead wrote, "and financed by them," Carrington was taken against her will "to a sanatorium run by nuns" (2017: 121). Carrington was told by two doctors that a solution to her troubles had been found in the seaside town of San Sebastian, where she would be able to walk along the sand and enjoy the sunshine. Where she would finally be free.

The doctors were lying.

During the car trip to San Sebastian, Carrington was given a drug and taken to a mental hospital in Santander, on the north coast of Spain. Sedated but surging with adrenaline, Carrington wrote that she clawed her doctor, who "slapped and strapped me down and compelled me to absorb food through tubes inserted into my nostrils" (1944/1988b: 178). Her hands and feet bound by leather straps, Carrington was powerless against medical staff who, she said, carved "artificial abscesses" into her body (as cited in Winslow, 2017: para. 7). Adding insult to injury, Carrington was injected with Cardiozal, a drug once used to treat schizophrenia and affective disorders but now in disuse due in part to the intense seizures and fear patients experienced during treatment.

According to Elena Poniatowska, who knew Carrington and researched the artist's life for her award-winning novel, *Leonora*, Cardiozal "provokes something akin to an epileptic attack" (2011/2015: 172). Poniatowska imagined what Carrington went through during repeated treatments at the asylum in Santander: "Leonora coughs, then yells. Her muscles contract, spasms race from her womb to her breast, her head is thrown back, her jawbone seems to be dislocated. Her mouth opens in an immense, terrifying grimace" (171). In Poniatowska's novel, during another treatment at the asylum, Jose, an orderly with whom Carrington had become friendly, confirmed that the injection of the drug induced a "fit [that] lasted for several minutes; convulsed, hideous, every part of her body, including her arms and wrists, her breasts and belly, were becoming twisted and deformed" (172). What happens to a person inside who is treated in such a manner? "Do you know what Cardiozal is?" Carrington asks a lover, her voice imagined by Poniatowska:

> It is a form of shock therapy when they inject you with such a high dose of insulin that you end up in a comatose state. The truth is, they kill you. They call it a cure for schizophrenia, but Cardiozal really kills off all there is inside you. The agony of what they did to me I still carry here, and here … and she places her hand on her heart and then on her head. (410–1)

According to Moorhead, Carrington's narration of her time in the asylum in *Down Below*

> is a harrowing, and yet ultimately inspiring, combination of extreme vulnerability, and extraordinary resilience. She describes, in minute detail, where a human being has to go, and what she or he must cling on to, when there is absolutely nothing else left. (2017: 125)

Moorhead said the trauma Carrington experienced in the mental hospital in Spain would prove to "be the pivotal experience of her life" (126). "What it mainly did for me in a conscious way," Carrington said, was to make me "aware that I was both mortal and touchable, and I could be destroyed" (as cited in Moorhead, 2017: 127). However, like Varo's silence around her traumas,

> even in her nineties, Leonora was never comfortable with talking about what happened in Santander in 1940: a shadow would cross her face if it was mentioned, and she would quickly light another Marlboro, inhale deeply, and suggest a change of subject.
>
> (Moorhead, 2017: 126)

And, like Varo's investment of her distressing experiences as the *prima materia* that yielded her painted transformations, Carrington worked with her trauma in the alchemical vessel of her art.

To be tortured and traumatized, held down and cut open—these were a few of the experiences that Carrington wrote about in *Down Below* as she worked to process the traumas and to heal. In 1951, Carrington painted her felt experience in *Down Below*, an oil on canvas in which the artist imaged an alchemical gathering of five figures on the lawn in front of a sprawling facility meant to evoke the mental hospital in Santander. At the back of the imaginal portrait of five figures is a naked, blackened woman in a state of *nigredo*; in front of her is a whitened woman, also naked, with the head of a bird—symbolic of the liberated soul and recalling Carrington's flight in *Crookhey Hall*, but now on the ground, her freedom gone. There is a male figure with long red hair but without arms who sits in the foreground with a voluptuous female in sexy garb but with a garter around her mouth, silencing her—an image of the depotentiation of both the masculine and feminine. At the right edge of the painting a fifth figure, a woman dressed in a blue gown and a winged headdress, looks at the four other figures— the display of Carrington's inner condition—with dismay. Yet, we might also say, her presence entering the situation brings the alchemical bluing of *imaginatio*, and thus the possibility of transformation.

Recall Carrington's alchemical attempt to metabolize an initial condition— the sickness of violence and war—and to restore things to a new state of health. In *Down Below*, Carrington wrote that she stopped menstruating for a time, her body's way of "transforming my blood into comprehensive energy—masculine and feminine, microcosmic and macrocosmic—and into a wine that was drunk by the moon and the sun" (1944/1988b: 177). Carrington's statement articulates her experience, as alchemical adept, of the link between personal psychospiritual transformation and the mysterious transpersonal process identified by Jung. But Carrington goes further in her implicit sense of the alchemical unity of body and psyche, in contrast to the Cartesian, patriarchal split between the two. No longer menstruating, it is as if she is pregnant. In her womb—like the metaphoric egg that holds immortality and absolute realization—a new possibility is forming in which the personal, transpersonal, and divine, the masculine and feminine, are transmuted into a wine for both the lunar psyche that shines from the dark and the solar ego. Wine ferments ingredients, dissolving the separations between them into nuances of flavor. In her transformative work, by yielding wine, we can imagine Carrington's amalgamation of masculine, feminine, personal, cultural, and cosmic energies to have dissolved difference "into shadings, tonalities, possibilities, implications" (Hillman, 2010: 194).

From an imaginal point of view, Carrington's experience is a twentieth-century reenactment of Persephone's rape and abduction into the underworld. In distress, Carrington discovered her psyche and body as an alchemical vessel, a somatic site of social antagonisms, a crucible for the human transmutation of archetypal forces (annihilation and war). In Spain, Carrington's encounter with the Dutchman, an agent of the German Fatherland—the Third Reich being the diabolical epitome of the patriarchal will to power—is charged with the culturally enforced traumatic nature of female experience within patriarchy. As a maiden, she is abducted and raped. Then, alone and isolated, she is imprisoned in the asylum of the underworld. In the asylum, the treatments of Cardiozal were administered to convulse Carrington's head back into sanity—silent acceptance of the unacceptable. Such invasive imagery evokes the threatened beheading of Varo in the dream of the executioner. Both images reflect the determination of "powerful people and government authorities" to silence the threat the women pose to patriarchy (Varo, 1997/2018: 94).

Destruction as the cause of coming into being[2]

Were Carrington and Varo, working in resistance to their denigration, chosen to heal a world made sick by the atrocities of war and the patriarchal silencing of women? Psychologically, it is possible that one or both women were in a state of inflation—that is, they were identified with their own importance as a way of compensating for feeling powerless and victimized in their lives. It is also possible that painting, writing, and working with life experience through the body and with painted images was an unconscious attempt to resolve issues related to trauma and persecution. After all, both Varo and Carrington had been confined against their will and mistreated.

But from the perspective of the cultural complex, there is another possibility to consider. What if the image of the executioner does not relate to Varo's personal psychology? What if the image in the dream is an attempt by the archetypal Self to symbolize the way a patriarchy responds to vulnerability at a group level? What if the rape of Carrington and her incarceration in an asylum were motivated and legitimized by the patriarchal group defense against vulnerability? Could the image of Varo's executioner and Carrington's distressed and depotentiated figures in *Down Below* be depictions of the way men in a patriarchy attack and annihilate that which is mysterious and thus beyond their ken and control? If so, Carrington's representations of her time in the asylum and Varo's encounter with the executioner suggest that what is dangerous to patriarchy is a feminine perspective that brings about awareness of oppression and the potential for wholeness and love held symbolically within the arts of cooking, painting, and weaving.

To liberate the gold of the personality from the repressive forces of patriarchy, both Carrington and Varo processed their degradation by destructive external forces in a quest for the sovereignty of the archetypal Self. From a Jungian perspective, destruction is a crucial experience as the ego surrenders to the Self in the death of how it has previously conceived of itself. Few people like this experience, which is often painful and almost always uncomfortable. Psychologically speaking, however, there is a method to the madness. "The experience of the Self," wrote Vladislav Šolc and George Didier,

> is essentially initiatory and transformative. It heralds the initiate into the deeper mysteries of the archetypal underworld where one discovers new aspects of their human identity and myth that seek incarnation. Of course, this brings about the relativization of the ego [and the] death [of the ego's] previously cherished structures. (2018: 201)

If one is "to fully experience the numinosum," Šolc and Didier added,

> one must humbly submit to the power (tremendum) of the inner other, or the holy; or one may be forced to submit by fate. It is in submitting to the Self that one is stripped of grandiose pretenses and opened to the possibility of a new identity. (201)

Seen in Varo's egg and Carrington's woman in blue in her painting *Down Below*, the women's engagement with the imaginal and numinous gave new meaning to their experiences of personal and cultural trauma, and opened the possibility of a transformative, holistic identity.

Regarding the relationship between painting and her psychological evolution, Varo once said of her discovery of Surrealism in Madrid in the 1920s that exposure to paintings, lectures, films, live theater, and the work of Federico García Lorca catalyzed her creative growth. Exposure to surrealist expressions allowed her to put everything she saw and felt into her own creative efforts, furthering a process she called "the initiation of the personality" (as cited in Arcq, 2010: 47). From a personal standpoint, Varo and Carrington painted in a conscious attempt to shape the raw contours of their inner lives, which for both women included more than their fair share of psychological pain and trauma.

For our purposes, there is also meaning in the way in which the relationship between the two artists helped each woman respond to the traumas of Fascism and patriarchy at a cultural level. Their friendship formed an alchemical vessel, like an egg or womb around them, in which the women stimulated, encouraged, and helped each other heal. Both were reborn into a new identity within the crucible of friendship. Friendship gave each woman the support needed to integrate the shadow and its archetypal, numinous aspects, informing their painting as a practice with purpose.

Painting, for Varo, was a search for self-discovery, a female quest to shape a world from the wonder and love that can be extracted from deep suffering. Both Kaplan and art historian Luis-Martín Lozano examined *Souvenir of the Valkyrie*, a 1938 Varo gouache painting on plywood that is virtually unknown and is well outside the fame of Varo's mature works. Varo, in "a rare example" of "making direct reference to a literary episode," titled the painting after

> the woman warriors of Norse mythology and more directly to Brunnhilde, the Valkyrie of Richard Wagner's *Nibelungen Ring*, whose punishment for disobeying the goddess Fricka was to be made a mortal woman and to be "left sleeping on the mountains with a wall of fire around her which only a hero could penetrate."
>
> (Kaplan, 1988: 59)

The image, painted while Varo was living with Perét in France, features an empty white corset laying on its side at the bottom of a well. A weed, or tendril of wild ivy, emerges from the corset, which has been "abandoned in a stark landscape" and is "surrounded by a curving wall of clouds or smoke" (59). The wall of the well, a symbol of protection, or of a boundary marking off the outside world from that which is within, has "begun to melt" (Lozano, 2000: 35). The heads of two women peer above the water-line. "They cannot see, they cannot speak, and they might not breathe" (35). Who are the women? Will they drown in the flood that is coming? With Varo's experience of misogynistic and male-dominated Surrealism in mind, Lozano questioned: "Might this not be a metaphor for subordination?" (35). "One only has to imagine," Lozano reflected,

> what it must have meant for Remedios Varo, as perhaps for Leonora Carrington, to be a woman trying to survive tied to the unchangeable condition of her gender (like a wild weed) and more so, to stand before the intellectual flood of the surrealists' discussions, which at times must have suffocated her and hidden her true identity and potential. (35)

Like Varo, Carrington painted, in part, to protest the manipulation of female imagination and archetypes of the divine Feminine by misogynistic male surrealists and patriarchal cultures determined to demonize women as inhuman monsters. "Men," wrote Sady Doyle, "define humanity, and women, insofar as they are not men, are not human. Thus, women must necessarily be put under male control—and to the extent that we resist this control, we are monstrous" (2019: xiii). "By constructing patriarchy," Doyle explained, "men make monsters: the twisted, slimy, devouring, mutating, massively powerful images of female desire and sexuality and motherhood that take place outside of patriarchy" (xix).

In patriarchy, men are terrified of women, whose bodies give and take "life without permission" (xix). "Fear of women," Doyle wrote, "may be the most important truth of misogyny" (xv).

> Men's dread of this power has given rise to countless, bluntly anatomical nightmares: corrupting uteruses, poisonous blood, women who have slimy, serpentine tails instead of vaginas, or snakelike, elastic jaws that swallow men whole, or "castrated" women whose bodies are open wounds. A monster is a supposed-to-be-subjugated body that has become threatening and voracious—a woman who is, in the most basic sense, out of (men's) control. (xix)

Terrified of women, and of his own disavowed inner feminine, the patriarchal man imagines the female as a monster, a terrorizing primeval force who threatens to bring about the end of the world. "In Greek," Doyle wrote, "*apokálypsis* means 'uncovering,' the revealing of a hidden truth: it means finding something powerful and important buried underneath what we think we know" (xx).

In revealing hidden truth, gestating transformative connections in her body and her work, Carrington, like Varo, painted not only for herself but for the benefit of others. As expressions of archetypal Feminine forces pressing for purchase and embodiment in human affairs, Carrington's paintings, wrote Gloria Orenstein, "become talismans and amulets bearing special powers designed to unlock hidden energies in the viewer" (as cited in Warlick, 2017: para. 3). Presumably, these hidden energies are ones needed to unmake a patriarchal power structure that inflicts upon women what Doyle called "the daily, grinding violence of subservience and loss of self" (2019: 108).

With all of this being said, we can consider the paintings of Varo and Carrington not only as works of art and as symbolic representations of inner processes of growth and transformation, but also as pieces of propaganda intended to expose and transform the ubiquitous presence of injurious psychological complexes at work on a cultural level. Through our amplifications, we endeavor, as Jung suggested, to illuminate the dynamics of the complexes not by imagining figures of light, but by making the darkness conscious (1954/1967: para. 335). In alchemical psychology, this means a return to the beginning, to the blackening.

This is precisely where Varo's dream of the executioner takes us: into the underworld, where we are invited to take part in an intimate engagement with death. Part of what the image of the executioner seems to be saying is that death is the first part of birthing new life. Put psychologically: coming into the light requires learning to see in the dark. Following a section on the *nigredo* in his essay "The Seduction of Black," Hillman observed that "the two [alchemical] processes most relevant for producing blackness—putrefaction and mortification—break down the inner cohesion of any fixed state" (2010: 88). In this process, the conscious suffering of the rot and shame produced by the projective defenses of the patriarchy creates a blackening that "breaks the paradigm; it dissolves whatever we rely upon as real and dear. Its negative force deprives consciousness of its dependable and comforting notions of goodness" (88). "By deconstructing presence into absence," Hillman reflected, "the *nigredo* makes possible psychological change. Each moment of blackening is a harbinger of alteration, of invisible discovery, and of dissolution of attachments to whatever has been taken as truth and reality, solid fact, or dogmatic virtue" (89). The eye, made dark and sophisticated by the *nigredo*, sees through what is literal to what is mythological and imaginal. "Thus, black often becomes the color of dress for the underworld, urban sophisticates, and the old who have seen a lot" (89).

Notes

1 Kaplan quoted Rich from the poem "Re-forming the Crystal," in *Poems: Selected and New, 1950–1974* (1975; New York, NY: Norton).
2 From Sabina Spielrein's essay "Destruction as the cause of coming into being" (*The Journal of Analytical Psychology, 39*[2], 155–86).

References

Aberth, S. (2010). *Leonora Carrington: Surrealism, alchemy and art*. Burlington, VT: Lund Humphries.
Arcq, T. (2010). Mirrors of the marvellous: Leonora Carrington and Remedios Varo (M. Suderman, Trans.). In S. Begley (Ed.), *Surreal Friends* (98–115). Burlington, VT: Humphries.
Assa, S. (1991). Gardens of delight, or what's cookin'? Leonora Carrington in the kitchen. *Studies in 20th Century Literature, 15*(2), 213–27.
Berland, R. (2010). Remedios Varo's Mexican drawings. *Journal of Surrealism and the Americas, 4*(1), 31–42.
Carrington, L. (1944/1988a). *Down Below* (K. Talbot & M. Warner, Trans.). New York, NY: New York Review of Books.
Carrington, L. (1944/1988b). *The house of fear: Notes from down below* (K. Talbot & M. Warner, Trans.). New York, NY: E. P. Dutton.
Carrington, L. (1988). *The seventh horse and other tales* (K. Talbot & M. Warner, Trans.). New York, NY: E. P. Dutton.
Chadwick, W. (1991). *Leonora Carrington: The Mexican years*. Albuquerque, NM: University of New Mexico Press.

Doyle, S. (2019). *Dead blondes and bad mothers: Monstrosity, patriarchy, and the fear of female power*. Brooklyn, NY: Melville House.

Gilligan, C., & Snider, N. (2018). *Why does patriarch persist?* Medford, MA: Polity Press.

Hillman, J. (2010). *Alchemical psychology*. Putman, CT: Spring Publications.

Jung, C. G. (1954/1967). The philosophical tree (R. F. C. Hull, Trans.). In H. Read et al. (Eds.), *The collected works of C. G. Jung* (Vol. 13, 251–349). Princeton, NJ: Princeton University Press.

Jung, C. G. (1937/1968). Religious ideas in alchemy (R. F. C. Hull, Trans.). In H. Read et al. (Eds.), *The collected works of C. G. Jung* (Vol. 12, 2nd ed., 225–483). Princeton, NJ: Princeton University Press.

Jung, C. G. (1943/1968). Introduction to the religious and psychological problems of alchemy (R. F. C. Hull, Trans.). In H. Read et al. (Eds.), *The collected works of C. G. Jung* (Vol. 12, 2nd ed., 1–38). Princeton, NJ: Princeton University Press.

Jung, C. G. (1955–56/1970). *Mysterium coniunctionis* (R. F. C. Hull, Trans.) (H. Read et al., Eds.), *The collected works of C. G. Jung* (Vol. 14, 2nd ed.). Princeton, NJ: Princeton University Press.

Kaplan, J. (1988). *Unexpected journeys: The art and life of Remedios Varo*. New York, NY: Abbeville Press.

Kimbles, S. (2000). The cultural complex and the myth of invisibility. In T. Singer (Ed.), *The vision thing: Myth, politics and psyche in the world* (157–69). New York, NY: Routledge.

Lozano, L-M. (2000). *The magic of Remedios Varo* (E. Goldson & L. Valenzuela, Trans.). Washington DC: National Museum of Women in the Arts.

Mather, M. (2014). *The alchemical Mercurius: Esoteric symbol of Jung's life and works*. New York, NY: Routledge.

Moorhead, J. (2017). *The surreal life of Leonora Carrington*. London, UK: Virago.

Poniatowska, E. (2011/2015). *Leonora: A novel* (A. Hopkinson, Trans.). London, UK: Profile Books.

Šolc, V., & Didier, G. (2018). *Dark religion: Fundamentalism from the perspective of Jungian psychology*. Asheville, NC: Chiron.

Suleiman, S. R. (1990). *Subversive intent: Gender, politics, and the avant-garde*. Cambridge, MA: Harvard University Press.

Varo, R. (1997/2018). *Letters, dreams & other writings* (M. Carson, Trans.). Cambridge, MA: Wakefield Press.

Warlick, M. E. (2017). Leonora Carrington's esoteric symbols and their sources. *Studia Hermetica Journal*, *VII*(5). Retrieved from portfolio.du.edu/mwarlick/page/65131a

Winslow, A. (2017). Down below—Leonora Carrington [Book review]. *Full Stop*. Retrieved from www.full-stop.net/2017/05/02/reviews/aaron-winslow/down-below-leonora-carrington/

Chapter 11

Breaking out

Varo, Carrington, and blackening the patriarchal paradigm

Remedios Varo and Leonora Carrington are hardly old people when life hurts them deeply. In the preceding pages, we have reflected on the transformation and healing that painting, as a spiritual practice and as a depth psychological form of active imagination, brought to each woman's life and art. Now, we shift and widen our gaze. Jung believed that we gather the world to ourselves when we face our shadow and attend to dreams and other workings of unconscious life (1954/1969: para. 432). What happens if we apply this foundational Jungian idea to the creative work of Carrington and Varo?

The Terrible Mother and the voice of the eternal Feminine

With cultural complexes related to patriarchal power in mind, the images painted by Carrington and Varo can be considered as living symbols midwifed by the archetypal forces of the transpersonal psyche in a symbolic effort to begin the blackening of the patriarchal paradigm. In such a context, the suffering the women endured in their personal histories acquires teleological meaning and finds both the keyhole and the key to breaking out of a paradigm that traps women and men in a "deeply flawed" democracy in which "basic rights of intimate life are in political peril, issues of racial and gender inequality persist, and economic inequality worsens" (Gilligan & Richards, 2009: 11).

Returning to Varo's creative and symbolic use of the myth of Theseus and the Minotaur, we see in her painting, *Minotaur*, that she has rendered a different image, bringing out of the labyrinth the male's shamed and split-off inner feminine, experienced by men through projection as monstrous and devouring. The distorted perception of women as devouring has terrified men who fear their own inner feminine throughout human history. Folk tales from multiple cultures offer stories of the *vagina dentata*. From the Latin meaning *toothed vagina*, old stories of the vagina dentata evoke the lethality of women, whose genital opening is said to contain teeth—the perfect implements for castration of the man's penis and testicles and for the annihilation of his masculine core (in part through the elimination of the ability to produce semen). Some of the folk tales of the vagina dentata may have been told to discourage rape. In others, the image of the vagina dentata seems to express a feminine archetypal rage at male domination of women and a violent patriarchal response to that rage. Erich Neumann mentioned a folk tale that told of a fish who lives in the vagina of a Terrible Mother. "The hero," according to Neumann, "is the man who overcomes the Terrible Mother, breaks the teeth out of her vagina, and so makes her into a woman" (1955/1963: 168).

With her image of the Minotaur, Varo dissolved the projection onto women of the unconscious distress of the shamed male and his fear of dismemberment by the presence of the inner, archetypal Feminine—Neumann's Terrible Mother. Varo began this psychological process in *Dead Leaves* by withdrawing from the labyrinth of the unconscious the blue thread of imagination that led the heroic male, Theseus, to the Minotaur. In her painting, Varo reveals the Minotaur she has drawn out from the labyrinth as the numinous Feminine. Her *Minotaur* is female, with the bluish light of the *imaginatio* radiating from the crown of her head.

In the artist's painting, behind the once monstrous but now reborn and redeemed creature, there is a keyhole in a black crack in the wall of a small room. In the female Minotaur's right hand is a key. With the key that fits into the keyhole, Varo seems to suggest the alchemical intercourse between the archetypal Feminine and Masculine. The union, or inner marriage, of these different but complementary forces turns out to be crucial to Varo's vision of a world where cultural complexes can be softened, and men and women liberated from adversarial roles as combatants in a war between sexes. Varo's vision, hinted at in her painting of a female Minotaur, is for the making of a world in which men and women—accessing within themselves the Feminine, Masculine, and Other—work together as conscious collaborators to nourish the soul of all beings and the cosmos in which life unfolds. From a Jungian perspective, the message Varo is sending us through her imagery seems clear enough: The Feminine holds the key to the re-making of the starting condition, which must be freed from traumatic suppression and repression of external and internalized patriarchal influences.

Gilligan and Richards cited trauma research that clearly identified "loss of voice as the psychic core of traumatic experience, an inability to tell one's story" (2009: 165). They found this traumatic core of female experience, in which patriarchal demands silence the female voice, embedded in the Freudian origins of depth psychology, typically marked by the publication of *The Interpretation of Dreams* in 1900. In *The Deepening Darkness: Patriarchy, Resistance, and Democracy's Future*, Gilligan and Richards examined "Freud's increasingly fraught relationship to women patients" (168). In his early work, "Freud had come to astonishing discoveries about the human psyche and invented a method to unravel its secrets, a method that freed women ... to know and to say what they knew" (166). As he developed psychoanalysis, Freud

> not only listened carefully and responsively to what women said in free association but also accorded them ultimate authority in the process of discovering the conflicts underlying their neurotic symptoms, thus undoing the initiation that had led them to substitute a father's [patriarchal] voice for their own. (166)

Over time, according to Gilligan and Richards, Freud's initial sensitivity to women faltered as he disavowed his "unmanly" sensibilities for relationality and "deep human sympathy" in a bid for recognition within the field of psychiatry (Freud, as cited in Gilligan & Richards, 2009: 166). At the expense of his female patients and the countless women whose treatment he influenced, Freud sought success in a societal structure that responds to vulnerability with misogynistic superiority and ruthless subjugation of anything that threatens "the fundamental rule of patriarchy: the claim on the part of the father to authority" (2009: 162).

For a time, Freud had attuned himself to bringing women back in touch with parts of their experience that had become dissociated, that is, held apart from consciousness. However, faced with numerous unresolved issues, including the death of his father, Freud, a son traumatized by loss, shifted course dramatically. Once devoted to connecting women with their own knowledge, Freud began to ignore, and thus mute, the voice of his female patients. As Gilligan and Richards observed, "We hear him discrediting women's experience and overriding their claims to knowledge with his own" (2009: 168).

What was it about women's hysteria that threatened an androcentric society? "The most common symptom of hysteria, the loss of voice, carries the political message: I have been silenced" (Gilligan & Richards, 2009: 177). Society, led by the field of psychology, responded punitively and self-protectively to the psyche's distress at having been silenced, imprisoning women involuntarily in asylums—now not only the voices but also their bodies removed, gone. In patriarchy, Doyle wrote, "female sexuality can exist only with male permission, in answer to male need, and in fact, female desire is so inherently subversive that it's best to just pretend it doesn't exist" (2019: 78).

Psychologically, Gilligan and Richards concluded,

> The riddle of femininity in patriarchy ... arises from the confusing perception that to be a good woman in patriarchy, a woman must become

selfless: She must sacrifice her voice for the sake of relationship—a sacrifice that poses a nonsense riddle because psychologically it cannot be solved. Without voice, one is not present; there is no relationship, only the chimera of relationship. The human desire for relationship becomes in itself an act of resistance to loss of voice, meaning to trauma. (2009: 168)

All of this means, as Jean Baker Miller asserted, that "women, by *their very existence*, confront and challenge men because they have been made *the embodiment of the dominant culture's unsolved problems*" (1986: 58, emphasis in original). At the same time, women struggle with the introjected presence of the patriarchy—as internalized strictures that both protect their sociopsychological survival and persecute the inner voice that would threaten it. When, as women, Miller concluded,

we can think only in terms given by the dominant culture and when that culture not only does not attend to our own experiences but specifically denies and devalues them, we are left with no way of conceptualizing our lives. Under these circumstances, a woman is often left with a global, undefined sense that she must be wrong. (58)

What does Freud's capitulation to patriarchy and the silencing and devaluing of women and feminine relationality have to do with the friendship between Remedios Varo and Leonora Carrington? For the two women, friendship formed a space in which they could each receive acceptance and healing through embodied experiences of being seen, heard, and known by the other person. Neither woman would have called herself an activist. Varo and Carrington both considered themselves artists. By whatever name they identified, their friendship and their art offered the women a way to find and use the female voice to produce images that speak volumes about women's experience and the numinous and mysterious powers of goddesses and other Feminine forces.

Did the artists intend their painted images as protests against "cultural forces that attack, demean, and silence women" (Gilligan & Snider, 2018: 84)? We do not know if the artists were conscious protestors of patriarchy. What we *do* know is that Varo and Carrington were artists who studied and experimented with the numinous power of symbols to channel and express living archetypal energy. Consciously or unconsciously, then, the women made art that serves symbolic and subversive social purposes. In this way, Gilligan and Richards noted, the women were fulfilling an archetypal imperative: "Since patriarchy rests on a suppression of voice and a rewriting of history, artists can perform the vital function of speaking the truth and shifting the framework" (2009: 198).

Woman Leaving the Psychoanalyst: Challenging the authority of the father

Varo depicted the female quest to break free from patriarchy in *Woman Leaving the Psychoanalyst*, a composition the artist completed in 1961.

In the painting, a woman wearing a green cloak walks through a cobblestoned courtyard. In her right hand, the woman carries a basket filled with what Varo described as "psychological waste" (1997/2018: 109). With her left thumb and forefinger, the woman holds the severed and shrunken head of a man upside-down by the hairs of a long, tapered, beard. The movement implied in the image suggests that the woman is about to drop the man's egg-shaped head into a small well set at ground level in the stonework of the courtyard.

Symbolically, a detail in the background of the painting is important to the message Varo is trying to send in the painting. Behind the woman, on

Figure 11.1 Woman Leaving the Psychoanalyst, Remedios Varo, oil on canvas, 1961. © Artists Rights Society (ARS), New York. Photo credit: Private Collection, Christie's Images/Bridgeman Images.

the wall in a doorway, is a plaque bearing the letters *FJA*. "As a surrealist painter," wrote Jacquelyn Yvonne White, "Varo was greatly influenced by ... psychoanalysis and the development of the connection between the conscious and unconscious mind" (2014: 28). Given Varo's interest in and dedication to engaging with unconscious forces, the letters on the plaque clearly point to Sigmund Freud, C. G. Jung, and Alfred Adler, the three founding fathers of depth psychology.

In her essay on Varo for Syracuse University, White suggested that Varo's painting symbolized the artist's attempt to liberate herself from the authority of the patriarchal power at the head of her own family: her father, Rodrigo. In the painting of the woman leaving the office of her "shrink," the small ghostly head of a man symbolizes the reduction of "an unhealthy relationship, which is one of the many things that are affecting the woman psychologically" (White, 2014: 29). The issues troubling the woman have been exposed in her visit to the psychoanalyst; as she leaves his office, a symbol of the dominion of the patriarch over the female, the woman "is able to remove it from her basket of troubles" and lower one of the veils that had been concealing her true nature (30).

With these insights in mind, White implied that Varo's image of a woman dropping the head of a man into a well is a multivalent symbol referring to the artist's father, to three of her psychological fathers, to patriarchal male authority in general. The dropped head refers to the attempt of the woman, as a projected version of Varo herself, to leave all these influences behind as she walks boldly, even defiantly, "in search of her independence" (White, 2014: 29). White further explored Varo's cultural experience as a woman who chafed under the lack of agency granted by patriarchal power structures in Spain:

> The symbolism in tossing away the head of a man becomes even more powerful when Varo's Spanish background is taken into account. During the twentieth century, the traditional Spanish family was patriarchal. In Varo's own family, the head of the household would have been her father. The life of a woman was ultimately controlled by her father until she married, when the power was transferred to her husband. By tossing her father's head into the well, the woman in the painting is metaphorically breaking free of the restraints put on her by a patriarchal society. (29)

In a similar vein, Carrington, in the painting *Down Below*, located her distressed figures and the blue-gowned, winged woman who brings hope into the picture outside the gates of—rather than within—the asylum that looms in the background. These acts of separation from patriarchal forces are essential to a woman's ability to know herself from a non-patriarchal perspective. Assigned inferior status by patterns of male domination, Varo and Carrington needed to break free of "the dominant ethic," which as Jean Baker Miller highlighted, "often induces women to view themselves and their own attempts to know, and act on their needs—or to enlarge their lives beyond the prescribed bounds—as either attacking men or trying to be like them" (1986: 17).

In the context of the synergistic and catalyzing nature of the relationship between the two artists, we notice that the imagery in *Woman Leaving the Psychoanalyst* also tracks into the mythological terrain of the patriarchy that underlies the foundations of psychoanalysis. "For Varo," Kaplan wrote, "dropping the father was a reversal of the traditional Oedipal drama that was the stock in trade of the male surrealists, as seen in such work as Dalí's *The Enigma of Desire: My Mother, my Mother, my Mother*" (1998: 115). Rejecting the myth of the daughter's penis envy and desire for the father, Varo defiantly has her female character leave behind the edifice of a patriarchal psychology, with the head of male authority cut off and discarded as psychological waste.

Mythologically, the painted scene can also be extended to suggest a reversal of the psychoanalytic interpretation of the story of Electra, who, in love with her father the King, conspired to murder her mother in revenge for his death. Turning the story on its head frees women from the patriarchal myth in which women devalue the Feminine and their own creative source in favor of the Masculine as King and keeper of the dominant order.

A feminist Surrealism

Multilayered in the "defiance of established authority" with which Varo imbued her art, *Woman Leaving the Psychoanalyst* also may have been Varo's way of asserting independence from the patriarchal influences that pervaded Surrealism (Agosin, 1998: 19). According to Kaplan, the painting of the woman who leaves the psychoanalyst's office conveys Varo's conflicted relationship with Surrealism, an artform grounded in Freudian psychology.

> Although she embraced the revolutionary energy of Surrealism, saying "Surrealism has contributed to art in the same way that psychoanalysis has contributed to the exploration of the subconscious," Varo's work is marked by an ironic, even taunting, ambivalence toward Surrealistic theory and practice.
>
> (Kaplan, 1998: 115)

In her essay "Subversive Strategies: The Work of Remedios Varo," Kaplan observed that, by dropping the shrunken head of the man into the well in her painting, Varo was externalizing her inner need to differentiate from the openly misogynistic men whose gender afforded them the authority to limit gifted women artists like herself and Carrington to the role of muses.

Their autonomy, creativity, and agency as artists in and of themselves was dismissed, and they were seen solely as agents of inspiration for the male artists.

> Key to Surrealist theory, which devoted considerable energy to defining the role of Woman in the creative process, was the image of the *femme-infant*, the naive woman-child whose spontaneous innocence, uncorrupted by logic or reason, brings her into closer contact with the intuitive realm of the unconscious. In thus equating woman's creativity with youth and innocence, Surrealist theory left little room for maturity or motherhood or the aging process among the women artists in the group. (1998: 121)

In the face of such virulent misogyny, it is "not surprising," Kaplan noted, "that Varo was able to produce her most significant mature work only years after leaving the circle of Surrealists in Paris" (122). Varo, Kaplan added,

> needed significant distance from its polemics and pronouncements, especially its limiting definitions of women, before being able to develop her own vocabulary of images and meanings. In refusing the position of *femme enfant, femme fatale*, god[d]ess, or muse offered to women by Surrealist theory... Varo created a series of images in which her female characters exhibit significant courage and engage in solitary acts of daring. (122)

For Varo, *Woman Leaving the Psychoanalyst* was one such daring imaginal act. For the artist, the painting functioned as a profound and impactful ritual, an "assertion of independence" that was "crucial to self discovery" (Kaplan, 1998: 116). In her painting, Varo engaged in a visual and artistic process of self-analysis. The artist's alchemical self-treatment could hardly have been more successful based on the symbolic evidence we see in the image: Analysis of the unconscious shrinks the toxic authority of the father and enlarges the woman's sense of her own worth and well-being.

In her artistic revolt against patriarchal surrealist doctrine, Varo engaged a variety of techniques. One of her favorites, Kaplan said, "was to employ surrealist techniques but use them at cross-purposes to Surrealist intention" (1998: 116). In a number of her works, Varo featured a technique called *decalcomania*, a surrealist practice

> of blotting paint to achieve accidental effects, as in the woodland landscape, grassy carpet and trees of *Solar Music* (1955). But [when] ... she employed this technique, the chance patterns served merely as a starting point from which to elaborate highly-detailed, controlled and

pre-planned images. Turning surrealist technique against itself, she invited only chance to control it. (116)

In turning the tables on doctrine set down and enforced by male artists, Varo distinguished her alchemical, artistic, and psychological process from the one-sided surrealist preoccupation with the autonomy of the unconscious. Kaplan offered a prose example of the way Varo worked to both spoof and honor her surrealist roots:

> In a deadpan letter penned into her sketchbook, Varo took aim at Surrealism's vaunted allegiance to the concept of psychic automatism that was seen as the perfect method for releasing art from the conscious control of its maker. Writing as though addressing an unknown psychiatrist chosen randomly from the phonebook, Varo described a traumatic confrontation with automatic images. (116)

Varo wrote the letter in French, a language she learned in Paris. By using the native tongue of Surrealism (translated by Kaplan), Varo attempted to "lampoon" a cherished piece of theory:

> Monsieur, Permit me to write to you … my distress is great… It began six months ago. I was enthusiastically painting a scene with a lovely prairie, some sheep, some cows walking serenely … but then … an irresistible force pushed me to put a little ladder on the back of each sheep … and some piles of well-folded handkerchiefs on the cows … I hid this painting and began others but I always felt it necessary to introduce unexpected elements … until the day I accidentally spilled some tomato sauce on my pants and found this stain so moving that I quickly cut the piece of fabric and framed it … Is [this] a sudden triggering of my subconscious mind that wishes to free itself … or am I simply crazy?
> (as cited in Kaplan, 1998: 116–7)

Kaplan added that, "in this delicious spoof," Varo

> found a way to simultaneously mock, trivialize, and, yet tenderly honor, this basic tenet of Surrealist practice. This was often her stance. She did not reject Surrealism. Rather, hers was a "double allegiance" that valued the Surrealists' "subversive/parodic energy" while critiquing many of its attitudes. Her critique was particularly pointed around issues related to women. (117)

In particular, in her portrayal of the female writer's silliness, Varo directed a spoofing critique at surrealists' trivializing and dismissive attitude toward women. "Among Varo's contributions to Surrealism," Kaplan concluded, was a new vision of creativity with woman as active subject rather than passive object or catalytic muse for the creativity of others. She offered an alternative iconography specifically counter to traditional male-defined Surrealist theory in which the revolutionary power of Eros uses Woman as a conduit for Man. Varo's work, instead, is based on woman's psychology and experiences in which her access to the marvelous relies on the self as active agent without need for erotic displacement. (117)

Both Varo's and Carrington's brand of female-centered Surrealism moved beyond the autonomy of the unconscious, reaching into and through personal and cultural complexes toward transformation, wholeness, and healing in partnership with presences, images, and energies arising from the unconscious realm of the psyche. This opened the door for their articulation as women of the authentic Feminine, human wholeness, and the cosmic forces that indwell it and in which it dwells. For both women, the practice of symbolic alchemy through painting helped them make a multifaceted break from the psychological prison of the patriarchy.

Exposing the big con and the project of female empowerment

Late in her life, Leonora Carrington told art historian Whitney Chadwick that childhood and other experiences opened her eyes to what she called " 'the big con job,' meaning the historical suppression of all versions of history that did not serve the needs of those in power. And this suppression has included denying the rights previously exercised by women in many early cultures" (as cited in Chadwick, 1998: 102).

"Influenced by Jung's search for archetypal meaning," Carrington, like Varo, painted to evoke the presence and power of "female knowledge ... that bypassed book learning and enabled the expression of powerful states of feeling—in which women were especially adept" (Chadwick, 1998: 105, 107). "The presence of images of female power and authority in much of Carrington's work," Chadwick wrote,

> has been interpreted as evidence of her gynocentric vision, as part of a symbolic landscape, the specific images of which can be "decoded" and reconstituted as a symbolic mapping of feminine creative power. To some extent this is true, but it may be too simple an explanation for what happens here. Deeply committed to the search to recover a universal feminine archetype as a source of inspiration and creativity, Carrington remains convinced that the female images circulating today—whether produced by women or men—are largely the invention of men. She sees "a powerful female force rising" but warns against what she calls "vulgarizing interpretations," believing that to name a power is inevitably

to reconstruct it in patriarchal terms for that is the only language we possess. (105–6)

Varo, for her part, was also determined to paint from a place that produced images of female empowerment. "Although many of the characters in Varo's paintings are androgynous or asexual," Kaplan wrote,

> in these mythological transformations she was careful to delineate the female anatomy of her heroines. Thus transferring power across gender lines and conferring heroic authority on women, Varo sets her work in opposition to the circumscribed limits to women's sphere articulated by orthodox Surrealist theory. (1998: 117)

Wherever they found it, in themselves and their histories, in Jungian depth psychology, alchemy, and Surrealism, and in the larger world happening around them, Carrington and Varo were drawing on the archetypal Feminine to paint their way out of the prison of patriarchy.

References

Agosin, M. (1998). Introduction. In M. Agosin (Ed.), *A woman's gaze: Latin American women artists* (9–26). Fredonia, NY: White Pine Press.

Chadwick, W. (1998). Leonora Carrington: Visual narrative in contemporary Mexican art. In M. Agosin (Ed.), *A woman's gaze: Latin American women artists* (97–109). Fredonia, NY: White Pine Press.

Doyle, S. (2019). *Dead blondes and bad mothers: Monstrosity, patriarchy, and the fear of female power.* Brooklyn, NY: Melville House.

Gilligan, C., & Richards, D. (2009). *Deepening Darkness: Patriarchy, resistance, and democracy's future.* Cambridge, NY: Cambridge University Press.

Gilligan, C., & Snider, N. (2018). *Why does patriarch persist?* Medford, MA: Polity Press.

Jung, C. G. (1954/1969). On the nature of the psyche (R. F. C. Hull, Trans.). In H. Read et al. (Eds.), *The collected works of C. G. Jung* (Vol. 8, 2nd ed., 114–25). Princeton, NJ: Princeton University Press.

Kaplan, J. (1998). Subversive strategies: The work of Remedios Varo. In M. Agosin (Ed.), *A woman's gaze: Latin American women artists* (110–28). Fredonia, NY: White Pine Press.

Miller, J. B. (1986). *Toward a new psychology of women.* Boston, MA: Beacon.

Neumann, E. (1955/1963). *The great mother* (R. Mannheim, Trans.). Princeton, NJ: Princeton University Press.

Varo, R. (1997/2018). *Letters, dreams & other writings* (M. Carson, Trans.). Cambridge, MA: Wakefield Press.

White, Y. (2014). The surrealist woman: The art of Remedios Varo. *Syracuse University Honors Program Capstone Projects.* 744. Retrieved from surface.syr.edu/honors_capstone/744

Chapter 12

In the footsteps of Virginia Woolf

Humiliated Manhood and the re-visioning of the Feminine

Janet Kaplan noted that from the time of her first solo exhibition at the Galería Diana in Mexico City in the mid-1950s, Varo could not finish paintings fast enough to accommodate the waiting list of patrons wanting to own her images (1998: 112). Kaplan attributed the appeal of Varo's work in her adopted country to her status as a foreigner who painted "on the margins" of the Mexican culture in which she lived for the last two decades of her life (110–1). Kaplan differentiated Varo "as a foreign female easel painter, producing diminutive and highly detailed work," from muralists such as Diego Rivera who produced the large-scale works that had dominated Mexican art for decades (113). "Varo was positioned outside prevailing trends of Mexican artistic production" (113). Unlike the difficulties of being female in a misogynistic patriarchy, in the case of painting, marginalization proved to be an important supporting factor, not a hindrance, to the intense appeal art patrons felt for Varo's work. "Rather than undercutting the power of Varo's work, however, her positioning as an outsider can be seen as a source of her strength, her work embodying strategies of renegotiation through which both style and content become subversive sites of resistance" (111). Varo's mature work, with its "intimate tableaux," Kaplan wrote,

> invites us into a fantastic universe in which properties of the organic and inorganic, the scientific and the magical, the natural and the technological, interchange and overlap. Peopled by owl artists, insect geologists, wood nymph musicians and enchanted astronomers, it is a world that challenges preconceived assumptions about how things ought to work. (112)

A woman's war: Woolf, words, and the will to power

For art historian Linda Nochin, the visual alchemy of Varo and Carrington assumed a critical role in pushing back against the presence and power of a patriarchal paradigm that thwarts the agency of women and the feminine (as cited in Agosin, 1998: 10). With paintings that call forth the feminine and protest the pitfalls to women of patriarchy, Varo and Carrington travel in a terrain mapped by other women, including Virginia Woolf, who wrote novels and nonfiction pieces intended to express radical feminist ideas and "to expose the patriarchal roots of fascist violence" (Gilligan & Richards, 2009: 215).

Although language can be considered a form of image, the potent weapon Woolf brought to the feminist fight against patriarchy was her mind. In Spain, Germany, and Italy in the 1930s, "what Woolf came to see," wrote Gilligan and Richards, was "that the aggressive violence of Fascism was rooted in humiliated manhood" (2009: 215). For Woolf, misogyny was a will-to-power crusade that epitomized the patriarchal male fear of the shame, vulnerability, and defenselessness associated with women and the feminine and the resulting need to project unconscious powerlessness onto others through domination and annihilation.

How much can one creative woman do to change something so big, so unwieldy, and so entrenched, as patriarchy? "Woolf's idea," wrote Jane Marcus, a feminist literary scholar, "was that the gender issue was inseparable from the buildup to war and the power of Fascism to rule the state" (2006: xxxvi). Scholar Mark Hussey studied Woolf's evolution from writer to feminist icon. In his preface to *Three Guineas*, Woolf's 1938 book-length essay on war and women, Hussey wrote:

> As the political situation in Europe in the 1930s moved inexorably to its crisis in 1939, Woolf began to collect newspaper clippings about the relations between the sexes in England, France, Germany, and Italy. The scrapbooks she made became the matrix from which developed the perspectives of her penultimate novel, *The Years* (1937), and the arguments of her *Three Guineas* (1938). (2005: xvi)

An early feminist, Woolf used words and ideas to fight her personal war against patriarchy. "Thinking was her fighting," Marcus said (2006: xli). "By writing," Woolf claimed, "I am doing what is far more necessary than anything else" (as cited in Marcus, 2006: xli). *Three Guineas*, Woolf's "ferocious" political pamphlet, stands as "paramount in its verbally aggressive attacks on the enemies of peace and the origins of war in patriarchy" (xli, lvii).

Like Varo and Carrington, Woolf understood the collective roots of personal suffering. Woolf wrote *Three Guineas* as both a public protest against the economic domination of women by men and as a private lament over the death of her nephew in the Spanish Civil War. Expressing her rage, Woolf at one point targeted the sexism of the Third Reich: "There are two worlds in the life of a nation," she wrote, citing Adolph Hitler, "the world of men and the world of women. Nature has done well to entrust the man with the care of his family and the nation. The woman's world is her family, her husband, her children, and her home" (as cited in Woolf, 1966: 65). Woolf chafed at the subordinating violence patriarchy inflicted on women. "In naming [*Three Guineas*] for the coins minted with [Britain's] proceeds from African slavery, Woolf invests her text with outrage at the exploits of English imperialists and makes the connection between race, capitalism, and patriarchy" (Marcus, 2006: xliii).

For Virginia Woolf, social change came at a cost. Late in March 1941, the writer who had once appeared on the cover of *Time* magazine filled her overcoat with rocks and walked into the River Ouse behind her house in Sussex.[1] The word *patriarchy* did not appear in the writer's obituary or published biographical accounts as contributing to her death. But, according to Woolf's husband, Leonard, "the general strain" of a war financed and fought by patriarchal fascist forces had helped to wear away his wife's spirit to the point where drowning herself in the river seemed the only way to end unbearable suffering (as cited in Oldfield, 2005: xx–xxi).

The difference a friendship made

Turning from the experience of Virginia Woolf back toward our engagement with the life and art of Remedios Varo and her friendship with Leonora Carrington, we wonder: Did Varo reach a similar place in her life? What was it like for this woman artist to carry on making images meant as medicine, as artistic antidotes to personal pain but also to what Woolf called the poison of patriarchy? As seen in Varo's weaving of the egg in the dream of the executioner and her final self-portrait in *Still Life Reviving*, Varo's life and work arrived at an opus of love and creativity that left her with a peaceful acceptance of her death. Still, we might wonder, was Varo getting ready to die, giving away sacred items and other belongings, in part because she felt worn down by the weight of living in a patriarchal world defined and dominated by the disavowed vulnerability of men? During those times when she would withdraw from the world, did Varo question the value, meaning, and impact of what she was doing with her life? Poet, art critic, and curator Edward Lucie-Smith pinpointed some of what we know about the Spanish painter's experience:

> The meticulous paintings she produced during the last ten years of her life demonstrate her interest in the occult and in alchemy, and often contain hints of the alienation she felt as a woman trying to make a place for herself as a woman in a man's world. (1993: 102)

For Varo and Carrington, the ability to creatively endure and address the trauma and alienation they experienced was cooked and nourished in the cauldron of their friendship. "Leonora ... never regarded her relationship with Remedios as collaborative or twin-like: for her, it was about sharing ideas, and she reveled in their common way of looking at the world and dealing with it," as well as their "common vision of how life could be. And what that came down to, more than anything, was a belief in their own autonomy" (Moorhead, 2017: 218).

Remedios Varo and Leonora Carrington had met for the first time in Paris, home ground to Surrealism, late in the 1930s. The women met again in Mexico City in 1942. At the time, Carrington was still reeling from her torment in the mental hospital in Spain. Varo, of course, had endured confinement in a French prison camp. In Mexico City, the archetypal forces that tore the world apart now brought Varo and Carrington back together. This time, the women were determined to live, heal, and paint. "Their marriages," Moorhead wrote, "though an important part of their lives, never overwhelmed them: neither the high points or the low points, the romance or the rows, were ever allowed to become too absorbing or distracting" (2017: 219). Each artist, Moorhead added,

> saw marriage in a way that is more common among men than women: it was part of their lives, but it had its discrete space, and it could not and would not impinge on the part of them that was dedicated to ideas and art. (219)

During the years of their friendship in Mexico City, Varo and Carrington worked alchemically and artistically to challenge patriarchal "mechanisms that silence women" (Beard, 2017: xi). The artists were barking up a tall tree. For these mechanisms, writes feminist Mary Beard, have been "deeply embedded in Western culture" for "thousands of years" (xi). As we have seen, painting, for each artist, grew from the ground of alchemical, psychological, and spiritual practices of personal growth, and from a willingness to engage as individuals in the shifting of cultural complexes that perpetuate misogyny and male domination. The women were also working in their intimate heterosexual relationships to reposition the voice of women and the Feminine. By refusing to accept the inferiority of women in their relationships with men, Varo and Carrington were re-shaping a rigid gender dynamic in both personal and public ways. The women, as artists and wives, rejected the androcentric status quo in favor of transformational ways of being that highlighted female autonomy and empowerment. Like bread from an oven, Varo and Carrington gave birth in Mexico City to a brand of feminism that served friends and family and nourished an alchemical transformation of patriarchal culture toward the embrace of women and the Feminine.

Note

1 Woolf appeared on the cover of *Time Magazine* on April 12, 1937. The cover story, a review of her novel, *The Years*, had a scathing patriarchal tone: "She has

no children. Careless of her clothes, her face, her greying hair, at 55 she is the picture of a sensitive, cloistered literary woman."

References

Agosin, M. (1998). Introduction. In M. Agosin (Ed.), *A woman's gaze: Latin American women artists* (9–26). Fredonia, NY: White Pine Press.

Beard, M. (2017). *Women & power: A manifesto*. New York, NY and London, UK: W. W. Norton & Company.

Gilligan, C., & Richards, D. (2009). *Deepening Darkness: Patriarchy, resistance, and democracy's future*. Cambridge, NY: Cambridge University Press.

Hussey, M. (2005). Preface: Virginia Woolf. In M. Hussey (Ed.), *Three Guineas: Virginia Woolf* (ix–xviii). Orlando, FL: Harcourt.

Kaplan, J. (1998). Subversive strategies: The work of Remedios Varo. In M. Agosin (Ed.), *A woman's gaze: Latin American women artists* (110–28). Fredonia, NY: White Pine Press.

Lucie-Smith, E. (1993). *Latin American art of the 20th century*. London, UK: Thames & Hudson.

Marcus, J. (2006). Introduction. In M. Hussey (Ed.), *Three Guineas: Virginia Woolf* (xxxv–lxiii). Orlando, FL: Harcourt.

Moorhead, J. (2017). *The surreal life of Leonora Carrington*. London, UK: Virago.

Oldfield, S. (2005). Introduction. In S. Oldfield (Ed.), *Afterwords: Letters on the death of Virginia Woolf* (xv–xxx). Piscataway, NJ: Rutgers University Press.

Woolf, V. (1966). *Three Guineas* (M. Hussey, Ed.). Orlando, FL: Harcourt.

Chapter 13

Alchemy in exile

Varo and Carrington in Mexico City

In 1941, a year before Carrington arrived, Remedios Varo moved to Mexico City, a country that had opened its borders to those fleeing the European theater of war. "I came to Mexico," Varo reflected later, "searching for the peace that I had not found, neither in Spain—that of the revolution—nor in Europe—that of the terrible war—for me it was impossible to paint amidst such anguish" (as cited in Kaplan, 1988: 85). At the time, Varo was married to Benjamin Perét, "one of the most aggressive and unwavering surrealists" (Nadeau, 1944/1965: 25), a poet who "belligerently participated in every revolutionary cause" he could find (Hubert, 1994: 257). The couple had been living in Paris, the epicenter of Surrealism. For Varo, asylum in Mexico was a temporary solution. She fully expected to return to France after the war.

Not expecting to settle down in Mexico, Varo and Perét avoided established artists, a group dominated by muralist Diego Rivera and painter Frida Kahlo. Instead, they gathered with other artists who had been exiled, like themselves, from homelands across Europe. Varo was the glue that held the group together.

> Her house was always open to those who needed shelter; whatever money she could gather she willingly offered to friends. As one of the beneficiaries of her kindness later put it, "These were not just nice ideas—her head and her heart were united in an extraordinary way."
>
> (Kaplan, 1988: 86)

The first house that Varo and Perét rented in Mexico City was a "ramshackle apartment" that Kaplan described as "a seedy white-washed tenement to which entry was gained by climbing through a window" (90, 92). The house had "primitive plumbing and holes in the floors" that Varo and Perét, both smokers, used as ashtrays (92). Rats thrived in the place, even though Perét put out poison to kill them. How was this possible? Varo, Kaplan explained, slipped the rats cheese behind her partner's back, unable to bear seeing the rodents suffer. Outside the apartment, the dilapidated state of the artist couple's neighborhood was not much better.

The house was bordered on one side by an unpaved vacant lot where trash from a nearby hospital was thrown, including the human hand sticking out from a newspaper wrapping that Perét saw there one day, which prompted him to burst into the house to announce that Surrealism lived in Mexico. (92)

Despite the conditions, Varo and Perét felt welcome in Mexico and somewhat settled for the first time in a long time. Varo wasted no time filling the home with cats "and numerous birds in cages that dotted an open patio" (Kaplan, 1988: 90). She also used needles to hang drawings by Picasso, Tanguay, and Ernst, works that she and Perét had brought with them from France. Perhaps because it mirrored and housed art, including the portrait given to her by Victor Brauner, Varo transformed the apartment into a sacred space. She surrounded herself with stones, shells, crystals, and bits of wood—all carefully placed "to maximize the magic of each piece" (92).

Leonora Carrington "responded strongly to the magical atmosphere of Varo's home" the moment she climbed in through the window (Aberth, 2010: 60). In Mexico together, the two women "built a strong emotional and spiritual connection based on a deep sense of mutual trust, a sense that the pain and despair each had known would be understood by the other" (Kaplan, 1988: 93). During this time, the women met almost daily, sharing their dreams, nightmares, and secrets they told no one else. The two artists turned heads wherever they went:

> Two beautiful women with an extraordinary flair for living, they created a powerful presence together. Carrington, the willowy, flamboyant English beauty, and Varo, the smaller and more quiet of the two, who is remembered [by André Breton] "as a very slight woman with an elfin face, very white skin, a mane of red hair and enormous sparkling eyes." (94–5)

Curious about how life worked in their adopted country and eager to learn about their new home, the women set out to explore Mexico City. According to Kaplan, they found

> a fertile atmosphere where magic was part of daily reality: traveling herb salesmen would set up on street corners with displays of seeds, insects, chameleons, special candles, seashells, and neatly wrapped parcels with such mysterious labels as "Sexual Weakness"—all used for the practice of witchcraft by the *curanderas* (healers), *brujas* (witches), and *espiritualistas* (spiritualists), who outnumbered doctors and nurses. (96)

Together in Mexico City, the artists created what art historian Kelly Wacker called "a female-centered alchemy" (1995: 3). André Breton and the male surrealists, Wacker wrote, "had already expressed their interest in alchemy, the role of women, and magic. However, the male-dominated group considered woman as a being controlled by magic and acting as a muse for the male artist" (3). In their creative work, on the other hand, Carrington and Varo "portrayed women in full control of their magical and alchemical powers" (3). In addition to painting, Carrington wrote fiction and sculpted. Varo designed and sewed costumes for the theater. The women also wrote two plays together. According to Arcq, "both plays deal with subjects related to occult and spiritualist doctrines, and are peopled with mediums, witches, archbishops, sinister characters who 'steal energy' and celestial elixirs that allow 'the soul to visibly separate from the body'" (2010: 100).

Stirring the cauldron: Varo and Carrington in the alchemical kitchen

In addition to their explorations, Varo and Carrington cooked up potent alchemical recipes in the kitchen. According to Wacker, "both Carrington and Varo saw food, whether vegetable or animal, as having a distinctive life force" (1995: 2). The women, Wacker added,

> believed that all life forces were subject to changes and transformations and that, if food had a life force, then it too could be transformed into something entirely different. By this reasoning, the kitchen became a metaphor of the alchemist's laboratory and food the philosopher's stone. (2)

Wacker and other art critics and historians agree that Varo and Carrington began experimenting in the kitchen with specific alchemical and symbolic purposes in mind. "They consciously chose to use images of the kitchen because of its association with women and because many of the alchemical processes are described in recipe form" (3).

In the imagery they painted, and in other alchemical experiments with food, Carrington and Varo "were well aware that they transformed the kitchen, traditionally a woman's space, into a metaphysical laboratory" (Wacker, 1995: 3). Wacker added that their alchemical perspective "had political implications as well; Sonia Assa has noted that Carrington's work in particular shows female characters 'in search of a recipe, that by working on the inside of the body, would change the world outside'" (3).

For two decades, Varo and Carrington saw each other most every day, talking together for hours at a time, "discussing life, their views on religion, nature, the universe and art. Anyone who looks at the work of both Carrington and Varo," wrote Stefan van Raay, "can only conclude that they were very close indeed: the harmony of the universe, its explanation beyond the purely scientific, the origins of creation, alchemy, the esoteric and the supernatural all play a significant part in their paintings" (2010: 16–7). At times, the closeness between the women may have made the relationship "claustrophobic" with "both interested in similar subjects, both inhabiting the same corner of the same city at the same time" (83).

Yet, the women were actually very different. "Varo was as sharp as a knife, quick-witted, always ready to pick up on new ideas and trends"; whereas "Carrington had a first-class brain, but was less focused on success than Varo: her responses to life were more intuitive, less calculated" (Moorhead, 2010: 80). Moorhead described Carrington as "an impossible creature: a wild child, an unfathomable puzzle of a girl; a young woman who refused to be tamed" (2017: 1). Varo, the engineer's daughter, was precise and scientific, her passion for magic and the mysteries of hidden worlds contained in discipline and a meticulous, even obsessive, attention to detail.

As artists, the women were attuned to one another. Both women drew from having suffered the strictures of patriarchy as children. They had each been victimized by the trauma of war. Both were drawn to practices of personal growth. The work of each woman had been nourished by the surrealist belief in the liberating powers of imagination and the wisdom of the unconscious mind. The eyes and hearts of both were open to the eruption of the miraculous as experienced in everyday life. Yet, even as they grew from the same taproot, Varo and Carrington as artists could not have been more different. Moorhead juxtaposed the styles of the two artists:

> Leonora's work is instinctive, organic and flowing; Remedios' work is about structure, form and precision. Leonora's paintings often feel as though they have erupted on to the canvas from somewhere very deep inside herself; Remedios' work has been pre-ordained, considered, planned. Leonora's work is about letting go and giving oneself over to elements beyond human power: Remedios' is more controlled and the work of an artist who seems to want to remain in charge. That was never Leonora's ambition: she saw herself as a conduit, a channel. Where Remedios was an illustrator, an interpreter, a painter of reality— albeit at times a magical reality—Leonora was unbridled, free from rules, and her work reflected the chaos, complications, paradoxes and contradictions of the widest reaches of the universe. (2017: 215)

What are we to make of the possible effect of these differences between two creative women who were close enough to be sisters?

From a Jungian perspective, we can comment on the presence of alchemical salt at work in the stew that was brewing in the cauldron of the relationship. Jung related alchemical salt with "the function of *feeling*" and with Eros, the archetypal principle of relatedness (1955–56/1970, para. 330, emphasis in original). For Jung, "the most outstanding properties of salt are bitterness and wisdom" (para. 330). "Tears, sorrow, and disappointment are bitter," he wrote, "but wisdom is the comforter in all psychic suffering. Indeed, bitterness and wisdom form a pair of alternatives: where there is bitterness wisdom is lacking, and where wisdom is there can be no bitterness" (para. 330).

As each woman cooked her own experience of bitterness in the cauldron of their relationship, their work was seasoned with what Hillman called the salt of the "impersonal, objective ground of personal experience" (2010: 60). In this way, Hillman added, "Salt makes events sensed and felt, giving us each a sense of the personal—my tears, my sweat and blood, my taste and value" (60). For Hillman, "salt … makes possible what psychology calls felt experience. We must turn to this same ground to mine our salt" for wisdom (60). Salt is therefore a crucial ingredient in the cooking of new psychological substances. The polarities of fluidity and structure Varo and Carrington embodied between them informed the wisdom and transformations they mined from the bitter ground of experience. Their differences fed and filled out the vivid ways they imaged and gave voice to the feminine.

Moorhead's characterizations of the differences between the two artists mentioned above are alchemically insightful. Alchemically speaking, the relationship between the two artists, and between their creative approaches, is crucial to the creation of paintings that protest the perils of patriarchy—for it is not possible to bring opposites together in a new way until they have first been separated. Both women were engaging with archetypal forces in the transformational tension between freedom and containment: Carrington, a channel for the flow of unbridled instinctual and archetypal energies; Varo, an instrument through which the precision and nuanced elegance of numinous forces could be birthed through imagination into human life.

It may be that between them, a collaboration between the qualities of spontaneity and planning, fluidity and structure, fed the playfully serious experimentation the women engaged in. Sharing "an intensity of imaginative power that each found in no one else," Varo and Carrington played with tangible, experiential metaphors and the crafting of divergent etiologies, mixing substances together to pose as a different substance (Kaplan, 1988: 95). An often-cited example of the sort of mischief Carrington and Varo cooked up in the alchemical kitchen together is the time they dished up tapioca pudding as caviar for guests at a dinner party. The women playfully cooked the tapioca in fish broth and colored the substance with squid ink. Everyone at the party thought the "caviar" was delicious (Wacker, 1995: 3).

At home in Mexico City, Varo and Carrington spent a fair amount of time together in the kitchen. Sometimes the recipes they came up with were outrageous, even downright silly. But the women were expressing their alchemical imagination in any way they could. One recipe, written in Varo's hand, offered " 'advice for scaring away inopportune dreams, insomnia, and deserts of quicksand under the bed' " (as cited in Kaplan, 1988: 95). Another recipe in Varo's notebook was "specially designed to stimulate a dream of being the King of England," and called for "the use of a sable brush to paint egg white all over the dreamer's body" (95). In a third, Varo called

> for a witch's brew of ingredients with which to stimulate erotic dreams, a list that includes: "a kilo of horseradish, three white hens, a head of garlic, four kilos of honey, a mirror, two calf livers, a brick, two clothespins, a corset with stays, two false mustaches, and hats to taste." (95)

Kaplan described this recipe as being "in the tradition of the finest French haute cuisine," detailing "painstaking preparations of the various ingredients. But in truly surreal spirit it offers urgent instructions for preparing the cook as well" (95). The instructions for the recipe pair the suggestion that the cook should have an androgynous nature with a mocking of feminine and masculine social pretenses:

> Put on the corset and make it quite tight. Sit down in front of the mirror, relax your nervous tension, smile and try on the mustaches and hats according to your taste (three-cornered, Napoleonic, cardinal's hat, imitation with lace, Basque beret, etc.)... Run and pour the broth (which should be very reduced) quickly into a cup. Quickly come back with it to in front of the mirror, smile, take a sip of broth, try on one of the mustaches, take another sip, try on a hat, drink, try on everything, taking sips in between and do it all as quickly as you can.
>
> (Varo, as cited in Kaplan, 1988: 95)

Varo's death: Alchemy and the bath that kills and vivifies[1]

Varo and Carrington's spirited time together came to an end with Varo's death in the fall of 1963. Varo was nine years older than Carrington. Without her mystical sister, Carrington was bereft of a presence she did not know how to live without. "She is the animator," Poniatowska wrote, "the teacher" (2011/2015: 278). "Being together protects them, and they take shelter, holding each other by the hand" (279). For Carrington, friendship with Varo

> is like an open patio ... Remedios is her ideal foil, she finishes the sentences she can only begin, her smile embraces her, she is her twin sister. Nobody is of as much interest to her as she is, she longs to show Remedios her canvases, the short stories she has been writing, tell her

her life story. "May she love me—what I want more than anything else at this moment is that Remedios will come to love me." (279–80)

On the fall afternoon that Varo dies, as told in Poniatowska's biographical novel *Leonora*, Carrington goes to the wake being held for her friend, her lost sister. She cannot cry. She smokes one cigarette after another. People talk, hug, but she

> pays no attention, since she no longer hears even what she is saying to herself. She closes herself off inside her inner cell, and remembers the day when Remedios told her that they were like the fox and the Little Prince: "And when the hour came to depart: 'Ah!' said the fox. 'Now I shall cry.'" Leonora chews over every word in a rage. (404)

After the funeral, Poniatowska imagined,

> Leonora takes refuge in her studio. She paints *The Burial of the Patriarchs*: one figure holds up a crozier [a hooked staff carried by a bishop as a symbol of pastoral office] bearing the image of Hermes, who transports the souls of the patriarchs to eternal life in a canoe. She reads *Giordano Bruno and the Hermetic Tradition* by Francis Yates, and paints *The Burning of Bruno*. She admires the philosopher's challenge: "There is no need to seek for divinity outside of ourselves." (404)

In Mexico City, without Varo, Carrington was desolate with loss. She poured her pain into *The Hearing Trumpet*, the novel she wrote about an old woman, Marion Leatherby, discarded by her family and committed to an old folks' home. The novel seems to be a tribute to Varo and the history and passion they shared: echoing the experience of separation from family, internment, rebellion against an androcentric world, and the transformative power of alchemy.

In the novel, Marion Leatherby, who is 92 years old, surprises everyone, including herself, by undergoing a transformation that allows her to serve as "an active participant in the destruction of the patriarchal world" and the birth of a new community centered around women and animals (Wacker, 1995: 3). At one point in the story, Marion Leatherby

> descends into the basement of an ominous tower where she finds an old woman who resembles her stirring the contents of a large cauldron over a fire. She is coerced into the pot, and at the moment she feels the scalding pain, she is transformed into the woman stirring the pot, watching in amazement as her own body is dissolved into the stew. (3)

Leatherby's transformation in the cauldron "is most certainly derived from the traditional alchemical imagery of the king and queen copulating and dissolving in the bath that 'kills and vivifies'" (Coudert, as cited in Wacker, 1995: 3). Linking death with renewal in the cosmic cycle of life, Wacker noted that the image of the marriage of king and queen in the bath "symbolizes the union of opposites and spiritual rebirth" (3). Carrington, according to Wacker, "made specific reference to this imagery in her painting, *Cornelia and Cornelius*, in which three alchemists carefully watch over the crucible as the king and queen are dissolved" (3).

Interestingly, all three alchemists in the painting are androgynes, apparently having integrated within themselves the masculine and feminine in their approach to their alchemical work. The two alchemists who pour water over the heads of the couple are also composite figures, having incorporated into themselves and the work that which is other (more) than human. On the right, the body of the alchemist who pours water over the king's head appears black with deep blue highlights and filled with creatures. The body of the alchemist on the left, who pours water over the queen's head, is gold with a mandala heart of feathers. The third alchemist, pictured centered above the bath, pours water directly into it through crossed wands. We can imagine that Carrington was depicting herself and Varo as working together to create a healing bath for what had been torn apart in themselves and in their world by fear and cultural complexes. But why three alchemists? Could the third alchemist, with a blue and pinkish face—imbued with colors associated with imagination and nurturing love—be an image of who Carrington and Varo became together?

Late in life, in *Leonora*, Carrington, now an old woman herself, reflects on the experiences of her life. "Love," she says, "disrupts old values, hurls one into the unknown" (Poniatowska, 2011/2015: 410). For our purposes, there is a thread that connects the love Carrington is describing and the artist's painting intended on a symbolic level to expose the vulnerable underbelly of patriarchy. Behind the third alchemist in *Cornelia and Cornelius*, we see on the right two small figures, one leading the other out of the forest, and on the left two figures fleeing, one human and running, deer-like, leaping out of the scene into the beyond. At a foundational level, love, along with the unbearable vulnerability involved in the loss of love, is one of the qualities that patriarchy armors itself against most fiercely. "Patriarchy," wrote Carol Gilligan, "strikes at the heart of what makes repair possible: our sensitivity to the pain of losing connection and our ability to give voice to what we are experiencing" (Gilligan & Snider, 2018: 144). The unconditional love that Varo and Carrington felt for one another, an intimate partnership in which each was devoted to the other person, freed and nourished their imagination, pouring the dissolving and reconstituting alchemy of love into the body of their alchemical works.

Both Varo and Carrington believed in the presence and power of that which transcends the ego in the unseen forces of psyche, nature, and cosmos. Studying mystical disciplines and metaphysical texts, the women's obsession with the development of the spiritual self dominated their work. They sought spiritual meaning and a transformative order in their recovery of "a universal feminine archetype as a source of inspiration and creativity" (Kaplan, 1998: 106). They felt it crucial to differentiate this powerful force from the patriarchal female images produced by both men and women.

With unswerving devotion, the women fought, as Virginia Woolf did, not to find their place in a man's patriarchal world, but to transform that world into one that made room for the imaginative presence of women. Western society, Gilligan and Richards believed, must turn to, and even rely upon, artists to expose the problem at its roots: "the traumatic disruption of intimate sexual life through patriarchal gender stereotypes, which crush any voice that might reasonably challenge such disruption" (2009: 223). Gilligan and Richards added:

> Our reliance on the voices of artists to deepen and expand our argument reflects our view that through their use of associative methods, artists can undo or free themselves from the dissociations of patriarchy. Their access to the body, a body no longer divided from the mind, and to feelings that are joined with, rather than severed from, thought allows them to explore both the costs of dissociation and the wellsprings of resistance. (223)

Alchemically, the friendship between Carrington and Varo brought opposites together, creating what we might call a living conjunction. It was sometimes difficult to distinguish where one woman started and the other left off. "They talked of philosophy," Kaplan wrote, "shared their anxieties, and even filtered into each other's dreams" (1988: 94). As one example, in the third of the ten dreams Varo recorded in her diary, Carrington appears as a cat:

> I'm bathing an orange kitten in the sink of some hotel, but that's not so, it seems instead that it's Leonora, who's wearing a large coat that needs to be washed. I spritz her with a little soapy water and keep on bathing the kitten, but am very puzzled and disturbed, because I'm not at all sure who it is I'm bathing.
>
> (Varo, 1997/2018: 81)

By joining forces—Carrington the wild mare and Varo the engineer and scientist—each woman found free flow into the current of numinous imagery and containment in the revelation of a new structure. Armored by the fiercely feminine force of love against the harshness of male domination, the women stood together against the patriarchy. In this way, painting—for each artist—became a subversive and radical act of protest. By standing at their easels and releasing imagination, the women committed artistic treason against what Gilligan and Richards called "the fundamental rule of patriarchy: the claim on the part of fathers to authority" (2009: 162).

Note

1 The phrase "kills and vivifies" is from Alison Coudert, *Alchemy: The Philosopher's Stone* (131), as cited in Kelly Wacker, "Alchemy in Exile: The alchemical kitchen in the work of Leonora Carrington and Remedios Varo" (1995; *Ohio Northern University Monograph*, 44).

References

Aberth, S. (2010). *Leonora Carrington: Surrealism, alchemy and art*. Burlington, VT: Lund Humphries.

Arcq, T. (2010). Mirrors of the marvellous: Leonora Carrington and Remedios Varo (M. Suderman, Trans.). In S. Begley (Ed.), *Surreal Friends* (98–115). Burlington, VT: Humphries.

Carrington, L. (1974/1996). *The hearing trumpet* (L. Carrington, Trans.). Cambridge, MA: Exact Change.

Gilligan, C., & Richards, D. (2009). *Deepening Darkness: Patriarchy, resistance, and democracy's future*. Cambridge, NY: Cambridge University Press.

Gilligan, C., & Snider, N. (2018). *Why does patriarch persist?* Medford, MA: Polity Press.

Hillman, J. (2010). *Alchemical psychology*. Putman, CT: Spring Publications.

Hubert, R. R. (1994). *Magnifying mirrors: Women, surrealism, & partnership*. Lincoln, NE: University of Nebraska Press.

Jung, C. G. (1955–56/1970). *Mysterium coniunctionis* (R. F. C. Hull, Trans.) (H. Read et al., Eds.), *The collected works of C. G. Jung* (Vol. 14, 2nd ed.). Princeton, NJ: Princeton University Press.

Kaplan, J. (1988). *Unexpected journeys: The art and life of Remedios Varo*. New York, NY: Abbeville Press.

Moorhead, J. (2010). Surreal friends in Mexico. In S. Begley (Ed.), *Surreal friends* (70–97). Burlington, VT: Humphries.

Moorhead, J. (2017). *The surreal life of Leonora Carrington*. London, UK: Virago.

Nadeau, M. (1944/1965). *The history of Surrealism* (R. Howard, Trans.). New York, NY: Macmillan.

Poniatowska, E. (2011/2015). *Leonora: A novel* (A. Hopkinson, Trans.). London, UK: Profile Books.

Van Raay, S. (2010). Surreal friends: Leonora Carrington, Remedios Varo and Kati Horna. In S. Begley (Ed.), *Surreal Friends* (8–29). Burlington, VT: Humphries.

Varo, R. (1997/2018). *Letters, dreams & other writings* (M. Carson, Trans.). Cambridge, MA: Wakefield Press.

Wacker, K. (1995). Alchemy in exile: The alchemical kitchen in the work of Leonora Carrington and Remedios Varo. *Ohio Northern University Monograph*, 44.

Chapter 14

The way they loved each other

The crucible of friendship and the unmaking of patriarchy

Leonora Carrington and Remedios Varo were probably aware at some level that their images of powerful women were threatening to the patriarchal male who armors himself against the vulnerability of feeling and relationality with rigid values and dominating behaviors that silence a woman's voice and damage, or even destroy, her sense of self. According to Arcq, in their studies, the women found that "in ancient pagan religions and secret doctrines, women had wielded powers that were later denied them" (2010: 102). Carrington wrote: "Most of us I hope, are now aware that woman should not have to demand Rights [that] were there from the beginning; they must be Taken Back Again, including the Mysteries which were ours and which were violated, stolen or destroyed" (as cited in Arcq, 2010: 102).

Reclaiming the place of the Feminine

In splitting off the nonhierarchical feminine principle from cultural consciousness, the lens through which history has been perceived arises from and reinforces patriarchal assumptions that the nature of reality is competitive, violent, and hegemonic. Feminist scholars, including anthropologist Marija Gimbutas and cultural historian Riane Eisler, have challenged the interpretation that ancient goddess-worshipping societies were matriarchal and, thus, hierarchical. The work of these women has demonstrated the possibility that cultures in Old Europe (before 4400 BCE) were peaceful, earth-loving, harmonious societies without weapons, communities in which both masculine and feminine genders were valued (Eisler, 1995; Gimbutas, 1997). Gimbutas, according to Jacques Leslie, posited:

> It was marauding Indo-Europeans, the forerunners of Western civilization, who destroyed these societies … Making incursions from the Russian steppes starting in 4400 BC, the Indo-Europeans were violent, indifferent to nature and dominated by men. Those features, she says, have been part of Western civilization ever since and account for

the political and environmental crises that now threaten the planet. (1989: para. 3)

Although Gimbutas's work, which drew on folklore and mythology, has been criticized for going beyond archeological facts, mythologist Joseph Campbell saw Gimbutas as "one of the few people on the planet who understood the ancient world, because she could bring her imagination to it and not just act like a scientist" (McClintock, as cited in Leslie, 1989: para. 12). Gimbutas's work, in challenging the notion of a hierarchical matriarchy, reveals the importance of the imagination and its subversive nature, as well as the importance to the patriarchy of silencing women and the experience of the feminine.

In contrast to Gimbutas's claims, the idea that goddess-worshipping cultures were hierarchically matriarchal turns patriarchy on its head and remains encased within the will-to-power paradigm—disavowing the possibility of a fundamentally egalitarian culture, and occluding the possibility of a feminine, relational, inclusive, and cooperative paradigm shift. The idea that matriarchy is the opposite of patriarchy—a situation in which women dominate men—colludes with the patriarchal, fear-based need to exclude women, a situation that both Carrington and Varo, as artists strongly influenced by Surrealism, were familiar with.

In his essay, "Surrealism and Misogyny," commenting on Surrealism as "a men's club," humanities expert Rudolf Kuenzli wrote,

The Surrealists lived in their own masculine world, with their eyes closed, the better to construct their male phantasms of the feminine. They did not see woman as a subject, but as a projection, an object of their own dreams of femininity. (1990: 17–8)

"Women," Kuenzli added,

are to the male Surrealists, as in the longstanding traditions of patriarchy, servants, helpers in the forms of child muse, virgin, *femme-enfant*, angel, celestial creature who is their salvation, or erotic object, model, doll—or she may be the threat of castration in the forms of the ubiquitous praying mantis or other devouring female animals. (19)

Psychologically speaking, Kuenzli pinpointed the cause of male surrealists' misogyny as a virulent case of castration anxiety:

Faced with the female figure, the male Surrealist fears castration, fears the dissolution of his ego. In order to overcome his fears, he fetishizes the female figure, he deforms, disfigures, manipulates her; he literally manhandles her in order to reestablish his own ego. (24)

The distorted and dislocated Feminine: The surrealism of Wifredo Lam

We see—and feel—this male fear of women in works by Picasso. We most certainly experience a hatred of women, as the projected form of the man's fear of his own inner feminine, in the work of Hans Bellmer, a German artist best known for the life-sized pubescent female dolls he produced in the mid-1930s. But it is two works by Wifredo Lam that interest us at this point, as we work to complete our look at the synergistic friendship between Varo and Carrington, two women who painted, in part, to address complexes at work in the patriarchal culture around them.

Wifredo Lam was born and raised in Sagua La Grande, a village in the sugar farming province of Villa Clara, Cuba. His mother's parents were of mixed-race: his mother was the daughter of a Congolese slave and a Cuban mulatto father; his father was a Chinese immigrant. Lam's family pushed him to practice law. Lam wanted to make art. In the autumn of 1923, Lam ended up in Madrid, where he learned from Fernando Zaragoza, the curator of the Museo Nacional del Prado and teacher of Salvador Dalí.

At the outbreak of the Spanish Civil War, in 1936, Lam sided with the Republicans in their fight against General Francisco Franco's fascist forces backed both by Mussolini's Italy and Hitler's Third Reich on the rise in Nazi Germany. Involved in the creation of posters and propaganda, in 1937 Lam was drafted to defend Madrid. Incapacitated in battle, he left the war and arrived in Paris in 1938. A friend wrote him a letter of introduction, and almost instantly Lam had a new friend—Picasso—whose influence is easily seen in Lam's "surreal figures projecting almost shattering emotions and a puzzle of hodgepodge cubism with an almost other-dimensional magnetism" (Parkstone International, 2016: para. 2).

In his art, Lam depicted presences disfigured and torn apart by violence, a reflection not only of the world around him but also of the history of racist-fueled violence to which his forbearers were subjected (Richards, 1988). In his disconcerting—sometimes frightening—compositing of female, male, and nonhuman features amid the presence of knives, scissors, and horses (a symbol for this artist of female carnality), Lam seems to be struggling with the oppressive and deadly chaos, collusion, and conflict amid the forces and experiences that Varo and Carrington sought to free from the grip of patriarchy.

We have suggested that the friendship between Carrington and Varo helped each woman make art that protests problems associated with patriarchy, including cultural complexes that protect men as a group from their own disavowed inner life. In this context, let us look at two paintings by Wifredo Lam. Our hope is to engage with the images Lam painted, and then bring these works into dialogue with works on similar themes by both Carrington and Varo. We are working to mobilize and release both emotion and insight constellated in the unconscious substrate of the paintings *themselves*. From a Jungian perspective, we are working to bring "conscious control to the ordering and arranging" of the images (Siegelman, 1990: 15). Jung called this process *active imagination*. For Jung, active imagination

> was a deliberate attempt to work with the mysterious or ego-alien aspects of dreams or fantasy images and to set them in deliberate dialogue with the conscious attitude so that out of this work some new synthesis—a third thing—would be born.
>
> (Siegelman, 1990: 15)

Wifredo Lam painted *Annunciation,* an oil on canvas, in 1944. The figure symbolizing the Virgin Mary is at the viewer's left. Lam paints Mary, the mother of God,

> with multiple pairs of wings and a face that seems to divide itself between the masklike head sprouting hands and a snout topped by multiple candle flames and an inverted round head. Below there are several tiers of cloven feet, faintly drawn in, some in the high-heeled footwear that Lam uses to designate the profane world.
>
> (Sims, 2002: 55)

"The angel of the Annunciation," wrote Lowery Stokes Sims, a retired curator and art historian who has published extensively on the work of Lam, "is the awesome masked figure on the right" (2002: 55).

> Endowed with multiple facial planes and features, the figure is horned as well as winged and seems to be draped in a stippled leopard-skin garment, which, along with the horseshoe elements and repeated double horn, conveys an intense masculine power associated with spiritual entities such as Ogun, the orisha of war, and Chango, the thunder orisha in Yorùbá culture. (55)[1]

In *Annunciation,* the juxtaposition between the human (the Virgin Mary) and divine (the Angel of Annunciation) is clear. The figures are oddly shaped, and there is some dislocation of body parts. But the distortions Lam painted into the piece do not interfere with our ability to differentiate between or relate with the two figures. The felt sense of the painting is one of anticipation. We look for movement between feminine and masculine, between human and divine. And we wonder: What is going to happen next?

Lam engaged with these pairs of opposites again in *The Eternal Present,* an oil on canvas the artist completed in 1944, the same year he painted *Annunciation*. In this painting, the clear juxtaposition in *Annunciation* between the feminine presence of Mary, the mother of God, and the masculine power of West African thunder and war gods gives way to a decidedly darker composition that blurs the distinction between opposites.

Lam locates his vision of the archetypal Feminine—the Eternal Present—at the left of the scene. She is a sight to behold: a seated figure with few human traits, flanked on the left by a tall female form wearing a flowered hat, high heels, and garter; attire Sims said "suggests that she embodies" for Lam "the profane (i.e., earthly) elements" (2002: 56). At the center of the scene, the Eternal Present is larger than the other two figures and is unrecognizable as a human form. One of her feet twists backwards. The other foot is actually "a gigantic hand" that "extends out from under her skirt" (57). The arms cross, the right hand holding a ceremonial plate and reaching "out to cup a multiple-jointed horse's hoof extending from the torso of the hatted figure at the left" (56–7).

What are we to make of this female creature on the left, whose head looks like a horse and who has a "breast and testicles grouped around her muzzle" (Fouchet, 1976: 201)? Lam described this hatted female as a "whore … From her heart comes … an animal's paw … she evokes cross-breeding, the degradation of the race" (as cited in Sims, 2002: 57).

The figure at the far right of the scene "stands in profile; her buttocks flank a tail which ends in two digits" (Sims, 2002: 57). This figure, "endowed with multiple heads," holds a knife (57). "Her breasts are mimicked by the dividing ovoid forms at the end of the elephantine trunk that is her nose" (57). Symbolically, Lam explained, the knife is "the instrument of integrity, but he makes no use of it, he does not fight. He suggests the indecision of the mulatto, who does not know where to go or what to do" (as cited in Sims, 2002: 57). In other published remarks, Lam indicated that he was trying to say something in the painting about the instinct for life as lived by the lineage of deported blacks who survived generations of slavery and torture. The artist once told an interviewer that, in his works, he

> wanted with all my heart to paint the drama of my country, but by thoroughly expressing the negro spirit, the beauty of the plastic art of the blacks. In this way I could act as a Trojan horse that would spew forth hallucinating figures with the power to surprise, to disturb the dreams of the exploiters.
>
> (As cited in Richards, 1988: 91)

Amid the dislocations and bizarre reconfigurations of body parts in *The Eternal Present*, French writer and film producer Max-Pol Fouchet found a method to the artist's madness. In the upper central part of the composition, Fouchet wrote,

> under a crown of half-moons, a conical fruit shoots forth as if from the opening of a vulva. The movement at the centre, the immobility of the

figures at the sides, the forms engendering forms, the dangling hair and tails, the veining of the giant leaves and the spontaneous arrangement of the different elements give the canvas a powerful unity, suggesting that, through the jungle of the present, fruitfulness is maintained, the future advances. (1976: 201)

Yet it is significant that Lam's rendering of the feminine is disturbing, in part because of the way it distorts and fragments the female figures, especially the Eternal Present. The shapes in the work hint at geometric equivalents, without reducing them to the fractured forms that were a hallmark of Cubism. In Lam's painting, the distortion, dislocation, and reconfiguration of body parts gives the gestalt of the work a felt sense of distress, and the knife-cut of barely concealed anger. To look upon the feminine forms in Lam's paintings, to be with the figures, is to experience the anguish of alienation. The figures are not cohesive presences—their body parts are split off from the other places of the body where they are normally found. In both *Annunciation* and *The Eternal Present*, the form of the female figure is so distorted as to be unrecognizable. Is this perhaps what being a woman in patriarchy feels like?

Horns of the goddess: The Minotaur in the work of Varo, Carrington, and Lam

Along such lines, what meaning are we to make of Lam's imagery, related to the work created out of the crucible of connection between Remedios Varo and Leonora Carrington? Staying with Lam's image, we notice the small horns growing from the head of the distorted female figure to the left of the Eternal Present. These horns, art historians have suggested, connect Lam's painting with the Cretan myth of the Minotaur. As we discussed in Part I, in 1959 Varo created two paintings, *Dead Leaves* and *Minotaur,* related to the myth. Leonora Carrington reworked the myth in a 1953 painting, *And Then We Saw the Daughter of the Minotaur.*

   In her painting, Carrington recast the myth of the male hero, Theseus, helped by Ariadne's thread of feeling, to find his way out of the labyrinth after killing the Minotaur. From a Jungian perspective, the myth symbolizes the descent of the hero into the labyrinth of the unconscious, where the monstrous aspects of the personality are sacrificed to birth a more conscious and fulfilling way of being. Carrington's painted myth shifts the perception of women as gratifiers of male lust. In her painting, a dog (presumably male), who stands over a prone and submissive female dog, seems stopped by the vision of the illuminated, archetypal Feminine arriving on the scene. This shifts the focus from the male who kills what is threatening to the creative expression and numinous presence of the transpersonal Feminine expressing her gifts. We see in the painting a female dancer with a flower growing from her head entering from an illuminated doorway. Notice, also, a numinous white goddess clothed in a gown of pink, a divinely Feminine being whose head, shaped like the petals of a flower, seems to flutter in a breeze under a sky filled with silver clouds. In *And Then We Saw the Daughter of the Minotaur*, it is clear that Carrington is reshaping the mythological narrative in which the archetypal Feminine—represented by the Minotaur's mother, Queen Pasiphae, and Ariadne, the Princess of Crete—is powerless in the face of masculine forces that are blindly caught in the need to gain power over an adversary.

In the myth of Theseus and the Minotaur, the trouble starts when Minos, the King of Crete, refuses to return a prized white bull, a symbol of masculine potency, to Poseidon, the God of the Sea. Enraged, Poseidon punishes Minos by placing a spell on Pasiphae, the King's wife, who conceives a mad and irresistible passion to mate with the white bull. The offspring of this union is a monstrosity, the Minotaur, who must be hidden away from civilization at the center of a labyrinth so that Minos does not have to be reminded of his shame and the humiliation of his ultimate powerlessness at the hands of an archetypal force, Poseidon.

From a Jungian perspective, the imagery in the myth suggests that the shame of King Minos has to do with his inability, or unwillingness, to surrender his need to have power over the unconscious, symbolized by Poseidon's connection with the ocean, an image often used to evoke the water of the emotional life and the depths of the unconscious itself. In the myth of the Minotaur, we notice also the powerlessness of the feminine. Queen Pasiphae, for example, cannot control her lust for the white bull. Ariadne gives Theseus the ball of thread so that he will not get lost in the labyrinth, but then is left abandoned by the hero, who fails to honor his promise to marry her.

With these images in mind, consider the way Carrington, in her painting, transforms the female experience from one of powerlessness, isolation, and abandonment by men caught in the will to power to one of creativity and numinosity. Next, compare the empowering way in which Carrington evokes the feminine from the approach taken in the two paintings by Lam—works in which the breasts and buttocks of women are distorted, the exaggeration of form somehow caricaturing, and thus diminishing and even mocking—what the male artist called the *eternal presence* of the divine Feminine. In Lam's image, the female figures are distorted almost beyond recognition and are thus deprived of their personhood. The hips of one woman become the shoulder of another. Legs of a small woman merge with the upper body of another woman. Even the face of the shrine-like Feminine being at the center of *The Eternal Present* is so heavily abstracted Her presence is difficult to engage with.

Like Carrington, Varo's *Minotaur* shapeshifts from male to female, lightly shaded rounded circles giving her once-monstrous creature the hint of breasts.

Figure 14.1 Minotaur, Remedios Varo, oil on masonite, 1959. © Artist Rights Society (ARS), NY. Photo Credit: Private Collection, Christie's Images/Bridgeman Images.

Varo's divine being is a thin-legged hybrid who is both human and not human. She is dressed delicately in clothing that is meticulously cross-stitched to fit the figure's form. The face is Varo's—oval, with large eyes—surrounded by the hood of a cloak that frays at the ends with shimmering tendrils of a mysterious matter that could be stardust. Small white horns curve upward from each side of the figure's head. In place of hair, Varo has painted the crown of the creature's head as a tiny galaxy, a cosmos in which gossamer clouds of a blue-white material float upward, anchored by a small glowing orb in the center. Though ordinarily seen as a symbol of the masculine, this bull's horns are moon shaped, a symbolic link to the possibility that "the bull can also be as a lunar symbol, when ridden by a moon goddess. In this context the bull usually has the meaning of the taming of masculine and animal nature" ("Bull," 2001, para. 2). In Varo's re-imagining of the myth, her monster is not monstrous at all; she is both delicate and divine, holding in the tapered fingers of her right hand a golden key.

Alchemically, the symbolism of the painting suggests that the key is what is needed to unlock the golden nature of the personality, and to gain access to the numinosity and magic of the universe, aspects of creation that are held captive in the shadow, symbolized by the black door behind and to the left of the female Minotaur. In the center of the black door is a keyhole that appears to float in the space, a symbol, perhaps, of the fearful but also enlivening experience one can have when stretching beyond the limits of one's comfort zone. As we have seen, pushing into and traveling through narrow passageways is a common theme for Varo's characters, who travel into the darkness of the unknown in their efforts to explore and transform what is base in their nature and in the world.

That Varo creates a cosmos emerging from the female Minotaur's head seems important. Varo may have been drawn to the mystical, the mysterious, and the numinous, but she engaged artistically with the unseen forces that animate the universe through a precise and detailed scientific mind. With the image of a cosmos emerging from the mind of the Minotaur, Varo metaphorically depicts a movement crucial to the unmaking of patriarchy. In Varo's imagining, the Minotaur undergoes a radical transformation. In Varo's painting, the shameful son made monstrous by the contaminating power complex of his father, Minos, King of Crete, shapeshifts into an illuminated, divinely Feminine creature who brings the human and non-human together into her own being. Alchemically, Varo's image of the Minotaur re-incorporates the feminine imagination and feeling that King Minos had disavowed.

In Varo's creature we look upon the re-animated presence of Ariadne, daughter of Minos and Queen Pasiphae. Borrowing from myth, Varo's painting *Dead Leaves* shows us the thread supplied by an Ariadne figure. For Varo, the thread belongs to the feminine and is blue, a symbol of imagination, and thus carries with it the relational capacity to feel into another's experience. Theseus follows Ariadne's thread on the metaphorical journey to the center of himself—and because the story is a myth, to the center of the collective psyche as well. In the labyrinth of the unconscious, the compulsively masculine Hero kills the Minotaur, a symbol for the shameful presence that threatens the shadowed identity of the group that must be defended by individuals through projected hatred and persecution of others.

From one perspective, we might say that having destroyed the old form (the male creature made monstrous through shame), Theseus, the mythic future king, gains access to the feeling nature that grounds the archetypal Hero into his own humanity. However, from a different perspective, the blue thread of the feminine imagination is betrayed by Theseus, who breaks his promise to marry Ariadne, using the thread, in the end, solely for his own purposes. Had Theseus honored the integrity of his promise, might he not have engaged with, rather than killed, the Minotaur—discovering at the core of the devouring complex of shame and fear the archetypal form of Varo's *Minotaur,* a mediating moon goddess? Whereas the myth valorizes the forceful vanquishing of that which is Other as a threat to the ego and the social order, Varo's female Minotaur alludes symbolically to the process by which consciousness and society is enlarged through cultivation of one's imaginal and emotional life in relationship with that which is more than human.

Female sexual objectification and other problems of patriarchy

In the presence of Wifredo Lam's distorted depictions of the Feminine and the reshaped contours of the feminine painted by Varo and Carrington, a host of thoughts arise related to the efforts of all three artists to expose the problems of patriarchy. With the rigid gender demands of patriarchy in mind, one problem that emerges is the black-or-white cultural bias which equates woman with Feminine and man with Masculine. Within these imprisoning gender stereotypes, a man must be rational and superior, and a woman must be emotional and subordinate.

There is also the patriarchal practice of female sexual objectification to consider. In patriarchy, the female body and female sexuality are commodities. A woman's soul, her essence, the voice of her deep inner longings and insights, is unacknowledged, and thus silenced, by the patriarchal male who defends his superior status by seeing the woman as a sexualized caricature. In this way, women are not allowed to be individuals. Instead, a woman is reduced to a sexualized object, a collection of eroticized body parts. In refusing to see, let alone honor, the gifts inherent to the female way of being, patriarchy disembodies and dismembers women and the feminine. Adding insult to injury, the patriarchal power principle begets self-objectification, a strategy a woman is forced to adopt to gain agency in a marketplace where her most valued resources are her female body parts. Spanish poet Rafael Alberti evoked the anguish and alienation a woman can experience as a result of patriarchal objectification:

> The light, dead on the corners,
> and in the houses.
> Neither men nor women
> were there anymore.
> "Get out."
> My body remained empty,
> a black sack at the window.
> It left.
> It left, circling the streets.
> My body went out with nobody in it. (1928/1995: 15)

Prizing power and the perpetuation of privilege, and heavily defended against the vulnerability of relationship, patriarchal men dehumanize women through an ethos that perceives female power and the power of the female body as threatening—even, as in the *vagina dentata*, lethal. The creativity and fertility of a woman, wrote Sady Doyle, "is something patriarchy must demonize and control in order to secure its own existence" (2019: 18).

Patriarchy injures men, too. Patriarchy stifles, and even snuffs out, a man's feeling nature. Feelings, in the heart of a man trapped in patriarchy, make him feel submissive and therefore weak. This experience can lead to unbearable feelings of humiliation and shame. From this vulnerable place, a man who has disavowed his feeling nature mocks the emotionality of the "chick flick." Threatened by what he identifies as the uncontrollable nature of feeling, which he has dissociated from and then projected onto women, the patriarchal male harshly discriminates against his own unconscious distress by reducing a woman to a sexualized caricature, thus robbing her of her mind, heart, soul, and voice. Armored against vulnerability, patriarchal men become obsessed with soldiers, war, and inherently violent sports, such as boxing, wrestling, and football. From a psychological perspective, these contests can be considered a ritualized patriarchal form of combat. With a fear-based focus on force, violent sports enable a man caught in a patriarchal paradigm to avoid the threatening vulnerability of relationality that has been banished from conscious awareness. In boxing or cage-fighting, for example, there is no tolerance for anything but imposing one's will on the opponent. In effect, the psychological and cultural dynamics of patriarchy put men in a straitjacket in which they must dominate and control their thoughts, emotions, and body so as not to appear vulnerable or powerless. In distress, some men enact their anger and sadness at their own unconscious powerlessness, shame, and alienation on others, including women. For a woman, the patriarchy is often a violent and profoundly lonely experience in which she is divorced from herself and thus isolated from others. She cannot own her body, her embodied experience, or her voice, as this would threaten the legitimacy of the patriarchy and her social survival.

Note

1 Orisha is an African word for a male deity or god. Lam painted male gods sacred to the Yorùbá people, an ethnic group that inhabits western Africa, mainly Nigeria, Benin, Togo, and part of Ghana.

References

Alberti, R. (1928/1995) *Concerning the Angels* (C. Sawyer-Laucanno, Trans.). San Francisco, CA: City Light Books.

Arcq, T. (2010). Mirrors of the marvellous: Leonora Carrington and Remedios Varo (M. Suderman, Trans.). In S. Begley (Ed.), *Surreal Friends* (98–115). Burlington, VT: Humphries.

Bull. (2001). In *Dictionary of Symbolism*. Retrieved from umich.edu/~umfandsf/symbolismproject/symbolism.html/B/bull.html

Doyle, S. (2019). *Dead blondes and bad mothers: Monstrosity, patriarchy, and the fear of female power*. Brooklyn, NY: Melville House.

Eisler, R. (1995). *The chalice and the blade*. New York, NY: HarperCollins.

Fouchet, M. P. (1976). *Wifredo Lam*. New York, NY: Rizzoli International.

Gimbutas, M. (1997). *The Kurgan culture and the Indo-Europeanization of Europe: Selected articles from 1952 to 1993*. Washington, D.C. Institute for the Study of Man.

Kuenzli, R. (1990). Surrealism and misogyny. In M. Caws, R. Kuenzli & G. Raaberg (Eds.), *Surrealism and women* (17–26). Cambridge, MA: MIT Press.

Leslie, J. (1989). The goddess theory: Controversial UCLA archeologist Marija Gimbutas argues that the world was at peace when god was a woman. *Los Angeles Times*. Retrieved from www.latimes.com/archives/la-xpm-1989-06-11-tm-2975-story.html

Parkstone International. (2016). Cuba's Picasso: The surreal world of Wifredo Lam. Retrieved from parkstone.international/2016/09/15/cubas-picasso-the-surreal-world-of-wifredo-lam/

Richards, P. (1988). Wifredo Lam: A Sketch. *Callaloo, 34*(1), 90–2.

Siegelman, E. (1990). *Metaphor & meaning in psychotherapy*. New York, NY: Guilford.

Sims, L. S. (2002). *Wifredo Lam and the international avant-garde, 1923–1982*. Austin: University of Texas Press.

Part III

Symbols of transformation

The golden key, the black door, and the inestimable value of the living third thing

Chapter 15

Imaginal dialogues
The alchemical treasure of the Feminine

With culturally prescribed patriarchal dynamics in mind, how, we might ask, can progress be made toward softening misogynistic cultural complexes and unmaking the patriarchy? Touching on the paintings of Remedios Varo, Leonora Carrington, and Wifredo Lam, there is meaningful work to be done on the level of the imagination. For example, what happens if we engage with the female figures in *Annunciation* and *The Eternal Present* not from the point of view of the artist's ego, but from the lived experience of the figures *themselves*? What if we invite the female forms in the paintings to speak for themselves about what they need to shift their experience?

From this perspective, imaginal space is made for Lam's female figures to shift. As symbols of living archetypal presences, they are no longer confined within the misogynistic parameters of patriarchy. Perhaps this was Lam's unconscious intention: to show what patriarchy does to women and to the feminine; it distorts their real shape, sometimes beyond recognition. In this way, the contours of the actual woman's being are lost, silenced in the patriarchal man's attempt to protect his sense of self from the threat of becoming entangled with real women and with his own inner feminine. Perhaps what Lam is symbolizing in the two paintings we have looked at is the confinement of women and the archetypal Feminine in a distorted realm in which the inherent dignity of being and the authenticity of voice are lost and a woman is nothing more than a projected representation of the man's own disavowed inner feminine. Psychologically speaking, patriarchy allows no one, regardless of gender, to engage with the life-giving feminine presences who have their birthplace in the unconscious regions of the psyche.

From an archetypal perspective, it is possible that Lam painted the anguish of the patriarchalized feminine to invite us into her fractured experience. Consciously or unconsciously, the artist seems to have worked to disturb us, to make us uncomfortable enough that we are compelled to do something to alleviate, or even eliminate, the distress of women who lose their voice and being. "I knew I was running the risk of not being understood," Lam once said, "either by the man on the street or by the others. But a true picture has the power to set the imagination to work, even if it takes time" (as cited in Goizueta, 2014: 15).

In *Annunciation* and *The Eternal Present*, Lam evoked not only the distress of the distorted feminine, but also touched into the painful experience of the imbalanced masculine. In the figures of the angel of Annunciation and the Eternal Present, Lam gave voice to the upset men experience when caught in a culturally prescribed version of themselves that narrows the range of acceptable emotions to anger and lust. In patriarchy, a man who is not allowed to feel is forced to amputate his willingness and ability to relate and connect, to experience healthy attachment with others, and to foster a relationship with his own unconscious. A man caught in patriarchy sees, and experiences, a woman and the feminine as a danger he must armor himself against. For a man caught in patriarchy, relating with a woman can be dangerous, even annihilating—the *relating* in and of itself is experienced as castrating. To neutralize such a threat to his manhood, the patriarchal man asserts his superiority through rigid gender roles that afford him the privilege and power to reduce a woman's numinous nature to the point where she is a helpless damsel, an eroticized muse, or a misogynized object: a nice piece of ass.

With these thoughts and dynamics in mind, it is important to clarify that the imagery Lam painted and the artist himself are not necessarily misogynistic. There is no evidence to pathologize this male painter as a patron of patriarchal privilege. Rather, we invite Lam's images into the creative and imaginal space of our look at the works of Varo and Carrington for a particular purpose: to see what happens if the *images themselves* are invited to dialogue with each other. What words might pass, for example, between Mary, as the mother of God and The Eternal Present, Lam's seemingly anguished image of the archetypal Feminine? What value might be added to our look at the paintings of Varo and Carrington if presences from these artist's painted worlds are invited to talk to each other and to the ones in Lam's works?

To set the backdrop for these imaginal dialogues, we draw from two disciplines. First, from an artistic perspective, there is Susan Rubin Suleiman's notion of *dialogism*, a conversation "*staged* by the critic who juxtaposes works and makes them speak to each other, perhaps even inventing the very words one work might address to the other" (1990: 133, emphasis in original). For Suleiman, the difficulty of dialogism lies in the challenge of what she called the "double allegiance," that is, the art critic must be willing to engage with a work of art from both opposing points of view, in this case a feminist point of view but also from the misogynistic perspective—with each possibly seeing the other as offensive and hurtful (133).

In addition to dialogism, from a Jungian perspective, the imaginal dialogue between figures in a painting can be considered a form of active imagination, a method Jung developed to "heal the split between the ego and the unconscious by using the resources of the unconscious itself to help bring the dissociated material back gradually into a relationship with the conscious ego" (Singer, 1994: 288). From a Jungian perspective, "the object of active imagination is to give a voice to sides of the personality ... that are normally not heard, thereby establishing a line of communication between consciousness and the unconscious" (Sharp, 1991: 12–3). In Jungian psychology, active imagination is one way to bring about the transcendent function, the psychic mechanism that Sharp said "arises from the tension between consciousness and the unconscious and supports their union" (135). Constellated by "a tension charged with energy," the transcendent function produces a third idea or image that "typically manifests symbolically and is experienced as a new attitude toward oneself and life" (136).

What would it be like to build a world in which women can know what they know and say what they know? Imagine a meeting between the Daughter of the Minotaur, from the oil painting by Leonora Carrington, and Ogun, the god of war from Wifredo Lam's image, *The Eternal Present*:

"I look at her," says the Daughter of the Minotaur, referring to the Eternal Present, "and I want to look away. Can you not see what men do? Can you not feel the harm you inflict? We wish to love and be loved. As women, we are willing to suffer and to feel your hurt. But we tire of your unending fury. Will you please lay down your anger and speak with me?"

A silence is broken by the sound of a blade.

"The blade is sharp," the God of War says. "I use it to keep things away that I don't want to think about."

A second male voice, the Executioner, speaks from Varo's dream: "Why do you talk to her? The cut of the blade says everything."

A female voice answers: "I know you are afraid. So am I. But I have something for you."

A new scene comes into shape: a small room, a figure with stardust emerging from the crown of her head, a golden key in her right hand. "I will give you the key," says the creature. "But you have to put it in the keyhole yourself." The female Minotaur from Varo's painting turns to her left and gestures toward a black door.

Fear spreads across the face of the Executioner. He stiffens. He does not want to put down his weapon. Two or three moments pass. The Executioner does not attack or withdraw. "I could see she was scared," he says of the woman in the dream who asked for more time so that she might weave her destiny to the man with whom she wished to be connected for eternity. "I knew she was upset. I gave her more time because there was no reason not to."

"I know it meant a lot to her," the lady Minotaur answers. "Thank you for hearing her request, and for granting her wish for more time. Her life had been upsetting and lonely. The ribbons and the egg made it possible for her to feel at peace."

"You are very odd. How is it that your head glows?"

"The light you see is born from the suffering I have known."

"I don't need light. I have my blade."

"You are good at cutting. The golden key unlocks the door to a place where things fit together differently."

"This room is small. I feel trapped in here. I want to go back to the dream. In the dream I use my blade and things are either one way or another."

"You are free to leave. I hope you stay. I like talking with you."

The Executioner turns to leave. He stops, realizing that the only way out of the room is through the black door. He stiffens again, gripping his weapon.

"Death is simple," the female creature says. "Your blade makes it so. A person is alive, and then they are dead. I wonder if you understand that things have changed. If you go back to the dream, things may not be as simple as you wish them to be."

The Executioner grips his blade and glares at the creature. "What are you talking about?"

"In the dream, the woman wishes to weave her destiny with a man. You give her more time to live. You realize: There will be another woman. There will be other requests. People want things."

"It doesn't matter what people want."

"Why did you give the women more time? You could have refused. Your blade was ready for use."

"You irritate me. You make things more complicated than they are."

"Things may already be more complicated than you want them to be."

"I want to go back to the dream now."

"I don't know the way. All I have is this golden key."

What are we to make of these imaginal interchanges? Will the executioner accept that he cannot go back to the dream? How much more abuse and injury can women endure from patriarchal men who cannot—or will not—surrender the authority of the blade (a symbol of patriarchy's need to execute emotions and imagination) in service to entering into a life-enhancing collaboration with the chalice (a symbol of the divine Feminine)?[1]

Self-preservation is the executioner's dream. Inside this fantasy of control he seeks as an agent of the male state to enforce the status quo, protecting himself and the collective from alien influences—such as the female Minotaur and the woman who dreams, paints, and imagines the weaving of an egg. The egg weaver and Varo's Minotaur offer the executioner an alternative: the courage (the French root of which is *coeur*, or heart) to face death as the way we come into being (Spielrein, 1994). Instead of self-preservation, the imagery offers him, as an agent of the collective (as we each are), the golden key to find within himself the dynamic drive centered in the feminine principle—a drive that strives for "change and the resurrection" of humankind through "the tendency to dissolve and assimilate" into new possibilities (174). This new social structure has at its core a relationship with the cyclical nature of death and birth, with Eros, and with Thanatos, the archetypal energy of Death. Embodied in the female Minotaur, and her weaving of the egg, the images speak to Varo's commitment to inclusivity and the well-being of all in a greater good founded in love, relationality, and the transpersonal creative cycle of life. Will the executioner realize that to use the key he will need to put down his blade? The future is unknown.

What we can say is that Remedios Varo and Leonora Carrington imagined worlds in which women embody the wonder of the universe and finger the blue thread of imagination that weaves love into the mantle of the earth. A message the artists sent through the images in their paintings is clear: There is magic in us and around us. Varo and Carrington saw the glow at the center of things, the need to relate to and partner with that which is Other, and to embrace, and be embraced, by the spiraling cycle of life. They suffered, healed, loved, and died. Their paintings are all we have left of the imagination that flowed, like water, from their hearts.

In a fundamental way, the feminine qualities the two women brought forth in their paintings are beyond calculation. They are priceless, beyond value. They are golden. At least this is the way a practitioner of alchemical psychology might see things. But alchemy is not practiced in a void. At some point we must put away the books and theories and engage with the world, and with ourselves. We must do as the prince in a fairy tale was instructed to do: When the king's men came to boil him in a pot, the prince was told not to let the men take him. He was told, instead, to run and jump into the cauldron on his own. The prince not only survived his brush with death, he emerged from the cauldron brighter in mind and more loving in heart than he had been before (Meade, 1993: 215). But, again, alchemical psychology is not practiced inside a story. Or is it? What if we can learn to live not just with our images, but *inside* them? What if we assign high value to the images that appear to us in our dreams, fantasies, and in metaphoric form in the moments of our daily lives?

Crossing into the terrain of human experience, what, we wonder, is the value of an image? In the summer of 2020, in a Sotheby's auction livestreamed due to the coronavirus, two Varo oil paintings sold for a combined $8 million. The year before, at a Christie's auction in May 2019, a collector paid $3.135 million for *Sympathy*, one of the four paintings Varo exhibited at the Galería Diana in Mexico City in the mid-1950s. Four years before, another Varo painting, *Vegetable Vampires*, sold at Christie's for $3.3 million. A fourth Varo piece, *Toward the Tower*, a work we examined earlier, sold for $4.3 million in 2014. What could be important enough in these paintings for someone to be willing to invest such large sums of money? What is it about Varo's work that people are willing to go to such great lengths to possess?

For Varo and Carrington, painting was a way to ritualize the wonder and love of invisible realms. But maybe the greatest gift these artists have to offer us today is not the tangible artifacts they have left behind. Maybe the women have something to share that cannot be bought at any price. What is this gift, this alchemical treasure hard to attain? Maybe the gift has to do with the way the women loved each other. For Varo and Carrington are living proof of what can happen when souls come together, and differences collaborate for a common good.

For one last image of Remedios Varo and Leonora Carrington, we turn to an artist of another time. In one of his last short poems, Sufi mystic Jalāl ad-Dīn Muhammad Rumi reflected on the love he felt for his teacher, Shams. The feeling of one man for another imagines into the same fertile field Varo and Carrington cultivated together:

> Those tender words we said to one another
> are stored in the secret heart of heaven
> one day, like the rain, they will fall and spread
> and their mystery will grow green over the world.
> (Rumi, trans. 2006: 14)

Note

1 The symbolism of blade and chalice is from Riane Eisler, *The chalice and the blade* (1995; New York, NY: Harper Collins).

References

Goizueta, E. (2014). Wifredo Lam's poetic imagination and the Spanish Baroque. In E. Goizueta (Ed.), *Wifredo Lam: Imagining new worlds* (3–20). Chestnut Hill, MA: Boston College.

Meade, M. (1993). *Men and the water of life: Initiation and the tempering of men*. San Francisco, CA: Harper San Francisco.

Rumi, J. (2006). *Rumi the card and book pack: Meditation, inspiration, and self-discovery* (E. Hanut, Ed.). North Clarendon, VT: Tuttle.

Sharp, D. (1991). *C. G. Jung lexicon: A primer of terms & concepts*. Toronto, Canada: Inner City Books.

Singer, J. (1994). *Boundaries of the soul: The practice of Jung's psychology*. New York, NY: Anchor Books.

Spielrein, S. (1994). Destruction as the cause of coming into being. *The Journal of Analytical Psychology, 39*(2), 155–186.

Suleiman, S. R. (1990). *Subversive intent: Gender, politics, and the avant-garde*. Cambridge, MA: Harvard University Press.

Index